GET A GOOD NIGHT'S SLEEP. . . EVERY NIGHT

With *Conquering Bad Dreams and Nightmares*, you can put a stop to bad dreams. Learn . . .

- Who suffers from bad dreams—and why
- What's causing your nightmares
- Which drugs and medicines affect your dreams
- How to interpret your bad dreams
- What common nightmares mean to you
- How to find the link between your bad dreams and your everyday life
- How reducing or eliminating bad dreams can reduce anxiety and depression
- How to overcome the Chronic Nightmare Disorder

THERE'S GOOD NEWS ABOUT BAD DREAMS—YOU CAN END THEM WITH A SIMPLE THREE-STEP CURE, AND THIS BOOK WILL SHOW YOU HOW!

CONQUERING BAD DREAMS & NIGHTMARES

A GUIDE TO UNDERSTANDING, INTERPRETATION, · AND CURE ·

BARRY KRAKOW, M.D. AND JOSEPH NEIDHARDT, M.D.

BERKLEY BOOKS, NEW YORK

The case studies mentioned in this book are based on the circumstances of actual people whose names and identities have been changed to protect their privacy.

CONQUERING BAD DREAMS AND NIGHTMARES

A Berkley Book / published by arrangement with
the authors

PRINTING HISTORY
Berkley trade paperback edition / October 1992

ISBN: 0-425-13211-0

A BERKLEY BOOK® TM 757,375
Berkley Books are published by The Berkley Publishing Group,
200 Madison Avenue, New York, New York 10016.
The name "Berkley" and the "B" logo
are trademarks belonging to Berkley Publishing Corporation.

PRINTED IN THE UNITED STATES OF AMERICA

10   9   8   7   6   5   4   3   2   1

To our parents
Bernard ז״ל and Marion   Cec and Ed

And to our families
Sandy, Cheryl, Tammy, Dale, Randy, Rich, Wendy, Jill, Heidi,
Peter and Whiteshell
Robert, Bette, Laurence, Penny, Wendy, Bernice, Jonathon,
Rebecca and Samuel

ACKNOWLEDGMENT

Foremost, we wish to thank our mentors Robert Kellner and Rolf Loehrich for their invaluable guidance and teaching; also, Richard Curtis, our agent, and Melinda Metz, our editor.

Thanks to those who contributed ideas and support, especially Marnie McDougall, Dan Sperling, Bonnie Stetson, Malcolm Weinstein. Also, Carol Cassell and Bruce Mann; and Irving Berlin, Sandy Chappell, Robert Engelman, Jan Evans, Tempe Evans, Leanne Gottfried, Mary Herring, Susan Jones, Lynn Joseph, Joan Koss, Susan McMeans, Steve Perls, Scott Shannon, Gershon Siegel, Eberhard Uhlenhuth, Tom Vosburgh.

We appreciate those who helped in our research, Dorothy Pathak, Dan Tandberg, Betty Bierner, Judy Legg, the University of New Mexico Departments of Psychiatry and Emergency Medicine; the library staffs at the University, the UNM School of Medicine and the Albuquerque and Santa Fe public libraries.

Also, thanks for special contributions from Carol Matthews, Frankie McCarty, Paul Roth, John Talley, Ellen Tallman. And John Allan, Claire Buckland, Ann Faraday, Glenn Hirsch, Ruth Mondlick, Pat Otto, Wolfgang Schmidt-Nowara. Also, Bob Conry, Janice Dalzell, Geoff and Janice Danzig, William Dement, Sheila Fodchuk, Ernest Hartmann, Cheryl Humphries, Susan and Rick Jeffs, Suyin Lee, Juanita Poole, and Gail Thomas.

I (E.J.N.) want to thank Whiteshell and my children for their love and support, and the Neidhardts, Roessels, and Gottfrieds. I (B.J.K.) want to thank all of the Krakow family for their *yedidut ve'chizuk*. Lastly, we are indebted to our patients who have so generously shared their experiences. Thanks to all.

Contents

Introduction

Whether nightmares trouble you once a year, once a week, or every single night, this book will supply the knowledge you need to deal effectively with your bad dreams.

There are three ways of coping with and eliminating troublesome dreams and nightmares:

- Increasing your knowledge about bad dreams in general
- Uncovering personal meaning in your own nightmares
- Curing your bad dreams with a specific treatment plan

These three approaches, separately or in combination, have helped people overcome their bad dreams. And, they will serve as a handy way to divide our book into sections.

First, we'll give you a comprehensive look at nightmares—from the bloodcurdling type that wake you up in a sweat to the anxiety type that disturb your sleep. You'll discover how bad dreams affect your mental and physical health and you'll also learn about the causes and meanings of nightmares.

Next, we'll show you how to find the personal meaning in your own nightmares. With our guidelines, you can dissect any dream or nightmare you've experienced and begin the very delicate, always intriguing, and sometimes complex process of dream interpretation.

Then, we'll teach you a specific method to put an end to your nightmares. People who've suffered chronic bad dreams for over forty years have achieved complete success with the technique we'll share with you.

Nightmares are one of the most vivid and dramatic experiences of the human mind. They evoke incredible images often compared to the world of movies. Yet no horror film, no

science-fiction fantasy, not even a slasher movie can upstage
the brutal images thrust upon us in our dreams. To portray
these images accurately, we'll explore the nightmares of real
people—mostly from our patients, as well as a few from our
colleagues, friends, and relatives.

We will explore the bad dreams of those who may have
suffered nightmares only twice a year and those who have
had them as often as twice a night, every night. Throughout,
we will maintain confidentiality for those who have so generously contributed their stories and dreams. We have done
so by altering their names, their jobs, and where they live.
Occasionally, we have altered the events unfolded in their
dreams. In a few instances we have combined the problems
of two people to capsulize valuable information. And, in
rare cases, we've created a character or a dream to detail a
particular point.

Let us further point out that many of these people have
worked for months and, in some cases, years, on a specific
emotional problem highlighted by their dreams and nightmares.
Their breakthroughs were filled with much joy and valuable
insight, but getting there required some pain and anguish. Yet,
their very real stories, which comprise a meaningful part of
their lifetimes, must be condensed into a few paragraphs
or a few pages at best. This is an irony that must not go
unstated.

The frontier of nightmare research has only been crossed
in the past two decades. While thousands of books and
articles have been written about dreaming, little has been
published about bad dreams. In fact, it was not until 1987
that the American Psychiatric Association finally listed
the occurrence of frequent nightmares as a distinct sleep
disorder.

Like most of you, we have had our bouts of nightmares
and difficult life experiences. We have also had a good deal
of medical and psychiatric training and practice which has
allowed us to witness the unhealthy impact nightmares have
had on other people. Through our work and research we have
been fortunate to learn how to deal effectively with nightmares,
and have helped many individuals who've been troubled by
their dreams. We believe this book will help you approach

your disturbing dreams in a healthy way.

As our patients and friends have enriched our lives with their generosity and sharing, we now wish to share what we've learned with you.

PART I

Nightmares:
Fact, Fiction, and Fantasy

CHAPTER 1

To Sleep, Perchance to Dream

WHEN WAS YOUR LAST NIGHTMARE?

Or, when was your most recent troubling dream?

A month ago? A week? Perhaps last night.

Whenever it was, you probably recall something about it. Maybe the nightmare was a horror story with monsters or wild animals, or the slasher type with blood and guts. If so, you may have awakened in the middle of the night with a racing heart and a feeling of panic or terror. For many others, the dream itself may not have awakened you, yet remembering it later that morning produced a strong reaction—grief, disgust, revulsion, anger, fear, depression, frustration, or, most commonly, anxiety.

These emotional reactions to bad dreams produce lasting effects, some of which hang over you throughout the day, if not longer. The term "nightmare hangover" has been used to describe these unpleasant feelings which persist long after the curtain has come down on your disturbing nighttime drama. For some, the nightmare replays itself—the horrible dream images resurface, conjuring up the same fear and dread throughout the day. For others, there are only vague memories of the dreams, yet they are plagued by feelings of depression, fatigue, and anxiety.

Whatever form the nightmare hangover takes, the effects are often similar—fatigue throughout the day, fear of going to sleep at night, recurrent anxieties and unpleasant feelings intruding into your life which disturb your effectiveness at work and disrupt your family life at home.

The nightmare hangover isn't the only problem caused by bad dreams. Adding insult to injury is the commonly held belief that having nightmares, frequently or even occasionally, somehow means you're crazy, mentally unbalanced, or in some way abnormal. Why would anyone have such horrible or disturbing dreams if there wasn't something wrong with their personality and mental health?

This view is widespread. Most of the chronic nightmare sufferers we work with and even those with merely an occasional bad dream assume their disturbing dreams imply a mental abnormality. And, most people are firmly convinced, in a strange way, that the nightmares represent a means of dealing with this so-called unhealthy state. Even people who suffer troublesome dreams once or twice a year still worry about their nightmares, convinced the dreams reflect badly upon themselves.

Fortunately for nightmare sufferers, chronic or otherwise, these theories are being challenged. New and exciting research questions the link between nightmares and abnormal mental health. The most intriguing theory—one which we have been actively researching—contends that nightmares are the *cause* of anxiety, depression, and assorted other mental health symptoms.

Eliminate the nightmares and many of these symptoms disappear!

Consider Emily, a thirty-three-year-old courtroom stenographer. She'd suffered from nightmares three times a week for several years before she enrolled in our studies on the effects and treatment of nightmares. She had this nightmare one month after she began recording her dreams.

"I am sitting on a couch with a girlfriend after playing racquetball. We compare shoes. She knows a good shoe repairman. I ask if she would take my shoes to him. She agrees, but then she promptly pulls out a map of the Middle East. I ask what she's doing and she says to follow her. We meet a blond woman held hostage by male captors. I realize we are now hostages.

"They put us all on stretchers—I'm third in line. We're going in for operations—my friend first. A doctor cuts into the side of her throat over the big artery, and then slices across her windpipe. All this fluid and blood gush out and my friend dies instantly. The blond is next. They make the same cuts on her throat, but nothing happens, so they sit her up and give her oxygen. Her eyes roll back in her head and then fluid and blood gush out. Only she doesn't die. She tries to scream, but she can't because of the slashes in her throat. The doctor says, 'This is just a reflex action,' and the blond collapses.

"Now it's my turn. They come and wheel me into the operating room. A masked doctor holds up the scalpel in front of his face, examining the shining steel blade. He moves the blade toward my throat. Slowly he moves his face down, using his free hand to stretch the skin on my neck. I see the blade moving closer . . .

" . . . I awaken, clutching and protecting my throat, crying out, 'Stop!' My heart is pounding. I am sweating all over. I can't go back to sleep."

Emily suffered from this ghastly type of nightmare as well as a variety of equally upsetting dreams. But, two months after working with the treatment we detailed for her, the nightmares ceased. And now two years later, they've not returned.

Not only does Emily no longer have bad dreams, but many of the effects of those nightmares have vanished as well. Listen to her own words six months after the troubling dreams stopped. "I feel so completely different . . . so *up* about things. I'm much less anxious than I used to be. I sleep better and I have more energy than I can ever remember having. Now that the bad dreams are gone, I can see how negative they were and how they'd been affecting my whole life. Thank goodness they're gone!"

Although we understand why scary dreams are so upsetting, many nightmares, perhaps the majority, are not as violent or as graphic as Emily's. Many dreams are not even considered distressing when retold by the dreamer to another person. But who determines whether or not a dream is a nightmare is the *dreamer* and the dreamer alone. If a dream upsets you for whatever reason, then call it a nightmare, because the anxiety, fear, or terror *you* feel is what defines it as a bad dream.

This point is so important, please allow us to repeat ourselves. Dreams are a very personal thing. Many are so personal you are unwilling to tell them to your best friends or loved ones. Even if a psychiatrist or professional dream interpreter doesn't find your dream the least bit frightening or anxiety-producing, *if you* do, then your dream certainly qualifies as a nightmare.

WHAT'S THE DIFFERENCE BETWEEN A NIGHTMARE AND A BAD DREAM?

There is very little difference. For both nightmares and bad dreams, the universal feature is unpleasantness—in the strongest sense of the word. In some way the dream disturbs you. This disturbance may be great or small, but it will always include a troubling emotional response. In Emily's dream a threat to her life produced enough fear to wake her from sleep.

It is just as common, if not more so, for a person to have a bad dream without awakening. But when you remember your nightmare in the morning, you experience the unpleasantness and bad feelings that were present while dreaming. If you don't awaken during the episode, the term *anxiety dream* is sometimes used instead of nightmare.

Sheila, a part-time secretary, had this anxiety dream. "It's dark outside the front of my house. I have a bunch of packages in my arms. I'm fooling with my keys, trying to find the one to the door. I go to stick it in the lock, but it won't go. I try another key and it won't go. No matter what key I use, I can't get them to work. I can't even get one to slip inside the lock.

"Then I hear something—not sure—but it's a creaking noise. I listen closely, but I can't figure out what it is. It doesn't get louder. It just keeps creaking. I try the keys again and they still won't work. I feel anxious and nervous because I'm locked out of my house and I don't know what I'm going to do. The creaky noise won't stop." When Sheila awakened in the morning, she vividly remembered this dream and relived the same anxiety she felt while dreaming.

Although we've used two terms—nightmares and anxiety dreams—we consider them the same thing. We've worked with people who've suffered just as much from either nightmares or anxiety dreams. Throughout our book we will use the terms interchangeably, regardless of whether the person wakes up from the dream or not.

Another nightmare experience involves *delayed anxiety*. The dream feels enjoyable, or at least doesn't cause you any distress, yet produces anxiety afterwards. A common theme for delayed anxiety is dreaming about sex with a parent or a sibling. During the dream, the encounter neither disturbs nor awakens you. However, when recalling the events in the dream, you may feel anxiety and disgust.

Philip, a middle-aged business executive, suffered a delayed anxiety dream involving aggression. "I'm working late in my office. The janitor comes in and mops the floor. He ignores me when I tell him I'm working. I stand up to tell him off but he turns the mop handle toward me and starts poking me. I grab the handle and wrestle with him. The handle breaks and I get the bigger end and hit him. I really pound him hard, bloody him good, and knock him out." When Philip remembered his dream upon awakening, he felt revulsion at his uninhibited violence.

The modern psychiatric term for nightmares is *dream anxiety attacks*. This is an excellent term because it indicates the unpleasantness found in all nightmares. *Nightmare, anxiety dream, and dream anxiety attack*, then, are variations in name only—they refer to the same thing and all of them can be treated successfully with the same method.

CAN NIGHTMARES KILL?

Nightmares cause physical and mental distress which is quite real and sometimes dramatic. In the classic, terrifying nightmare, like the knife at Emily's throat, it's clear how stressful the episode can be. In medical terms we call this the "fight or flight" discharge from the nervous system. It is the ultimate stress reaction, gearing you up to fight off a saber-toothed tiger or climb a tree as fast as you can.

Nowadays, lions and tigers and bears may chase you in your dreams, although your daily confrontations with the boss, a spouse, or your children can stress you out as well. Whether awake or dreaming, these acute stress reactions cause your heart rate to double. Your breathing becomes shallow and increases to twice its normal rate. Your blood pressure rises and you perspire all over. The pupils of your eyes dilate and your body trembles. And somewhere, best described as the "pit of your stomach," you have feelings of panic.

Sleep lab recordings of nightmare sufferers reveal these changes building up gradually while you are still asleep. As the nightmare progresses, your vital signs crescendo to a peak just as you awaken. These physical and mental changes can also be induced by nightmares without frightening images. Sheila, whose nightmare seems more eerie than scary, experienced a reaction similar to Emily's. Her heart raced and a terrific rush of anxiety coursed through her body when she recalled the dream.

So the harmful effects of nightmares are largely the effects of stress. Researchers in the fields of psychology and medicine have investigated the effects of stressful conditions over the past 30 years. The conclusion has always been the same—stress can lead to illness and death. This view of stress is especially valid in modern times because of the increasingly hectic ways in which we live and play and work.

Stress may also produce a vicious cycle by causing more nightmares which in turn cause more stress. One of the major predisposing factors for nightmares is physical illness—an obvious form of stress. People suffering from high fevers, those undergoing operations, or individuals suffering from heart and lung conditions may have a greater propensity for bad dreams. The stress of nightmares to those individuals suffering from serious illnesses is likely to add another burden to their already compromised health.

More research is needed to understand the effects of the negative emotions we might feel in our dreams. No definite conclusions can be drawn now. However, for some nightmare sufferers our research indicates that nightmares may be more of a *cause* of mental health symptoms than previously thought.

When we evaluated specific complaints in our patients, such as anxiety and depression, we found people improved markedly after the nightmares were eliminated. We had only instructed them on the method for abolishing their bad dreams. They received no additional psychotherapy to treat the anxiety and the depression. Still, after their bad dreams were conquered they felt better and their psychological test scores confirmed significant improvement several months later.

We cannot be certain about the degree of stress caused by nightmares because people react differently to their bad dreams. The one thing we can be very sure about is that a lot more people suffer from bad dreams than is usually believed. While "sweet dreams" is a classic bedtime refrain, the facts suggest otherwise.

WHO SUFFERS FROM BAD DREAMS?

Bad dreams are almost a universal experience. Everybody has them, some people more than others. At least twelve million adults in this country suffer from chronic nightmares, that is, they have at least one bad dream a week which awakens them from sleep. Usually these people suffer more frequently. They often experience troubling dreams several times a week or, in severe cases, every night or several times each night, and typically, for years. But this number only includes the chronic nightmare sufferers as determined by the psychiatric definition for the Chronic Nightmare Disorder.

What about people who are troubled by anxiety dreams that may not awaken them, yet leave the same destructive feelings of depression and anxiety in their aftermath? Or what about the people who do awaken from their troublesome dreams but feel too embarrassed to talk them over with anyone? Or maybe they confided in someone, but were left with a hopeless feeling that no one understood what was so disturbing.

We suspect millions of people have had such experiences. In fact, most people experience distressing dreams routinely. This was highlighted by the studies of Calvin Hall, a psychiatrist who wrote *The Meaning of Dreams* in the 1950s. He reviewed the content of a large number of dreams in *normal* people and discovered that "the unpleasant emotions of fear, anger and sadness are twice as frequent as the pleasant emotions of joy and happiness. Dreaming, on the whole, is not a pleasurable pastime."

Other experts on dreaming have written about this tendency toward bad dreams. In researching our book, we've reviewed hundreds of so-called regular dreams in these other texts. Many of the dreams have morbid or terrifying or anxiety-producing aspects. In reviewing the popular book, *Dream Power*, by Ann Faraday, we need look no further than the first page of the introduction. She recounts her childhood dreams in which she's pursued by "men wearing long white coats" and by another man with a "skin disease down one side of his face."

This is not to say we don't also have wonderful dreams which are truly inspiring and uplifting as well as funny or silly or bizarre. So, not every dream is bad. However, for whatever reasons, negative feelings and disturbing images appear frequently in our dream worlds.

Children are the largest group consistently to suffer bad dreams. Nightmares are so common in childhood that some psychologists view them as a natural development in a child's growing-up process. In the children's section, we'll describe a few nightmare themes which reflect mental growth stages in kids.

Interestingly, while children tend to ask their parents about their nightmares, adults are not so open. There is one major reason why adults are reluctant to discuss their bad dreams:

We are scared and embarrassed by the horrible and crazy things we dream in our nightmares.

We wonder if this doesn't suggest something awful about ourselves. Are we crazy? Are we repressed homicidal maniacs? Are we bad people? Time and again, we've heard people ask the question, "If I dream such awful things, doesn't that say something awful about myself or about my mental health?"

To date there has never been any convincing research to prove there is a relationship between having nightmares and mental illness. We've worked with patients who report suffering from nightmares every week for forty years. These same people have functioned at a healthy level in their jobs and family lives.

TAKING BACK THE NIGHT

We'll briefly outline how this book is organized so you can get the most from it. Those of you with severe, chronic nightmares may wish to start with the treatment program in Part III. If you are reading for more general information about understanding and interpreting nightmares, you'll find the first two sections very useful.

In the remainder of this first section, we'll provide a great deal of general information about bad dreams, focusing on the causes and meanings of nightmares—the common ones and the not-so-common. And, for those of you with frequent nightmares, we've devoted an entire chapter to the Chronic Nightmare Disorder.

In the next section, *How to Interpret Your Bad Dreams and Nightmares*, we will teach you a step-by-step method for analyzing your bad dreams. Whether you have nightmares a few times a year or a few times a week, this section will help you dissect your troubling dreams. Here, you will learn how to gain valuable insights from your nightmares. And, for some, interpreting your bad dreams will prove to be the only cure you need to conquer them.

In the third section, *Turning Nightmares into Dreams*, we will teach you a scientifically proven method for eliminating bad dreams. In our research at the University of New Mexico School of Medicine, we have shown that a simple, three-step technique can successfully treat nightmares. In fact, more than half the people we've treated have virtually eliminated or markedly reduced their nightmares within a few weeks of using this method, and that includes individuals who've had disturbing dreams several times a week for forty years or longer!

The final section, *Wrapping Up the Night*, contains two special chapters. We'll talk about the nightmare's "cousins,"—nightmarelike experiences including sleepwalking, night terrors, sleep paralysis, posttraumatic nightmares, nocturnal seizures, sleep panic attacks, and the REM behavior disorder, a recently described condition similar to sleepwalking. We'll focus on the different medications and psychotherapy often needed for these problems.

In the last chapter, we'll talk exclusively about children and how to work with them to overcome their nightmares. We'll also discuss other childhood disturbances, including night terrors, sleepwalking and sleep-talking, confusional arousals, and head-banging.

Throughout this book we'll tell you about many individuals and their bad dreams. We owe them a great debt for their willingness to share their stories so others may learn from their difficult experiences. If you suffer from chronic nightmares, we believe these cases will support you in your attempts to deal with your own troubling dreams. For those reading because of a more general interest in nightmares, this book will provide you with new insights and new ways of thinking about bad dreams.

One note of caution must be added here. As physicians, we are obligated to inform you that some patients with serious mental health problems may have nightmares. Likewise, some people with bad dreams may develop serious mental health problems.

If you have troublesome dreams you cannot cope with, or if you have frequent nightmares that cause you significant problems, then you may need professional counseling. In writing a book, we cannot communicate with you directly to know how to advise you. Some of you may need to take additional measures in approaching your dreams. We must leave this to your judgment.

We do not wish to scare you with this thought, but we feel it is necessary to dispense this advice early in our book for those who may need psychotherapy while they work with their nightmares. That should be a relatively small number. The majority of people who suffer from nightmares will find this book highly informative and very helpful in dealing with their troubling dreams.

Now let's explore the inner workings of our minds during sleep so we can understand how nightmares unfold.

CHAPTER 2

Nightmare on REM Street

This is the only technical chapter of our book.

It contains useful information to help you understand how dreams and nightmares occur in your sleep. If you find some of the material difficult, try to get the gist of our discussion about REM sleep, but don't worry about all the details. Following this chapter, we'll describe nightmares from several patients to demonstrate how bad dreams are caused.

LET'S GO BACK TO SLEEP

Sleep encompasses more than a quarter of our lives, yet the science of sleep medicine has only been established in the medical community during the past decade. In fact, REM sleep (*r*apid *e*ye *m*ovement) was not discovered until the 1950s. Eugene Aserinksy and Nathaniel Kleitman first noted rapid eye movements in sleeping babies and adults in 1953. In 1957, William Dement and Kleitman linked REM to dreaming. Researchers in this burgeoning field of sleep disorders medicine now divide sleep into two different worlds: the REM state associated with dreaming, and the non-REM state (abbreviated NREM) where we snooze and generally don't dream.

In an average life span, you spend twenty-plus years asleep—REM accounting for five of those years. At birth we like the dream world best of all. The average infant sleeps up to eighteen hours a day and spends half of that in REM. By the time we've reached the age of four, our sleep has dropped to ten to twelve hours per day and our percentage of REM has dropped to 25 to 30 percent.

By late adolescence and adulthood, we spend less than 25 percent of our sleep in REM. Twenty percent is the average for most people. In a typical night's sleep of eight hours, you dream a bit under two hours. In the beginning of the night, your dreams are short, but as your sleep continues, dreams last longer—up to thirty or forty minutes by early morning.

So how can we tell the difference between dreaming in the REM state and genuine sleeping in the NREM mode?

We begin by observing sleep stages on a brain wave tracing which we call the EEG or electroencephalogram. The EEG is a monitor like the EKG which records impulses from your heart. Like your heart, the brain's electrical impulses produce unique wave forms. Recorded on the EEG printout, these wave forms resemble a doctor's handwriting—illegible scribble—yet, to the expert's eye, the markings distinguish between the various sleep stages and will also show when you are in the REM dream world.

If you spent a night in a sleep lab, we'd hook you up to several contraptions to monitor your sleep cycle. By attaching electrodes to parts of your body, impulses from the brain as well as your eyes and muscles are recorded.

To your scalp, we would attach electrodes to note the EEG pattern of the brain.

To your closed eyes, we would tape electrodes to measure eye movement on an EOG—the electro-oculogram.

To your chin and to larger muscles in your legs or arms, we would tape electrodes to measure muscle movement on an EMG—the electromyogram.

While awake with eyes closed, the EEG electrodes would record a lot of small, spikelike patterns called alpha waves. These alpha waves run together like a row of little peaks and valleys. You might view them as a series of VVVVVVVVVVs strung together with more wavy edges. About ten of these alpha waves will be generated in one second. This alpha pattern indicates a state of relaxed alertness and it will show more than 50 percent alpha waves.

Within several minutes of lying down, you'd be drifting off to sleep. Would you begin dreaming right away? Possibly, but usually not. Often, you pass through NREM stages before entering the dream world of REM.

NREM consists of four numbered stages. Typically, when you first go to sleep at night, you'll pass through all four levels—1 through 4, with Stage 4 considered the deepest phase of sleep. Then, you'll turn around and pass back through all four levels again—4 through 1. This may take two hours. Until you've completed this first NREM cycle, you're unlikely to enter REM.

To repeat, genuine sleep includes this whole series of NREM stages which are markedly different from the REM dream world. The four NREM levels show up on the EEG printout with many new wave forms. By the way, the printout measuring an average night's sleep runs the length of five football fields, or 1500 feet! The majority of that printout is filled with NREM waves. These forms have different shapes and sizes and occur at different frequencies. Some appear regularly every few seconds, while others occur several times per second. To a polysomnographer—a physician trained in evaluating EEG findings—these different sizes, shapes, and frequencies indicate the brain's activity in a particular phase of sleep.

Stage 1 of NREM is the phase of falling asleep. It is a twilight zone of consciousness which is also called the hypnagogic (pronounced *hip - nuh - GAHJ - ick*) state. We spend little time in Stage 1. The only way to pass through this stage is through falling asleep or waking up. The Stage 1 EEG pattern is similar to the state of relaxed alertness with eyes closed, that is, there are many of the little peak-and-valley rows of alpha waves. However, the alpha waves are now less than 50 percent of the total wave forms. This distinction is not enough for some experts who don't consider Stage 1 to be real sleep; instead, they call it a gateway to the other NREM stages.

Still, our reactions to the outside world are diminished in Stage 1. In one experiment, college students had their eyes taped *open* while the EEG recorded their passage through Stage 1. Despite being able to "see," they could not recall anything from the outside world. Also, in this light phase of falling asleep, your mental activity drifts and you may see brief dreamlike images—dreamlets—in your mind's eye.

The problem in accurately describing Stage 1 is that it lasts such a short time—perhaps a few minutes or, in some cases, as little as thirty seconds. This is why we receive so many different responses from people when they are abruptly awakened from Stage 1. Some individuals clearly believe they were more awake than asleep.

Stage 2 of sleep is the real thing. We spend more time in Stage 2 than in any other phase—50 percent or more of our total sleep time. Despite spending the most time in this phase, we know little about it. On the EEG, new patterns emerge called K-complexes and sleep spindles. These patterns may represent arousal activity; for example, they appear if a sound is made near the sleeper. This suggests an alerting response in your sleep. On your first cycle of NREM sleep, you don't spend a long time in Stage 2 because your body seems to need deeper sleep to restore itself.

If you continue your natural sleep cycle, you next arrive at *Stage 3* and *Stage 4* which are lumped together (Stage 3/4) because they show so many delta waves on the EEG. Delta waves are large, wide spikes about five times the size of the small alpha waves. Delta waves are also termed slow waves because their frequency is much less than other wave forms. They occur at only one or two per second and therefore Stage 3/4 is given the initials *SWS* for *s*low *w*ave *s*leep.

Our bodies use slow wave sleep as the time for recuperation. Looking at physiological indicators during these deep stages of sleep, the brain's temperature and blood flow are reduced—a clear sign of decreased activity. Our heart and breathing rates are at their twenty-four-hour lows. Not only are respirations and heartbeats reduced, they are also more stable. We seem to be truly at rest.

If you consistently exercise each day, you may need more slow wave sleep. Also, if you are deprived of SWS, you are more prone to muscle soreness in the morning as well as overall physical discomfort and sensitivity to pain. Presumably, SWS facilitates physical recuperation from the day's events, which may explain why your first stay in delta sleep is the longest. You might spend more than one hour there, but over the course of the night you would only require about 20 percent of your total sleep in Stage 3/4. This adds up to less than two hours in an eight-hour night.

Once you've completed your first passage through Stage 3/4, your sleep cycle reverses itself and heads backwards through Stage 2. Then, about ninety minutes from the time you initially entered Stage 1 when you went to bed, you'd be back at something which looks quite like Stage 1 again.

Only it *isn't* Stage 1; it's actually the REM dream state.

REM has many similarities to Stage 1 of NREM sleep. Both have a similar pattern with many peak-and-valley rows of alpha waves. These alpha waves make it difficult to distinguish between Stage 1 and REM on the EEG tracing. There are, however, two prominent aspects of REM that clearly distinguish it from Stage 1.

The first distinction, seen on the EOG, is rapid eye movements that directly accompany dreaming. The second distinction, seen on the EMG, is the near-total absence of voluntary muscle tone. In other words, you can move your eyes, but that's about all. In REM, you don't roll about the bed or change positions. In fact, if you suddenly become aware of yourself dreaming while you're dreaming, you might notice the sensation of being paralyzed, and for good reason—you literally *are* paralyzed!

You spend 20 to 25 percent of your total sleep in REM. Perhaps 80 to 90 percent of REM is spent dreaming. For the other 10 to 20 percent of REM time, it's unknown what's really going on. It does seem clear, though, that we're not always dreaming for every minute of REM. Interestingly, some dreamlike activity occurs in the other NREM stages of sleep; however, the amount compared to REM is considerably less and much different.

Each night, you experience four to six REM periods, which add up to less than two hours on an average eight-hour night of sleep. Among people who sleep for different lengths of time, the percentage of REM sleep will often increase. For example, in short sleepers (less than six hours), the proportion of both Stage 3/4 and REM sleep increases. And in longer sleepers (greater than ten hours), REM sleep also increases. Some researchers have postulated that this implies a need for dreaming.

In some ways, REM is more like being awake than asleep. Vital signs, such as pulse rate, respiratory rate, and blood pressure are irregular. Cardiac dysrhythmias—irregular heartbeats—can actually increase during REM and the blood pressure can shoot up 40 points. This cardiac instability has led some experts to speculate that REM may be instrumental in the triggering process for heart attacks which occur during sleep.

Other signs of activity include increased brain metabolism. During REM, the blood flow to the brain increases, as does temperature and the use of glucose. In men, full or partial penile erections also accompany REM sleep, as does clitoral engorgement in women. Yet, with all this obvious activity of the body during REM, it is surprisingly difficult to wake someone from the dream state. At times, it may be more difficult to arouse a dreamer from the dreamworld than someone in the so-called deepest phase of sleep—Stage 3/4.

As you travel through your first REM phase of the night, you may only spend a few minutes dreaming. You would then cycle through Stages 2, 3, and 4, then back again until you arrived at your second stay in REM. Throughout the night, this continues with each cycle lasting between 70 and 100 minutes. Each portion of REM, however, will last longer, while your slow wave sleep of Stage 3/4 nearly disappears. The first time you go into REM, you may dream five minutes, whereas the last time you enter REM you might dream as long as forty minutes.

If you were to guess in what part of the night bad dreams occur, you might select the later episodes of REM, that is, later at night or early in the morning. These REM periods are longer and therefore give the dreamer extended opportunities to dream.

Your guess would be correct, although it's not clear why more nightmares occur within these longer dream periods. There is a tendency for dreams to start out pleasantly enough, then progressively worsen. In fact, the longer you dream, the more likely your dreams will turn into something unpleasant. Most dream anxiety attacks, then, occur near the time of awakening, that is, when you get up to go to work or go about the day's business. This is so for most people, including night-shift workers.

REM nightmares are also very easy to remember—too easy. This may be due to the threatening themes against our survival, security, or self-esteem. Or, it may be due to bad dreams occurring close to the morning when we are awakening. Regardless, when you wake up from a nightmare, it's difficult to forget the unpleasant details. Sometimes those details are so distressing that if you were to return to sleep right away, then awaken several hours later, you would have little difficulty in recalling the dream images.

If we had hooked up Emily, Sheila, and Philip—our dreamers from Chapter 1—to the EEG while they had their nightmares, we would have discovered that their bad dreams had occurred during a typical REM stage. However, everything that causes us distress in our sleep cannot be strictly classified as a REM nightmare.

Our nightmares have cousins—rather ill-mannered ones at that!

THE NIGHTMARE FAMILY OF TROUBLEMAKERS

The word *nightmare* derives from two words: *night* and *mare*. *Night* has a variety of ancient meanings which refer to sleep and death; while *mare* comes from the word *mara*, which means to crush. The crusher who caused nightmares was a demon known as the *incubus*, which sat on your chest to suffocate you in your sleep. Way back when, if you said you had a nightmare, you didn't mean you dreamt someone chased you with a knife or you were locked out of your house. These would have been called bad dreams, or anxiety dreams.

Perhaps the most famous painting to depict the nightmare experience shows the scenario of the dreamer crushed by a demon. Painted in 1781 by Henry Fuseli, "The Nightmare" depicts a woman lying paralyzed on her back with a demon figure squatting atop her chest. The woman lies partly off the bed as if she were struggling to break free from her paralysis.

For hundreds of years, *nightmare* referred to this specific incubus attack. Over the last century, the word *nightmare* has undergone changes in meaning. Now, it implies any kind of bad dream, as well as serving as a catchall term for other sleep disturbances.

This has created a problem because the extensive research in the field of sleep medicine now makes it possible to identify more than a dozen different disturbances, including nightmares and anxiety dreams, that occur while sleeping or in sleeplike states. These episodes can be filled with just as much terror and anxiety as any nightmare you'd *never* want to experience. What makes things more confusing is that the REM stage can account for some but not all of these sleep disturbances. Many of these nightmarish events do not occur during REM.

The larger problem is that these other processes occur so commonly—especially sleep paralysis and hypnagogic hallu-cinations—that people may experience both nightmares and one or more of these other nightmarelike events.

Sleep paralysis (SP) usually occurs while you're falling asleep. Because you're partly awake you become terrified when you realize you can't move. Hypnagogic hallucinations (HH) often accompany sleep paralysis. These hallucinations are often threatening images of sinister characters that appear more vivid than dream images. Although both SP and HH have REM-like properties, they seem to occur in Stage 1 of sleep.

Other disturbances such as night terrors occur in our deepest sleep—Stage 3/4. Victims awaken abruptly from sleep with wild screams and terrorized looks on their faces. Often they're completely disoriented, yet once they fully awaken, they have no idea why they were acting so frightened.

Any of these disturbances could be mistaken for a nightmare. And there are other nightmarelike disturbances as well—some more deadly than nightmares. We've treated an adolescent with a sleepwalking disturbance who put his head through a glass aquarium and fell out of a second-story bedroom window. A colleague of ours has treated a patient with the REM behavior disorder who acted out his dream by diving under a tidal wave, only to break his neck by smashing his head against a wall.

Other disturbances include the Old Hag experience, narcolepsy, sleep-talking, sleep panic attacks, nocturnal seizures, daymares, and flashbacks. All these nightmarelike occurrences must be approached and treated differently from REM nightmares and anxiety dreams.

Because this rather large "field of bad dreams" is broad, we know there are some readers who may suffer from one of these problems as well as nightmares. That's why we've devoted an entire chapter in our final section of the book to detail the relevant points you need to know. If you suffer from one of these other disturbances, you may want to review that chapter now, and then return to our next topic—the causes of nightmares.

CHAPTER 3

The Many Causes of Nightmares and Bad Dreams

BEFORE THE COMMON ERA: THE DREAM INVADERS

Although "dream invaders" might suggest a new video arcade game, we're really talking about a very serious belief held by many people more than two thousand years ago—a belief that dreams were caused by supernatural entities invading the body and mind.

One of the earliest cultures—the Greeks—evolved a ritual known as *incubation therapy*, which involved deities delivering cures to sick people in their sleep. Notice the similarity to *incubus*—the demon who caused nightmares.

During an incubation ritual, the ill person slept in a special temple while awaiting a god or spirit's visit in a dream. In some cases, the dream provided the full cure, while in others the deity performed an operation on the diseased body part. In still others, the dreamer reported the dream to a priest who interpreted it to find the cure. So before the rise of Christianity in Western civilization, belief in the relationship between dreams and deities was widespread and dreaming was taken very seriously.

Both terms—incubation and incubus—derive from the Latin word *incubare*, which means to lie on or lie upon or lie down on. Both terms are straightforward. With incubation, the dreamer *lies on* the special bed in the temple for receiving the dream. With the incubus, the demon *lies upon* the dreamer. Notice, however, that incubation suggests a positive relationship with the gods while incubus suggests a negative one. This difference may have come about through changing attitudes about sex and religion.

In classical times, many of the gods were thought to visit humans to procreate. There are numerous stories of women visited by the god Zeus in different forms—a swan, a bull, or a human. He made love to these women and spawned individuals with human and heavenly attributes. The classic examples are Alexander the Great and Hercules, both allegedly offspring of a god and a human. So, having sex with a god was not considered evil, although there was the possibility that the spirit was an incubus—a supernatural entity, such as a monster or demon. And these demons could terrorize or seduce their victims.

The negative perception about incubi may have been encouraged by religious influences. If people truly believed their dreams were caused by "higher beings" or they were visited by gods, it's easy to see how that idea would compete with certain religious concepts. In checking our history and etymology texts, we were unable to find any references to the incubus before the Common Era; whereas incubation therapy was well described long before the Common Era, dating back to 500 B.C.E. and probably earlier. Incubus attacks appear in literature repeatedly *after* the Common Era, especially in the Dark Ages, roughly between 500 and 1500 A.D.

The belief that invading spirits cause dreams—good and bad—still holds in some cultures in our world today. In Western culture, however, the dream invaders theory fell largely by the wayside with the rise of scientific thinking in the 19th century.

NINETEENTH-CENTURY VIEWS: WHAT'S IN AN OLD WIVES' TALE?

If you don't want nightmares, here's some quick advice:
Never eat avocados, cucumbers, cheese or beans.
Don't sleep on your back.
Don't go to bed with a full stomach.
Don't sleep with your head under a pillow.
Don't wear tight pajamas.
Don't sleep on your stomach or your side and definitely don't dangle your feet off the edge of the bed.
Oh, and don't go to bed hungry.
Many of these old wives' tales matched 19th century views that ascribed physical or mechanical causes to bad dreams.

Before the impact of Sigmund Freud, the prevailing theory to explain nightmares invoked a central idea—somehow the brain or nervous system was improperly stimulated and the result was a bad dream. Eating large meals before bedtime left your stomach too full. This blocked the circulation of blood to the brain. Conversely, leaving the stomach empty created intense hunger pangs that irritated the brain. Sleeping in certain positions cramped your lungs which led to poor air getting to the brain, again resulting in nightmares.

To prove these theories, experiments were performed using a variety of stimuli. The most well known tests were conducted by *and* on French researcher Alfred Maury, who published his work in 1861. A feather tickling his nose produced a dream of an awful torture in which a mask was stuck to his face then ripped away, peeling off the skin. In another, a hot iron was held close to his face. He dreamed of robbers extorting money from people by holding their feet to hot coals. Maury's most famous nightmare occurred by accident. He had a lengthy dream involving the French Revolution. At the end, he awakened as the guillotine fell upon his own neck, only to discover his headboard had landed on his neck.

So the 19th century view of bad dreams emphasized the physical causes. This reveals an interesting change from the past, because it allowed for dreams to have some internal basis within the person even if they were initiated by an external stimuli, such as food or feathers. This trend may have cleared the way for reconsidering the mental causes of dreams. We say reconsider because the notion of mental causes of dreams had been suggested almost 2500 years ago by Hippocrates and even earlier in Biblical and Talmudic references. But this view was not to take hold until the 20th century.

EARLY TWENTIETH-CENTURY VIEWS

In the early 1900s, ideas about dreaming changed radically. Psychological causes were advanced to explain how dreams were produced. The leading contributor to these theories was Sigmund Freud, a physician trained as a neurologist. Freud worked extensively with dreams—his own and his patients'. He established a theory that dreaming is the *guardian of sleep*. A dream is a complex drama played out in the sleeping mind as a means of disguising various thoughts that might otherwise awaken the person.

Freud believed the unconscious mind is filled with assorted desires and wants, mostly related to our natural drives such as aggression and sexuality. Consciously satisfying these *wishes*— a Freudian term—might throw us into turmoil, as many of these desires run counter to our morals and ethics. By disguising the wishes in dream form as a bizarre or nonsensical story, the wish can still be fulfilled, but the dreamer does not directly face the disturbing aspects of his or her desires.

This *wish fulfillment theory* explains how sleep is preserved through dreams. Simply put, dreaming about pushing *candles* into his *mother's purse* is a much less intense experience for a man than dreaming about making love to his mother. Or, a woman who dreams about driving her *father's car* and fondling the *stick shift* is less perturbed than if she dreams about a sexual encounter with her father. These symbols—candles, purse, car, and stick shift—are what Freud called the *manifest dream*, that is, the actual picture painted in your mind's eye. These symbolic dream forms allow us to continue sleeping uneventfully.

However, within the manifest dream is the *latent* content which provides the hidden meaning of the dream—sexual, aggressive, or otherwise. The manifest dream is the raw reported dream whereas the latent content will yield the thoughts and feelings that actually caused the dream. A teenage boy dreams he violently smashes a bottle of *pop* against a wall. We are not surprised to discover he is angry at his dad when we learn he calls his father, *Pop*-pa. This boy, like many adolescents, has trouble confronting his dad with hostile feelings. His dream has no such difficulty. Simplistically, the boy's anger is the underlying cause of his dream.

While there have been variations on Freud's theories and several newer ideas about dreaming, it is Freud who is rightly credited with giving our dreamworlds respectability in modern psychology and medicine. Freud, however, wrote little about nightmares. In his earliest writings, he called nightmares *failed dreams* because they do not disguise the anxiety-provoking images—the dream fails to guard the person's sleep and the dreamer awakens. Freud, however, was not satisfied with this view and over the next several decades he speculated on a variety of theories about nightmares.

One theory describes nightmares as *punishment dreams*. Suppose a woman feels a strong desire while awake for an action she considers immoral, such as making love to another woman's husband. Instead of dreaming of this lovemaking, the woman may dream of being attacked by a man with a knife. Her real desire has been twisted into symbolic nightmarish form to punish her for thinking immoral thoughts. The nightmare, then, functions as a reaction and punishment to her immoral desires.

If we assume we have a *wish* to be punished for thinking bad thoughts, then punishment dreams fit well with Freud's wish fulfillment theory. Common accidents can be viewed in a comparable way, that is, spontaneous attempts at self-punishment. For example, you do something you think wrong— say, you yell at your spouse. You then "accidentally" punish yourself by cutting your skin while shaving or nicking your finger while peeling an apple.

Could a nightmare reflect your attempt at self-punishment for a deed you merely thought about? Sounds pretty stern, then again, many of Freud's theories evolved out of the Victorian Age. While plausible for some bad dreams, the punishment theory is difficult to reconcile with all nightmares.

Another explanation is that we have a conflict over something we've done in the past. Suppose the woman with adulterous thoughts committed adultery several years ago. The memory causes her anxiety which she attempts to suppress, blocking it out of her mind. While successfully avoiding the memory while awake, the conflict bubbles up in her dreaming mind. A nightmare unfolds where she dreams of sex with a man— in a public place! Instead of enjoying the encounter she is distraught about discovery. Contrary to wishing for punishment, this woman *consciously* tried to avoid facing the issues raised by her adultery. The nightmare, however, brought the past back and renewed her anxiety.

This could be interpreted as an *unconscious* wish to be punished, in which case Freud's view would still hold. Trying to determine the conscious versus the unconscious motivations of a person is an exceedingly difficult task. We cannot absolutely refute the Freudian theory of punishment dreams, nor can we completely agree with it.

Still later in his career, Freud suggested anxiety dreams were caused by neuroses. In general, neuroses are unhealthy behaviors and patterns of thinking which people develop to deal with problems or conflicts. For example, a woman may be unable to express her anger. She represses it and becomes anxious and depressed as a result. This is called neurotic depression. Because she's developed this habit of repressing the anger, she never learns how to deal with it and can expect anxiety and depression to return on a regular basis.

The same anxiety and depression produced by her neuroses could cause anxiety dreams which would then fit Freud's belief that "anxiety in dreams is an anxiety problem and not a dream-problem." Since the basis of a neurosis, according to Freud, was often a result of a sexual conflict, the basis of the dream could be sexual as well.

This idea was carried to the extreme by Freud's colleague and future biographer, Ernest Jones, another psychoanalyst. In 1911, he published the first part of his famous text, *On the Nightmare*. Jones focused on the old definition for nightmare, that is, incubus attack. According to Jones, a nightmare included three characteristics: an agonizing dread; a sense of oppression or weight on the chest which interfered with breathing; and a helpless paralysis. This sounds a lot like sleep paralysis, so Jones probably was basing his theories on more than just typical REM nightmares. Even so, his ideas are very intriguing.

Jones insisted nightmares were *always* caused by an unconscious sexual conflict relating to an incestuous desire. If we return briefly to the ideas behind the incubus attack, we can see how Jones' ideas took shape. These supernatural entities such as monsters or demons wanted sex from their dreaming victims. The incubus or male demon visited women. Likewise, a *succubus*—derived from Latin *succabare*, to lie under—the female demon, visited men in their sleep.

Down through the ages many people have reported incubus and succubus attacks. Sandra Shulman's book, *Nightmare: The World of Terrifying Dreams*, details several incidents involving incubi. One story recounts a fellow who had a forty-year romance with his succubus and allegedly preferred prison to renouncing her. Another man, who ran a brothel filled with succubi, was condemned to death in Bologna in 1468. Then there was the story of the 15th century bishop who claimed an incubus had taken on the appearance of the bishop himself while accosting nuns in bed.

For many people with traditional standards of sexuality—perhaps the majority in our society—an incubus or succubus attack could represent a horrifying encounter. In fact, the sexual repression of the Victorian Age was probably at the heart of Ernest Jones' theories. His ideas were complicated—some would say, convoluted—but in essence he attached to these demons specific sexual attributes which correspond to our growth patterns as children.

For example, if you had a nightmare about a werewolf biting you, Jones felt this was connected to the sexual sadistic stage in your early childhood where you learn to bite. This would also be incestuous because biting is linked to early breastfeeding experiences.

According to Jones, the nightmare of the werewolf unfolds through *projected repressed impulses*. Both psychological terms *projection* and *repression* refer to *defense mechanisms* which are mental ways in which you defend yourself against unwanted *thoughts* and *emotions*. As an infant, you learn biting hurts other people. You learn this by responding to another person's pain or you learn it by getting spanked. Either way, you *repress* the desire to bite because you discover it is unacceptable behavior.

As an adult you still have the desire to bite, but you repress this oral need or perhaps find another outlet, healthy or otherwise, like smoking cigarettes or sucking on lollipops or singing opera. *Repression* prevents you from renewing the infantile biting behavior which would cause you considerable anxiety and problems in your relations with others. By keeping your jaws shut, you have *defended* yourself against the conflicts inherent in biting behavior.

While you're chewing this over, let's move on to *projection*. Here, you unconsciously take your own impulses or emotions—usually unpleasant ones, such as anger—and project them onto another individual. If you are an angry person, yet you can't deal with your rage, you might point your finger at a friend or colleague or perhaps someone you don't even know, then accuse that person of having too much anger. Why would you do this? Again the answer is to *defend* yourself from having to deal with the issues and conflicts underlying your own anger.

You might use other *defense mechanisms* besides projection to avoid dealing with anger. Suppose you're angry and frustrated because you're unattached and not sexually satisfied. You could *displace* these feelings by hitting golf balls. Or, you could *sublimate* the feelings by writing romantic short stories. Or, you could *humor* yourself by cracking jokes about your sexual frustration. These three defenses are more socially acceptable and relatively healthy because they would help you adapt to a frustrating situation. Projection is usually not healthy because it is an attempt to deny the problem. It is a type of *denial*—the ultimate defense which leads you to believe no problem or conflict exists.

Now let's see how Jones' theory relates to these defenses. The werewolf is the *projection* of our *repressed* incestuous and sadistic biting impulses. As an adult you can expect to harbor certain repressed feelings about your sexuality. With some oversimplification, we might suggest that if you had not integrated your oral-sadistic phase—biting behavior—in a healthy manner, you might have nightmares about werewolves or other animals nipping at you.

According to Jones, such figures as demons, witches, vampires, and the devil were all creations from our minds—notably our dreaming minds. They represent our repressed feelings towards sex and incest. These creatures symbolize various forms of incest as well as infantile sexual impulses such as sucking, biting, defecating, and urinating. While this might seem farfetched to many people, Jones surveyed a wealth of human experience, history, and literature to prove his point.

He was an inveterate scholar and discovered an incredible overlap in the folklore behind fairy tales and superstitions in various societies and civilizations. For him, it was too much of a coincidence that so many of these tales described similar types of repressed and projected impulses.

Jones recognized as well that much of this went beyond mere fairy tale as he pointed to the gruesome events of the witch trials in the seventeenth and eighteenth centuries in Europe and America. Nowadays, we need look no further than our movie theaters to see how consistently successful horror and monster movies have become in this society. Our culture has progressed so much we can now spend five or six dollars to watch our worst nightmares on a giant silver screen!

We accept some of Jones' ideas, especially the historical point of sexual repression at the turn of the century. Jones' scholarly work provides an explanation for some nightmares. We would, however, like to offer an additional viewpoint that might also explain Jones' observations. Namely, child abuse in the form of sexual abuse could cause many of the same findings. We wonder if Jones was witnessing the incestuous desires of the parent—not the child—directed at the child.

A child's memory of these very real incestuous attacks could easily be transfigured into horrible images and monsters in the night. Considering that an open discussion about child abuse has only occurred in the last ten to twenty years in our society, it's possible that child abuse was overlooked as a cause of nightmares in earlier times. We speculate on this because several of our patients have described childhood sexual abuse prior to the start of their nightmares.

There is considerable truth to the theories of Freud and Jones. However, most psychologists and psychiatrists today would not consider purely sexual themes as the underlying basis of all nightmares.

CURRENT VIEWS:
THE NEW BIOLOGY OF DREAMING

While there have been many other dream investigators in the 20th century, including Carl Jung, Alfred Adler, Calvin Hall, and Fritz Perls, to name a few, rarely do they spend much time discussing nightmares in their writings. They talk about anxiety in dreams and conflicts which arise within these dreams, but they do not focus on nightmares as a distinct process.

There was not much new on dream research until the breakthroughs in the early 1950s when REM was discovered. When it was apparent that nightmares occurred during the REM phase of sleep like other dreams, research on anxiety dreams became more extensive, although so-called normal dreaming has continued to receive more attention.

One of the most intriguing speculations came in 1977. Hobson and McCarley published a controversial paper titled,

"The Brain as Dream State Generator: An Activation Synthesis Hypothesis of the Dream Process." Or: What causes us to dream? The article was published in the *American Journal of Psychiatry* and generated huge controversies in the fields of psychology and psychiatry. More letters to the editor were written about their article than for any other previously published in that journal.

The paper outlined new ideas on the workings of the central nervous system, suggesting that dreams may be generated by a primitive part of the brain called the *brain stem*. If you peered through a skull with x-ray vision, you could see the brain stem inside the lower portion of the skull, connecting the largest part of our brain above—the cerebral cortex—with the beginning of the spinal cord below.

Hobson and McCarley pinpointed an area in the brain stem called the *pons*. The pons generates impulses which act as a pacemaker for the REM state. Since modern neurophysiology presumes the pons does *not* generate thoughts or emotions, this pontine theory contrasts sharply with Freud's ideas. Instead of thoughts and feelings from our highest centers in the brain— the cerebral cortex—inducing our dreams, there is some other instigator, perhaps an automatic signal from the pons. Such a signal from the brain stem would not conduct conscious or unconscious wishes, and therefore would negate Freud's theory.

Their research views dreaming as a three-step sequence. First, the brain activates the process of dreaming through biochemical and neurophysiological pathways which somehow trigger REM cycles. Second, once REM is begun, information must be gathered to create the dream images. And third, we respond to our dreams, either during the dream itself or after awakening. Hobson and McCarley's original article addresses the first two phases of this dream process. Their work did not focus on our responses to the dream.

The first step of activation begins in the pons. About the size of a walnut, the pons sits below the cerebral cortex roughly at eye level. It affects many nervous system functions, including eye movements, balance and orientation, muscle tone, sensation, and muscle movement on the face and hearing. In dreaming, the pons serves a pivotal role. When the brain's internal clock registers that it's time for REM, a signal activates the pons and a series of events unfold in four areas of the brain.

First, all the nerves beneath the brain stem in the spinal cord are inhibited; that is, a message temporarily blocks or cuts off the spinal reflexes. In effect, our muscle tone is gone—we are paralyzed.

Second, the oculomotor region which contains nerves controlling eye muscle movement is activated. The eyes respond by moving back and forth rapidly in the characteristic motion called Rapid Eye Movement.

Third, that part of the brain receiving input from sensory organs in our body, such as from the skin or ears, is inhibited. In other words, our normal responses to noise or touch or other stimuli from the external world are reduced. This makes it more difficult to be awakened while dreaming.

Fourth, the cerebral cortex is engaged to produce a dream story from a variety of information.

What kind of information?

Unfortunately, we don't know. It is as if the pons were an activating system sending out random and periodic electrical impulses. Somehow the cerebral cortex converts these signals into new thoughts or images. As these new thoughts and images are exposed to older memories and thoughts stored in the higher brain, the material is compared and assimilated. Eventually, from both the old and new material, dreams are created.

When dream scenes shift rapidly, as they often do, the pons may be sending out a new batch of signals. Furthermore, dream images may be bizarre and chaotic because of the randomness of these signals. After receiving a series of random signals, the cerebral cortex must weave the chaos together. Perhaps this is why dreams also appear symbolic or metaphorical.

Some people have interpreted the pontine brain stem hypothesis as *mechanistic*—a theory that all things in the universe will ultimately be explained through our understanding of sciences such as physics and chemistry. This suggests that dreams carry no special meaning; rather, they are random neurochemically mediated events.

In fact, dreams can be produced with specific neurotransmitters—the chemicals that make our brain cells function. One neurochemical—acetylcholine—is thought to play the major role in initiating REM. Injecting animals or humans with a substance which acts like acetylcholine can induce a longer

REM period. Also, when humans are exposed to insecticides containing acetylcholine-type chemicals, they can suffer a toxic side effect of paroxysms of dreaming.

Conversely, the neurotransmitters norepinephrine and serotonin may act as inhibitors of dreaming or may somehow turn off the dream process. Antidepressant medicines probably suppress dreams by their actions on these inhibiting neurotransmitters.

Still, we don't think this proves all dreams are based on "meaningless" neurochemical interactions. We believe all mental activity has a neurochemical component; yet, we wouldn't suggest all thought is meaningless. Furthermore, we're not convinced of the so-called randomness of dream activity. We'll be discussing our view on the meaning of nightmares in the next chapter. We hold a combining view that dreams are neurochemically produced and they also possess meaning. Incidentally, Hobson has since revised his own theories to incorporate the deeper psychological significance of dreams.

In the future it's likely Hobson and McCarley's landmark work on the brain stem will lead the way to understanding *how* we dream; however, no one has answered the more perplexing question of *why* we dream at all.

BRIAN'S TRIP TO THE SLAMMER

To illustrate the newer biologic view towards dreaming and to recapitulate the various causes we've discussed earlier, let's look at an example of one man's dream.

Brian, a paramedic in his thirties, had a nightmare after watching a movie. "I am being carted off to prison for a crime. I'm to go to jail in Guadalajara and I don't have any chance for a minimum security jail. No one's listening to my plea about being a paramedic . . . that I could work in the medical field while in jail. I'm afraid of being raped in prison and that I'm not going to make it out alive. My crime is a felony, but I don't know what. The whole thing scares the crap out of me.

"I make a phone call to a woman—my ex-girlfriend—and find her insensitive about my going to prison. I have to hang up on her. I think about how I didn't get a good lawyer for the trial and that there was no plea bargaining. I'm frustrated. I still don't know the crime I've committed. As I wake up I give praise to God this is just a dream and that I'm not going to jail."

Earlier that day Brian had seen *Tango and Cash*, a movie with Sylvester Stallone and Kurt Russell. They're good cops who get framed and end up in jail. They plea-bargain so they can do a little time in minimum security, but the bad guys kidnap them and haul them off to a hard-core jail with all of the criminals they had previously arrested and put away over the years. They fear for their lives.

These are Brian's initial thoughts about his nightmare. "I guess the movie had more impact on me than I thought. I really felt like I was going to prison. It wasn't until the end when I woke up, that I realized I was dreaming." For Brian, this would be the end of his search for a cause. He views the world mechanistically. As far as he's concerned, the events of the movie he watched while awake had a strong impact upon him, thereby creating the nightmare in his sleep.

We would ask, however, what caused Brian to have this *particular* nightmare?

Neurochemically speaking, let's look at the REM phase of sleep. The dream is initiated through the pons which in turn would send all its signals to the other parts of the brain. These impulses trigger old and new information to be evaluated by the brain for use in the dream.

So what new information might be available? Brian recalled he recently thought about a trip to Mexico. He considered a number of resort areas, including Guadalajara. He intended to go without his current girlfriend. He claimed he needed a break from everything; his girlfriend felt he was breaking away from their relationship. At first glance we have some idea of the residues floating around in Brian's mind which provided the major images of the nightmare.

Upon further exploration of the dream's story, however, Brian admitted to a fear of losing his freedom, particularly concerning his view toward women. The particular woman in the dream was not his current girlfriend. This other woman had been a previous girlfriend who had desired a closer relationship than Brian was willing to consider. As he reflected on his need for freedom, he realized he also felt an obligation to be married and have children. He admitted to a sense of guilt for not having fulfilled this responsibility. He suddenly realized he had committed a crime—the crime of omission, that is, *not* getting married—for which he was being punished.

So at this juncture we can point to several causes of Brian's nightmare. Through neurochemical transmission, his memories of the recent past were turned into a bad dream. So it was merely a chemical reaction in his brain, right?

Or, could we say Brian had an unconscious wish to punish himself for not fulfilling his obligation as a family man?

Or, might Brian's conflict over intimate relationships with women be the source of the nightmare? By suppressing his feelings during the day, a significant conflict surfaced in his dreams.

Along these same lines, could we speculate that the anxiety Brian felt in his nightmare is really an anxiety problem—not a dream problem—stemming from conflicts in Brian's personality?

Lastly, could the sexual impulses conveyed in his fear of rape and his fear of entanglement in a relationship have caused the nightmare?

There is one more possibility. We neglected to mention that Brian ate bean and cheese tacos with guacamole for dinner that night.

Is one of these theories more correct than the others?

Each clearly has some validity. Our view is to look at the conflicts in the dream. In Brian's dream story, the conflicts about relationships and loss of personal freedom are clear, especially since we've looked further into his background. He is an independent person who's obsessed with his freedom. He's never been married and though he has an active social life, he often breaks off his relationships with women because he claims they want to tie him down.

In our view, Brian's nightmare could have been caused by his fear of losing his independence. The feeling of being trapped or imprisoned could easily have run through Brian's mind as he watched the movie; then his unconscious simply found the perfect vehicle to highlight this conflict to him during his sleep.

Incorporating events from the day into the night's dreams is a common occurrence in dreaming. A significant percentage of your dream images will be drawn from your daily activities and thoughts. Freud called this *day residues*. This raises the question of whether or not Brian would have had a prison dream if he had not seen the movie. He may not have, but he still might have had a dream where he felt trapped.

Let's pretend that earlier in the day Brian left his keys in his car only to discover them later. When finding the keys in his unlocked car he might have had a passing thought: "I'm glad I didn't lock the keys in the car." Later that night he could have dreamed he was locked inside his car unable to open the doors. Perhaps in this version his old girlfriend sits in the next seat, unperturbed by being trapped in the vehicle as Brian anxiously searches for a way out.

Brian might have attributed this anxiety dream to his fear of being "locked" into something. We would point to the same underlying conflict—his fear of losing his freedom—as the basis for the nightmare. The events during the day simply provided the material to work with—be it a movie or leaving keys in a car.

Many nightmares will not offer such easy explanations. You may have to work longer to find the meaning in the symbols and action portrayed in your dreams. The content of the dream will obviously come from a variety of old and new inputs received into your brain. These include factors such as genetic material, cultural and social influences, belief systems, religious views, psychosexual development, traumatic events, sexual abuse, defense mechanisms, and emotional conflicts, to name a few.

All this information will be considered in light of your current life situation and your past experiences. We don't know how these factors are represented in the brain, but we do know they can have a large impact on the third step in dreaming—your emotional response. Unfortunately, our scientific knowledge about this response is incomplete. All we can say is the obvious—while the images are created in the visual cortex of the brain, the emotion-generating parts of the brain respond to the images.

The emotional response, though, varies for different reasons. Some of us are genetically predisposed to be more reactive. Others may have greater sensitivity to sensory input and will produce more intense images in their brains. This may lead to more intense reactions. In some cases, you may suffer an intense response to a traumatic event—an accident, assault, natural disaster, or war-related event. The traumatic episode may impact so heavily upon your nervous system that a small stimulus reproduces the whole response again. This can occur during sleep as nightmares and during wakefulness as the experience called *flashbacks*.

Traumatic nightmares highlight the difficulties in trying to find exact causes of bad dreams. On the one hand, we have the situation where an obvious event precedes the onset of the nightmares. Yet, not everyone who suffers trauma will develop bad dreams. Exploring traumatic nightmares yields some surprising insights into the causes of any nightmare.

TRAUMATIC NIGHTMARES

John is married—at least he comes home to his wife. Twenty years ago things were different. He returned from Vietnam and promptly wed, then he and his wife had two kids, born one year apart. He managed fairly well with the usual work pressures, but he would be jumpy occasionally with haunting memories of Vietnam. Overall, though, there was enough positive in his life to keep out most of those intrusive flashbacks.

Several years later his world deteriorated. It had been going downhill for some time, and it's difficult to determine which problems developed first. Did his wife become independent through a healthy maturing, or did John push her away with his own isolation? Was there really no longer a challenge to his job, or had he become alienated to most things in his life, including work? Were his kids going through adolescent rebellion, or had they become hostile by his lack of affection?

John's posttraumatic stress disorder (abbreviated PTSD) had reared its ugly head. Depression, anxiety, insomnia, and nightmares were now common occurrences. He lay awake at night not wanting to sleep. One particular nightmare kept recurring. "Someone is coming through the door. I reach for my gun. It's empty and I awake in a panic." The king-size bed kept his wife safe from his flailing arms, but John began calling out again as a more grisly nightmare recurred, too—the one where he shoots a boy running at him with a grenade. The young boy falls and the grenade explodes, mutilating his body. John sees all too clearly the horror-stricken face of the boy.

When John returned from Vietnam, he deluded himself into thinking he didn't need treatment. He'd gone through many gruesome events during the war and he felt putting everything behind him was the best medicine. When John finally received treatment for PTSD fifteen years after the war, he did very well. But he had to start down a painful path by reliving many of his experiences which brought him back in touch with all his feelings—the good ones, too. As John got better, his nightmares went away.

John's story shows how people often go through a cycle with PTSD. First, they try to ignore or deny the problem, then they try to live with it as they go to pieces. Unfortunately, everyone doesn't do well in treatment. Many people suffer alcoholism, drug addiction, joblessness, depression, and suicide. The treatment is too painful for some people. And many don't make it through treatment or even to treatment.

The posttraumatic stress disorder may begin with posttraumatic nightmares which can occur directly after the event. Often, however, there is a time lag before the victim seeks help. According to at least one researcher, Ernest Hartmann—one of the world's leading experts on nightmares—this is unfortunate, because the nightmares may respond to brief psychotherapy which might prevent the full-blown disorder. Though this approach remains unproven, Hartmann noted several cases where just talking about what happened over and over again seemed to prevent a more serious disorder.

Reviewing the trauma may be therapeutic because PTSD develops through a deadening of the emotions. Patients who develop the full-blown disorder know that emotional triggers set off flashbacks and disturbing memories. Unconsciously or otherwise, sufferers avoid people, places, and things which trigger these extreme responses. Over time, their emotional responses become so diminished, they may be incapable of expressing warmth or love for their family and friends.

When we hear about the specific traumatic or series of traumatic events suffered by patients, we might assume this is the reason they have developed the symptoms, including recurrent nightmares. While it's clear that trauma precedes the problem, many researchers speculate that the traumatic event catalyzes something festering within the victim. In other words, some people who develop PTSD are setups for the problem, with the trauma serving as a catalyst.

This theory is very useful for understanding how people develop nightmares. Could some nightmare sufferers be setups waiting for the "wrong" button to be pushed? One study examined threatening external stimuli in the form of movies as a cause of nightmares. In this study, young men were monitored for changes in their heart and breathing rates as they watched a film about primitive cultural practices of circumcision.

Some men showed increases in their vital signs, suggesting the movie images aroused anxiety or fear, while others were unperturbed. The ones who felt anxiety *during* the movie had more nightmares on subsequent nights. So does this mean that those emotionally affected had nightmares because ritual circumcision simply scared them? Or, could these young men have deep-seated conflicts about their male image which manifested as nightmares once exposed to the stimuli of circumcision? Then again, would a different movie—perhaps one about a serial killer—invoke nightmares in another group of men?

Traumatic nightmares have been well described by Hartmann in his book, *The Nightmare: The Psychology and Biology of Terrifying Dreams*. He details a variety of cases which begin with bad dreams and deteriorate to the posttraumatic stress disorder. In this process, an event occurs—an accident, a death, a fire, an illness or some other traumatic experience to the individual. Then, the person "replays" the event in his dreams.

Hartmann notes that victims' dreams may be very different than ordinary dreams. Sometimes they take on a memorylike quality as if the person is reliving the episode and not just dreaming about it. And sometimes one significant detail will be altered from the real-life event, changing the dream into something more nightmarish.

Hartmann studied two groups of Vietnam veterans, both of whom encountered the severe stress of heavy combat. One group developed posttraumatic nightmares and the other group never had any nightmares.

What was the difference?

There were two consistent findings. The nightmare sufferers had been a bit younger and, probably because of their age, they developed closer, perhaps adolescent, buddy relationships in Vietnam. Nearly every one of the young men who went on to suffer nightmares had suffered the loss of one of his buddies. The other group was, on average, a few years older, and they consciously avoided falling into the trap of forming close relationships with anybody during the war because they knew this could end in disaster.

How might losing a close friend in combat go on to produce nightmares? There have been many psychological theories suggested. At the root of these theories is a belief that the individual is vulnerable to the problem before the trauma.

Vulnerability is an important consideration when we try to understand disease. Do drugs turn people into addicts, or does their low self-esteem prior to using drugs steer them toward drugs? Does alcohol turn people into alcoholics, or are these individuals so biologically vulnerable that once they start drinking they are doomed to become alcoholics? Research suggests if you are genetically vulnerable to alcohol, it will act on you like a disease for which the only treatment is abstinence.

What might be the vulnerability of young soldiers passing through their adolescence under the ravages of war? Most likely, it is a problem of identity formation. This is the age in which you struggle with big questions about who you really are. You look around at other people, comparing yourself, and trying to find your identity. Sometimes you compare yourself to your father or mother, or your brothers and sisters. You'll see many similarities and differences which will help you to know yourself better.

When you make best friends during this period in your life, you often bond with people who mirror some of your own traits. This can be a way of reinforcing your identity. A problem can arise beyond the normal grief experience, however, when you lose a close friend. You've invested so much conscious and unconscious energy in identifying with the other individual that if you were to lose that person, you feel as if you've lost a part of yourself—a very big part of yourself.

Ultimately, we all experience death and losses throughout our lives, but in late adolescence and early adulthood where our identity is struggling to emerge, it is more difficult to adjust, because we experience the loss *too* personally. That is, when our best friend dies we may become confused to the point of believing we have "died" with the person.

This shows up clearly in nightmares. Hartmann describes two classic cases among veterans who had lost their best buddies in war. One man dreamed of having to go to the mortuary to identify dead bodies. "I identify a couple of guys and in my nightmare then—I identify myself! . . . I start to run and can't stop running until I wake up . . ."

Another man's dream details the events of his buddy's death. The soldier had escaped while his friend was killed in a tent. "When the shooting is over, I go to my tent. . . . There is a body in my bunk with a big bloody gaping hole in his chest. I try to see who it is, but I always wake up before I can see his face. I wonder, 'Is it me or my buddy?' "

In Freud's later years he spoke about nightmares as an attempt to gain control over the horrible events of the past. Individuals relive the traumatic experiences in their dreams so they can master the anxiety initiated by the real-life episode. Another psychological theory that fits well with those who lose a close friend in war is the phenomenon known as survivor guilt. Survivors wonder why they were spared and their friends or family members died. This was reported frequently in victims who survived concentration camps.

War and war-related activities are not the only causes of PTSD. Abused children as well as accident victims develop the same symptoms as well. Eileen, a housewife and mother of three kids, went through the windshield of her car during a Christmas-season accident. She woke up in the hospital two days later with cuts on her face and a brain contusion. Plastic surgery and her body's ability to heal left a small scar. But the mental scar from trauma was larger and, to aggravate things, she suffered headaches every day.

The nightmares of seeing the other car and the deafening crash left her exhausted when she awakened in the middle of the night. She tried to block out the memories, but the headaches were constant reminders. Eventually, she was treated with hypnosis to recall as much as she could about the crash. This reliving of the trauma helped put it behind her. She also used hypnosis along with medications to control the pain. Over the next three months the nightmares subsided.

In Eileen's case, her nightmares were virtually identical to the actual trauma. Other victims will awaken with a completely blank memory—a so-called white nightmare. They know they've been dreaming and awaken in panic, but have no recall of the events in the dream. This may be the psyche's attempt to blot out all memories of the trauma. Some studies show dreaming is reduced just after severe trauma, that is, there is less REM time. When REM returns, however, the person suffers a rebound effect with a greater preponderance of nightmares accompanying her normal dreams.

Is it possible that nightmares surfacing directly after a traumatic event represent a healthy way for the mind to integrate the events? Rhonda, a recent dental school graduate, got the bad news about her pregnancy far too late to consider abortion. The tests showed a baby that could not survive because of an uncorrectable abnormality of the brain. Still, the fetus's heart was pumping, and Rhonda would have to wait eight more weeks to deliver.

The infant died two days after birth and Rhonda started having nightmares a week later. They often focused on one thing—her other child. He is a four-year-old healthy boy, but in her nightmares he was always about to die in some horrible tragedy. Another catastrophe assaulted Rhonda two weeks after the death of her infant when her husband died in a car accident. Her nightmares continued for several months.

Rhonda is an intelligent and strong woman, but she needed help. Sensibly, she started psychotherapy to talk about her grief and losses. She still suffers from depression and insomnia and has remained in counseling as should be expected for someone who has lived through such mortal blows. But after six months her nightmares went away.

We are left with the question of why. What is there about Rhonda's psychological makeup that may have enabled her to use the nightmares temporarily to integrate the deadly assaults she'd suffered? And what other aspects of her mind enabled the nightmares to stop when they no longer served a purpose?

Very tough questions. We wish we could provide definitive answers. We can't. Many people suffer traumatic nightmares who don't go on to suffer the full-blown PTSD syndrome, just as many people who suffer trauma never develop nightmares.

We'll be looking more at individuals who've had chronic nightmares for long periods of time—some literally for decades. And we'll reexplore the issue of psychological vulnerability as it relates to these chronic sufferers. Now we'll look at one last but relatively clear-cut cause for nightmares—drugs.

MEDICATION- AND DRUG-INDUCED NIGHTMARES

Jordan is a twenty-nine-year-old sales manager. He makes good money at his job because he's compulsive, putting in long hours to serve his clients. Jordan's compulsiveness, though, has not always been to his benefit. He has a big sweet tooth and could often gobble up mounds of candy bars and other treats in the course of his long business days. It finally caught up with him, turning his sweet tooth into an aching one.

Eventually, abscesses set in and several root canals were required to save his teeth. If you've ever had a root canal or other dental work, you know the pain can be intense. Because of a vast network of nerves, the face and mouth are one of the more sensitive areas of the human body. That's nice for kissing, but not for digging up your teeth. Jordan became addicted to a narcotic painkiller in his futile attempt to control the pain. Shortly thereafter, Jordan's dreams changed dramatically.

"I am inside a box. It's a coffin. I am screaming at the top of my lungs and cannot move a muscle. I am surprised no one hears me because I know I'm screaming wildly and loudly. Suddenly, my friends appear by the side of the box. I'm glad to see them, but they start laughing. They have ropes in their hands and tie them around the box so tight it's cutting off my breathing. I'm suffocating and I can't scream anymore.

"My family shows up. I'm glad to see them, but they won't do anything to get me out of the box or undo the ropes. Another man who I don't recognize comes along with a machine gun. He points it directly into my chest and starts firing. I don't feel any pain but I know I'm dying. My family and my friends all apologize to me. They keep saying they're sorry to me. Just before I die I wake up."

Suppose we told you Jordan's dreadful nightmares went away as soon as he stopped taking narcotics. Would you assume the drugs caused the bad dreams? Or does Jordan have underlying conflicts which the painkillers somehow unmasked in his sleep? We don't have the answer. We know from talking with Jordan that he has a fear of death. He served in the army and experienced some difficult times.

When he developed the problem with his teeth, he had conflicts with his close friends and family. However, when he quit using the painkillers, the nightmares stopped, although his conflicts and fears continued until he went into therapy.

This example highlights the theory that some people may be more prone to nightmares. Two people may have the same underlying problem and yet only one of them has nightmares. Perhaps this is what occurs in drug-induced nightmares. We can't be sure, although drug-induced nightmares are fairly common. In our appendix, we've listed 30 medications that have the side effect of nightmares.

The types of drugs causing nightmares cover a range of health problems. Medicines used in the treatment of high blood pressure, Parkinsonism, depression, pain, insomnia, cardiac chest pain, and even the common cold have been known to cause bad dreams. Ironically, some drugs that work effectively in the treatment of anxiety and psychotic behavior may also produce bad dreams.

We've worked with one patient whose nightmares took the form of vivid hallucinations induced by anti-Parkinsonism medication. He often envisioned his own family members. The visions were so real that the only way he could sort them out was to wrap his arms around them and attempt to lift them up. If he could lift them, then they were the visions, because in real life he knew he was too weak to lift anybody. In this particular case, altering the medication was not effective, probably because many anti-Parkinsonism medications are known to cause nightmares.

With other drugs, altering the way you take the medicine or simply changing to another medicine may work. This is an approach to consider with drugs called beta blockers. These common drugs are used for a variety of heart conditions, including high blood pressure and angina. One study has shown that nearly 80 percent of people suffer bad dreams when they use beta blockers. Fortunately, there are many types of beta blockers. And because of their effectiveness, pharmaceutical manufacturers are attempting to synthesize new types. Having your doctor prescribe a different beta blocker may ease the problem of bad dreams.

Withdrawal from drugs is another cause of nightmares. This is common with alcohol, tranquilizers, and tricyclic antidepressants. The alcohol or medications alter the sleep cycle, markedly *reducing* the amount of REM sleep. When the drug is withdrawn, the body attempts to return to its natural sleep cycle; however, in readjusting, the body tries to catch up on the lost REM. This is called *REM rebound* and may require a physician's care. For people with addictions to alcohol or tranquilizers, medical consultation is often required to help ease the withdrawal symptoms, including the predictably terrifying dreams.

For those wanting to stop antidepressants, the most important consideration is how effective the drug has been in treating the depression. Obviously, if the side effects are too severe, the medication must be stopped or substituted, but when discontinuing antidepressants, the patient should be prepared for more nightmares.

Illicit drugs are also known to induce nightmares, sometimes through direct use as well as withdrawal. Marijuana, narcotics, amphetamines, and cocaine can cause bad dreams. Again, a physician's guidance may be critical to a successful withdrawal from the offending agent.

Many of the drugs that cause nightmares require a doctor's prescription and therefore should serve an important function. In some cases the side effect of nightmares may have to be tolerated. You should consult with your physician before changing or discontinuing any medications.

DOES CAUSE EQUAL MEANING?

We've discussed obvious causes of nightmares, including drugs and trauma. And we've reviewed ideas pertaining to biological and psychological causes. In many cases we may never find the exact cause of a bad dream. However, expanding on the theory of conflict as the cause, we can often clarify the *meaning* of the bad dream. This meaning as an expression of a conflict may have "caused" the nightmare. In reality, it's difficult to separate the cause from the meaning of your bad dreams. In many cases, the cause and the meaning are one and the same.

Usually, the meaning will convey something about an unresolved emotional conflict. The conflict may go back to your childhood, or it may be a current problem in your life. Because of the nature of the dreaming process, any conflict brought out in the nightmare is likely to encompass both the old and the new—the conflict from childhood as well as the current one.

For years Jack has been troubled by his relationship with his mother, so much so he resigned himself to putting it out of his mind. Even up to the point of his mother's death, she could not stop treating him as the youngest child in the family—the baby son. Jack married a few years after his mom's death and quickly found himself in a similar situation with his wife. She was more domineering and demanding than he'd thought, and much of her nagging reminded him of his relationship with his mother.

Jack developed anxiety dreams in the third year of his marriage. Here's a typical one: "I am camping by myself in a beautiful meadow. The stars are out and the air is crisp and clean. I feel very much at peace until I discover I'm not alone. On a hill above my campsite I see a large cow. This annoys me for some reason—I think because she has disturbed my privacy. But I resolve to go to sleep. I am charmed by a few birds singing in the distance. I hear the wind rustling through the tree branches, then I drift off.

"I wake up to a terrible bellowing noise—the cow is mooing. I try ducking my head into the sleeping bag, but the noise gets louder. I crane my neck outside the tent and see the cow coming towards me, mooing all the time. I'm exhausted, too tired to move my tent, so I resolve to wait it out. Now I stuff clothes and blankets over my head, but none of this works as the mooing gets louder. Finally I roll over in frustration—the noise is unbearable. At that moment I bump against my wife in bed next to me. She wakes up, then I wake up and realize I've been dreaming."

Jack had little difficulty associating the cow's mooing with his wife's nagging. He also recognized his own denial of the problem in his vain attempts to get back to sleep in the dream. But a closer examination of the dream revealed some additional content. In visualizing the dream, Jack recalled the oddly painted cow's hoofs—a garish lavender color. His association to this color was immediate. As a child he remembered his mother dressing up for a party, using brightly colored polish on her fingernails.

In this dream, Jack experienced the similar conflict he had

initially with his mother and then with his wife. The basis of Jack's nightmares, then, was this continuing conflict in his relationships with his wife and deceased mother. Can we say this caused the anxiety dream? Not exactly, because we know that every person who has a conflict with his or her mother or spouse will *not* express these conflicts through nightmares.

This returns us to the question of why some people experience nightmares as a way of processing information about themselves. Is it that their conflicts surface in their sleep because their normal defensive barriers may not function as well to keep them repressed? It's frustrating that no one has a definitive answer to this question. We are left with the notion that some people are more prone to nightmares and that their bad dreams often reflect conscious and unconscious concerns or stress about important emotional conflicts in their lives.

While looking for causes is interesting and insightful, we must realize that our present level of knowledge does not provide all the answers we'd like. If, instead, we turn our attention to looking at the meaning of our nightmares, we may discover a more fruitful way of looking at bad dreams.

CHAPTER 4

The Meaning of Nightmares and Bad Dreams

WHAT DO *YOU* THINK YOUR NIGHTMARES MEAN?

When people hear we are studying nightmares, they often tell us one of their bad dreams. Then they ask, "What does it mean?" No sooner have they asked the question than they answer it themselves with another question: "Does it mean I'm crazy?" Or, "Does it mean I'm going to get sick?" Or, "Does it mean I ate the wrong food?"

People have different expectations about what their nightmares reveal. Tom dreams he's walking out of a bar. A huge biker takes a swing at him, belting him in the stomach. Tom awakens doubled up in pain. He'd been to a restaurant that night and was suffering a minor bout of food poisoning. According to Tom, the nightmare reflects his churning stomach. His unconscious sensed his physical discomfort, then incorporated the pain into the dream.

Jody has nightmares of a dog chasing her. This dream crops up whenever she's under stress. As an infant, Jody was attacked by a German shepherd. The dog bit her heavy snowsuit, frightening her without causing physical injury. Jody believes the recurring nightmare relates to this childhood experience. Now her unconscious matches up any current anxieties to those similar anxious feelings aroused years ago by the attacking dog. If she labors under stress during the day, the dream dog revisits at night.

These are straightforward examples which suggest simple meanings to the nightmares. This next one is more complex. Elizabeth believes dreams convey symbolic messages. She dreams of diving into tropical waters only to be chased by a shark. Elizabeth feels the water is a symbol for her unconscious.

To the shark, she associates her own anger and aggression.

Elizabeth thought the dream meant she was afraid of her own aggressiveness. It was easier to keep her anger repressed—underwater. This fits with Elizabeth's conscious fears. She was always frightened by her father's bad temper. When she noticed her own uncontrollable anger as a young adult, she tried to smother the feelings. Now Elizabeth rarely expresses her anger. Her nightmare suggests she's done too good a job of repression.

Let's look at one more example. Raymond, a grad student in biochemistry, thinks nightmares are caused by neurochemical reactions in the brain. Raymond had a nightmare of running for a train to escape from gangsters, but the train left the station before he could hop on. When the bad guys assaulted him, he awoke terrified. He found no personal meaning in this dream and assumed it had none. This little drama unfolded in his unconscious because of neurochemical discharges in his brain cells.

These four people—Tom, Jody, Elizabeth, and Raymond—experienced similar neurochemical discharges and they experienced similar physical and emotional responses—racing hearts and anxiety. Yet, the meaning for all four related to their personal understanding and perspective on dreams. They experience the nightmare as meaningful or not in their own particular way.

Each of these four views has validity. We would suggest you consider all these perspectives in your efforts to interpret the meaning of your own nightmares. This will prove more satisfying and insightful. Now we'll explore these viewpoints in depth by answering the questions dreamers often ask about their nightmares.

IS MY BRAIN PLAYING DIRTY TRICKS ON ME?

Raymond advocates various biochemical theories about the functioning of the brain to prove his point that dreams mean nothing at all. And he goes a step further and states that dreaming is an *outdated function*. He compares this to an appendix which serves no function in our abdomens.

The appendix is thought to be *vestigial*—a small remnant of a larger structure in the digestive system which no longer serves a function in humans other than to land us in the hospital with a life-threatening surgical emergency!

Could dreaming be a vestigial process?

Let's reconsider Tom's food-poisoning dream where he's slugged in the belly. If dreams are a series of biochemical interactions, then the first step in producing Tom's dream story is to process at least two pieces of information. First, he feels sick to his stomach from the food he's eaten earlier. Next, on TV that evening, perhaps he watched a crime story showing a mugging. Tom's unconscious then incorporated these two pieces of information into the dream.

Freud talked about how the unconscious incorporates both internal and external information. In Tom's case, the brain senses an internal stimulus—the queasy stomach—and tries to involve it in the dream so the dreamer doesn't have to awaken. This doesn't always work. Take the example of an alarm clock ringing. Though you may dream of pealing church bells, eventually you will awaken to the reality that it's time to go to work.

The external stimulus—a mugging on TV—provides another example of *day residue*. To re-illustrate, if you chopped onions for dinner, you may incorporate elements of that process into your dream that night. Your brain can select the *knife*, the *onion*, the *chopping motion*, or the *cutting board*, as well as a thousand other relatively unconscious details your mind notices. If you look close enough you will find day residues in a large number of images in your dreams.

When Tom sleeps, his brain processes the information about his stomach and the mugging. When his REM cycle begins, his unconscious puts the two items together and suddenly Tom has a nightmare about using his stomach as a punching bag. If we take this at face value, we could say the incorporation of day residues and internal stimuli produced a nightmare with no meaning whatsoever. It is an expression of random information. If we stop here in our analysis, the nightmare has no meaning.

We're not inclined to accept this point of view. We wonder why Tom's brain chose those two pieces of information to include in the dream. Out of the thousands of pieces of input, why did his unconscious select what it did? Is it a case of the squeaky wheel getting oiled—his irritating stomachache? We think not, when you consider this: The overwhelming majority of stimuli are never incorporated into your dreams and night-mares. For example, when dreamers have been touched or stimulated in some way with feathers, oil of cloves, shining lights, or even ringing bells, they usually do *not* include this input into their dreams.

Furthermore, think about the times you might have had a nagging physical symptom or illness—a headache, sore throat, stuffed-up nose, sore back, or, like Tom, severe indigestion—can you remember the last time one of these symptoms appeared in a dream, let alone caused you a nightmare? Rarely, if ever, is the answer most people tell us.

This highlights the essence of Freud's view about day residue incorporation into dreams. Regarding both the external stimuli from the day as well as the internal stimuli while sleeping, Freud strongly believed the selection of *specific stimuli* for dream material is an incredibly complex process we can barely begin to fathom in our study of human psychology.

In our view, the perspective that dreaming is an outdated biological function lacks substantial evidence. To the contrary, it raises the much larger question of why do we dream at all? And why do so many animals, notably mammals, experience REM sleep and, presumably, dreaming? Based on evolution, we can safely assume dreaming has occurred for millions of years—perhaps up to two hundred million years.

How do we know this? The REM cycle has been demon-strated in a wide range of animals—goats, sheep, cats, monkeys, rats, rabbits, and opossums. Much knowledge on dreaming has come from animal studies. When we watch cats "chasing mice" in their sleep this occurs in a REM period. Likewise, when we hear dogs whimpering in their sleep, it's possible they are experiencing a disturbing dream.

Many of these animals share common ancestors. According to evolutionary theory we would *not* expect each species to develop the REM cycle on its own; rather, the REM cycle would be present in common ancestors. Furthermore, processes that span so many species are more likely to serve adaptive and useful functions.

Considering the human appendix, a similar structure is found in a variety of species, including horses and some monkeys. In these cases, however, the structure is larger and serves as an aid to efficient digestion, while in man the appendix is thought to no longer aid digestion. Regarding dreaming, then, it would be most unusual for all these different species to possess this function in their brains and for it to be vestigial in every one of them, especially after millions of years of natural selection.

Furthermore, why do newborn human infants as well as newborns in other species have REM periods lasting 50 percent of their sleep time or longer? Something important seems to be occurring. Perhaps REM processes valuable information about the environment and about self. Or, it may involve another activity essential to brain development. In fact, babies in the uterus demonstrate the REM state as early as the 27th week of pregnancy. And, it is several months after birth before the percentage of REM drops.

Could essential genetic information be translated to the newborn through images created in dreaming? If so, could this account for the learning of valuable behavioral instincts in animals as well? Might dreaming be an integral part of all learning? Experiments have shown that people deprived of REM sleep have more difficulty learning new tasks or solving problems. Another study has demonstrated a possible link between dreaming and learning a foreign language. People studying French were asked to maintain dream diaries during the semester. Those students who dreamed the soonest *in French* after beginning the course or who had more French language content in their dreams were consistently more proficient in speaking French.

Recent studies by Pavlides and Winson have yielded considerable support for a relationship between REM sleep and memory. These two researchers studied individual neurons or nerve cells in the brain of a rat cycling through several waking and sleeping stages. They monitored two separate neurons, each coding distinct information about the rat's position or space. Specifically, each neuron mapped out a distinct, nonoverlapping position in the environment.

When the rat was exposed to one position, then the first neuron discharged vigorously, mapping the space for future reference. Because the second neuron did not code for this position, it remained virtually inactive. Next, the rat was monitored while asleep and minimal discharges were noted from either neuron. However, when the rat entered the REM phase, the first neuron fired again at a much higher rate, suggesting that the earlier waking information was now being reprocessed during REM. The second neuron remained essentially inactive during REM. This reprocessing of data during REM could represent a crucial link to understanding the brain's capacity for memory.

One footnote to this theory regards a small mammal known as the echidna—a small, spiny anteater—which is distinct for *not* incurring REM while asleep. As Winson has theorized, this mammal diverged from the evolutionary tree prior to the development of REM physiology. Therefore, instead of learning while asleep through reprocessing, the echidna evolved something different—a huge prefrontal cortex, that is, the front part of the brain.

By comparison, humans and other mammals which possess REM actually have a much smaller proportion of this front part of the brain in proportion to the total brain. So according to this theory, our human brain did not require some bold new structural design to assist in learning because it already possessed a very functional design which included the ability to undergo the REM state.

In summary, then, we think dreams and nightmares serve a purpose—several in fact; however, sorting out these various functions is not so easy.

ARE NIGHTMARES THERAPEUTIC?

Let's examine Jody's recurrent nightmares of attacking dogs. She's put together the connection between her initial attack as an infant and her recurrent bad dreams whenever she feels stressed. Jody believes the nightmares are helpful by letting her experience the stress and anxiety in a well-recognized setting. When she awakens, although clearly disturbed by the nightmare, she realizes instantly it's a dream and only a dream.

She asks the question: "What would happen if I didn't have these nightmares? Would my mind require some other way of releasing stress? Would I be more uptight and anxious during the day if I didn't release this stuff at night?"

Many people share this concern about nightmares. It is as if they were attached to their bad dreams. When we question people who hold these beliefs, it's clear they feel the nightmare serves some purpose. Most believe this is a function of the unconscious mind. They prefer to ignore their bad dreams, or, as in Jody's case, assume the nightmare has performed its stress-releasing function.

What evidence is there to support this as the real meaning of nightmares?

We mentioned Freud's later theories about traumatic nightmares; he called it the *repetition compulsion*. A person experiences a traumatic event which then repeatedly plagues his or her dreams because the mind is attempting to master the trauma. Reliving the event as a nightmare reproduces the anxiety from the trauma, and, by reliving the anxiety, the victim attempts to master it by repeating the experience over and over again. Mastering trauma through dreams supports the idea of the unconscious providing therapy for the individual.

There is a crucial question raised by this reasoning. If you abolished your nightmares, would your mental health worsen? Would you have to unleash your negative emotions in another way? For example, maybe your angry feelings would escalate or perhaps your daily anxieties would worsen. These are important and interesting questions. Surprisingly, few authorities have attempted to answer them.

In a few older reports, some researchers have noted that schizophrenics may get worse if they are deprived of dreams and nightmares. These researchers speculated that nightmares facilitate a release of anxiety at night, promoting better mental health during the day. These reports, however, were based on what in research we term anecdotal information or case reports; that is, a few observations on a few patients and not a scientifically controlled research study on many patients. In other words, the observations remain theories and are not proven.

One psychiatrist, John Mack, briefly addressed these questions in his book, *Nightmares and Human Conflict*. In one case of traumatic war neuroses, he speculates that the sufferer has recurrent nightmares to compartmentalize his anxiety and guilt. By reliving a deadly war scene in which he failed to save his buddy, the dreamer only has to suffer the experience in one short nightmare instead of feeling anxious and guilty all day. By represssing the horrible events during the day, he can function normally. This sounds similar to Freud's theory of punishment dreams as an unconscious way of absolving guilt.

At present, there is no clinical evidence to support this theory. In fact, repression might lead to worse symptoms, such as

PTSD. Moreover, we have demonstrated the opposite finding in a number of our patients. Banishing their nightmares has made them feel better and healthier. This might be from improved sleep. Or, perhaps they feel more confident in having conquered their nightmares. Or, could it be that recurrent nightmares were the sole problem these patients suffered from? That is, there were no deeper, underlying mental health conditions causing the nightmares. If so, eliminating the nightmares was the solution to the problem.

We promise to return to this discussion in our section on treating nightmares. In our research, no patients who have banished their nightmares have later complained of worse mental health. We know of many patients who have felt markedly better after putting an end to their bad dreams.

DO MY NIGHTMARES MEAN I'M CRAZY?

Simply put, no!

Many normal people have nightmares, as do a few people with serious mental disorders. Some people who develop problems such as depression, schizophrenia, or other forms of psychosis may also manifest a problem with nightmares either before or during their illnesses.

However, many patients with depression or schizophrenia never suffer from disturbing dreams or nightmares. In the psychiatric literature there are a few cases which suggest that bad dreams may herald the early stages of mental illness. And because nightmares can be so bizarre and scary, many experts have wondered about a link between nightmares and the hallucinations experienced in psychosis. Still, there has never been any systematic study to prove any correlation between them.

The first distinction you must make is how frequently you have the nightmares. If you suffer from chronic nightmares you may be more prone to symptoms such as anxiety. We'll delve more into chronic nightmare sufferers in the last chapter of this section.

If you suffer occasionally from nightmares, or if you've noticed an increased frequency of late, you might ask yourself if these disturbing dreams represent a mental health barometer. They may in fact lead you to some important insights about your feelings which in turn may indicate a need for counseling.

However, to repeat, there is no convincing evidence to suggest that a particular pattern of disturbing dreams dictates a diagnosis of serious mental illness.

NIGHTMARES AND PHYSICAL HEALTH

Sam was a great athlete in school; he made the football team in college. At six foot three and 250 pounds, he was a terrific linebacker. His aggressiveness served him well on the playing field, but twenty years later Sam's mean streak proved inappropriate. He took out his aggressions and anger on his family and he rarely exercised beyond his television armchair quarterbacking. He also stuck to his youthful diet, which now turned his inactive body into more fat than muscle. Sam was a setup for the heart attack he had at the age of forty-six.

Two months prior to his heart attack he recalled having had the following nightmare: "I am playing football in the Rose Bowl. I am chasing the ball carrier. He goes off the field and I pursue him. Suddenly, I find myself on a tennis court where a tennis match is under way. The referee starts yelling at me to get off the court. So I leave the stadium and head down a street. I glance up . . . a large truck bears down on me. There is no escape. I wake up in a panic."

Sam, who rarely remembers any of his dreams, recalled this one because it awakened him. What is the meaning of such a dream? We can't be sure without a lengthy analysis, but we can raise a question relating to this *type* of dream: Does dreaming about death signal important information about your heart?

Robert C. Smith investigated this exact relationship. Men with heart disease were evaluated to look for a connection between their dreams and the severity of their illness. Smith measured the pumping ability of the heart and discovered that the men with poorer functioning hearts had more bad dreams about death. A similar finding was noted among women heart patients who had dreams about separation or loss of a loved one. They also showed worse functioning of their hearts.

We can't say Sam could have prevented his heart attack by considering his dream. But this theory about nightmares raises the intriguing question of whether bad dreams might provide information about the risks of heart disease. There are well-recognized risks for heart attacks, including smoking, high cholesterol, and lack of exercise, to name a few. Could dream analysis provide another useful predictor in patients with known heart problems?

Some nightmares may be harmful to the heart. Another study examined the dreaming behavior of patients suffering from cardiac chest pain. The most interesting observation was that two patients developed chest pain repeatedly while dreaming. Cardiac chest pain or angina is caused by constriction of the heart's blood vessels, the coronary arteries. It is well known that stress can cause people to have angina attacks. Do anxiety dreams therefore create enough stress to produce angina episodes?

One expert has raised the possibility that nightmares could precipitate cardiac arrests. John Mack described a patient who dreamed "giants were chasing the little people and stepping on their chests." This patient had experienced a cardiac arrest and was successfully resuscitated with CPR. Shortly thereafter, he recalled the dream about the giants. However, it is impossible to know when his dream occurred—before, during, or after the cardiac arrest.

Dream content and medical illness in hospitalized patients have also been surveyed. In men, dreams referring to death, and in women, those referring to loss and separation, showed worse outcomes 6 months after they were discharged from the hospital. In this study Smith looked at a variety of illnesses including heart disease, cancer, infections, lung disease, drug abuse, seizures, and depression. So whether we are talking specifically about heart disease or ill health in general, anxiety dreams and nightmares may imply added risks, or they may predict worsening health.

Understandably, the information about dreams and sickness is likely to make some of you anxious. We hope we can set your minds at ease by stating that your personal experience with bad dreams must be evaluated on its own merits. Dreaming about death or separation from a loved one certainly does *not* mean you have heart disease or your health will deteriorate.

If, however, you have a pattern of bad dreams prior to a hospitalization, we suggest you discuss this with your doctor. Maybe the dreams are indicating you require more attention and care during your hospital stay. If so, address that issue with your physician. Likewise, if you are known to have heart disease and you regularly dream about death or separation, you may need to discuss that with your doctor. Or, maybe you need to ask yourself if you're doing everything to improve your heart problem. Have you stopped smoking? Are you exercising regularly? Is your diet lower in fat? Perhaps the nightmares serve as an early warning device to let you know you can do more to help yourself.

In other illnesses the nightmare may go beyond its warning mode to produce a vicious cycle. Patients with ulcers can secrete more acid during their REM cycles which may aggravate ulcers. People with high blood pressure may have more dreams of aggression which in turn might cause the blood pressure to rise. Lastly, men with increased anxiety in their dreams may have less REM-stage erections, although there is nothing to suggest that nightmares cause impotence.

Do nightmares actually cause direct harmful effects? Or might they serve as a helpful warning device? Theories about the effects of dreams on physical health remain speculative. Further research is needed to find the answers to these questions.

NIGHTMARES IN PREGNANCY AND LABOR

Francine is a forty-two-year-old woman who works at our hospital. She knew her biological clock was ticking, and she and her husband wanted a third child. They had two boys— the younger was big and strong; the older one was slender and sensitive, which sometimes worried Francine.

When she learned of her third pregnancy she was excited, then two weeks later she developed vaginal bleeding. The doctor consoled her, trying to tell her she would still be able to get pregnant again if she miscarried. This did not ease her worries and an ultrasound could not clarify the picture because the pregnancy was only a few weeks old. By the third month of gestation, however, everything was fine; she started to show.

Francine had worked with physicians as a research methodologist and knew much of the jargon. She knew that viability was at or around twenty-eight weeks, but at twenty-five weeks she had this nightmare: "I can see right inside my uterus. I can see this small form moving—like a shell. It's pressing with one end up and I hold my hand against it. I start saying, anxiously,

'You're not ready.' It continues to push and it makes a bulge. It has a mind of its own and it turns slowly into a shrimp with fins. The fins are sharp enough to cut through the uterus and the skin. It is very much alive, but is it viable? I panic and push it back in, then I wake up."

Francine felt silly worrying about this nightmare. After all, she didn't really believe dreams predicted the future, but she couldn't help wonder if this meant she would have an early labor. She was worried about having to undergo a cesarean section and about the baby's health.

When reviewing this nightmare with Francine she just shrugged her shoulders at "Why a shrimp?" Ten minutes later the discussion turned to her older son and she admitted to her overprotectiveness towards him. Then she suddenly recalled his nickname—"Shrimpy." The connection to her current pregnancy now dawned on her. She admitted to her worries of the baby being small and helpless like the older son. What if it was premature? She was reminded she had been assertive in the dream and had pushed the baby back inside her uterus, suggesting she might deliver at the right time.

In a further attempt to ease her anxieties, we offered her information concerning research which had been done on nightmares and pregnancy. Many women report an increase in unusual dreams during pregnancy, including an upsurge of nightmares.

Studies have also looked at the relationship between dreams and labor. In general, women who fight back in their nightmares or who have higher levels of anxiety and more pronounced threats in their nightmares have easier labors. One researcher explored whether nightmares related to length of labor, and discovered that if the woman is more assertive in the nightmare, the labor is sometimes shorter. Another study suggested that if dream anxiety and the threat in the dream are greater, the length of labor is reduced.

These studies were conducted in North America. We've also discovered some interesting tidbits in a study conducted with women of a Zulu tribe in Africa. Zulu women who have a lot of anxiety dreams of flooding have a high rate of fertility, whereas women who have dreams of still waters have fewer children.

These studies provide evidence that dreams and nightmares are meaningful for women regarding labor, delivery, and fertility. Undoubtedly, however, there are many women who have had no nightmares and delivered healthy babies without complications.

Much of this information consoled Francine and we are happy to report she delivered a healthy boy. Her labor was a bit longer than she'd hoped for, but she avoided her biggest fear— a C-section. She thinks we should now do a study to investigate the relationship between nightmares and C-sections.

CAN NIGHTMARES PREDICT BAD THINGS?

Ricky works at a ski basin in New Mexico where he drives a snowcat machine for grooming powder on the mountain. The machine is dangerous because of the heavy blades which churn up the snow. Ricky's beloved dog of eleven years, Magic, often trails alongside the machine, frolicking in the snow but keeping a safe distance. One night Ricky dreamed Magic was running alongside the machine as Ricky went up and down the slopes. Then with one wrong turn, Magic got caught, chopped up badly by the blades. Ricky awoke in a sweat and from that day to the end of the ski season, he never took Magic to work.

A premonition in a dream?

Let's look at another example. Ellen was finishing her Ph.D. in psychology in Wisconsin when she had this dream: "I'm in a courtroom. The judge holds a huge document. It reminds me of my dissertation. He puts down the papers and looks them over as if he were weighing a decision about admitting the document as evidence.

"From the back of the courtroom someone comes in. I know this person. It is Mr. L. whose case study I've included in my dissertation. Mr. L. looks at me with hostility, then the judge gavels the court into session and I wake up feeling anxious."

Ellen worked with Mr. L. as a patient during her last year of training in psychology. He provided an interesting example of the obsessive-compulsive disorder which Ellen wanted to use in her dissertation. When Mr. L. consented, everything seemed okay. However, over the next few months, Ellen noticed a change in their sessions. A friction developed. When Ellen referred to the dissertation, Mr. L. turned colder. Was Ellen's nightmare foreshadowing a hostile patient who might demand a new "hearing" about his case in the dissertation?

She decided to speak with him about it. In exploring Mr. L.'s feelings about the dissertation, she discovered he felt used. He thought Ellen was more interested in her dissertation than in him. Mr. L. recalled an incident when he was younger. His mother insisted he play the piano for her friends. Despite the warm reception from this small audience, he resented his mother's pushiness and felt used.

Eventually, Mr. L. gained some insight into his reluctance toward sharing his abilities in any public way. A new accord was reached and Ellen went on to use his case material in her dissertation.

We will never know the true predictiveness of these dreams. Magic might have been killed by the snowcat machine and Mr. L. might have sued Ellen sometime in the future. What's revealing is that the dreamers took action because of their dreams.

Ricky said it was instinct. "I didn't give it a second thought. I just told myself Magic won't be coming to work." Ellen's situation seemed to require more thought. She did not want to confront Mr. L. initially because she sensed he would deny he was upset. He often denied other things in therapy. Ellen knew she could drop his case from the dissertation and find another one; however, she knew it would be bad therapy to drop the whole thing without working through the matter with Mr. L.

Still, with all this effort to make the right decision, Ellen's response is similar to Ricky's. "This will sound funny, but I don't pay much attention to dreams probably because I don't recall many of my own. I'm also more interested in other areas of psychology where dream interpretation doesn't play a big role. But I must say, that dream left me with anxiety for weeks until I worked out the problem. From the moment I woke up from it, I knew I would have to face a tense situation with Mr. L."

These examples demonstrate how seriously some people take their dreams, which raises a question: How do you know which dreams to take seriously and which ones to ignore?

In our culture, prophetic dreams have fallen by the wayside. In the past, prophecy dreams were held in high regard. The Old

Testament records some of the earliest prophetic dreams in the stories of Joseph and Daniel. The ancient Greeks also had views about prophetic dreams. One of the most famous books ever written about dreaming was *The Interpretation of Dreams* by Artemidorus of Daldis sometime in the second century A.D. He labeled prophetic dreams *oneiros*, and distinguished them from ordinary dreams resulting from too much or too little food or from some irrational desire of the dreamer.

The *oneiros* predict the future either for good or bad. According to Artemidorus, some dreams come true exactly as they are dreamed while others carry symbolic prophecies. To interpret symbolic dreams, we must know about the personal history and culture of the dreamer. In other words, the same dream could be interpreted differently, depending on who dreamt it and where the person lived.

For example, "You must interpret all [dreams of] vomiting blood, food, or phlegm as indicating benefits for the poor and harm for the rich. For the poor could not lose anything unless they have previously acquired something to lose. But since the rich already possess something, they can lose it."

Consider the case of the perfume dealer who dreamt he had no nose, obviously a nightmare for someone who makes a living smelling scents. This perfume dealer lost his business after this dream. Later, the same man had another dream of losing his nose. According to ancient Greek culture this dream could express "losing face." Subsequently, the man was caught forging a signature and had to flee the country. Finally, during an illness this same man dreamt of losing his nose once again and this time he died shortly thereafter. On this occasion the dream foretold his death because "The skull of a man has no nose."

In our society, some would scoff at these tales. We have learned to have greater respect for these notions after listening to the prophetic nightmares of our patients.

Belinda had this dream on Christmas Eve a few weeks before she entered our research study. "I am in a building and I climb to the top. When I look outside I notice there is a fire, so I hurry down to get out. But as I descend, the building is getting shorter. Finally, at the bottom I'm trapped in a stairway. I don't know what to do. I try to escape through an elevator, but the fire is getting worse. I wake up sweating."

That morning, Belinda's daughter, Geraldine, also awakened from her own nightmare. "I am walking down an alley. I see a red glare in the distance. I run to see what it is, but as I get closer, I get scared. I finally see it's a fire. I'm not sure what's burning, but I think it's a house. I feel helpless and worry that somebody might be inside, but I turn away because I don't know what to do. Then I wake up."

Christmas night, approximately twelve hours after Belinda and Geraldine had their dreams, their neighbor's house a few doors down the street burned to the ground. Fortunately, no one was injured. Were their nightmares premonitions, or did Belinda and her daughter possess some unconscious knowledge about the tragedy which befell their neighbors? Did they somehow know the house was at risk for fire? It's hard to reconcile what happened. Belinda and Geraldine vaguely remembered talking about their neighbor several days earlier, but it was only in passing. The last time they had entered their neighbor's house was six years ago.

This next case proved more disastrous. We encountered a woman who telephoned our clinic. She declined to come in for counseling, but she wanted advice on a disturbing dream she'd experienced. The woman's son was scheduled for a hernia operation and she had a nightmare in which he died during the operation.

The boy had the hernia since he was two and it hadn't bothered him, but the doctors told the mother it might push out and get stuck, causing worse problems. The woman was in a panic, especially because she had previously experienced a fateful premonition about a flying trip. She'd been scheduled to visit Vancouver Island, but experienced a waking premonition that caused her worry. She canceled her trip and discovered later the flight crashed.

This was a most difficult situation. Not knowing what to advise her, we suggested she heed her warning and talk to both the anesthesiologist and the surgeon. Then, if the worrisome feelings persisted, she should consider postponing the surgery. She talked to both doctors—surgeon and anesthesiologist—and felt relieved, so she consented to her son's surgery.

The boy died two days after the operation. No obvious cause was uncovered. This is one of those dreadful stories that leave you feeling empty and sad. Your heart goes out to this mother and you ask yourself if there was anything else you could have done, said, or advised. Was it all just a horrible coincidence? It is impossible to reconcile.

Fortunately, not all cases end so tragically. We recount a true story from a book entitled, *All for the Boss*. The incident took place in the 1920s in New York City. A very religious Jewish woman, Aidel, had this dream. "I dreamt I heard heartrending sobs coming from a room. I found the knob of the door, opened it, and peered inside. The room was empty except for a casket on the floor. On a chair, near the casket, sat a woman dressed in a long, black dress with a black kerchief covering her head. Even though she was seated, I realized she was the tallest woman I had ever seen. It was she who was weeping uncontrollably.

"Suddenly, I heard a whisper in my ear. 'In the casket lies Abraham, the Patriarch, and sitting near him is Sarah, the Matriarch, mourning his death.' As soon as I heard who they were, I rushed into the room and began to weep and cry. In my hysteria, I ripped my clothes and shrieked, 'I will not leave this room until you promise me my prayers have been answered.'

"As I stood there, the top of the casket slid open. Abraham's face appeared with eyes closed, but with tears coursing down his cheeks onto his long, white beard. Sarah grasped my hand and said to me, 'You can go now. Your prayers have been answered.'

"I awoke then, but the dream was so vivid and frightening that I could not stop weeping."

Aidel's husband, Yosef, was considered an expert in dream interpretation, but he was deeply disturbed upon listening to her nightmare. For one thing, the Biblical reference to Abraham and Sarah was reversed, that is, the Bible records that Abraham mourned the death of Sarah. The dream had switched this. After further contemplation, though, Yosef said it was a good dream because her prayers, whatever they might be, would be answered.

But a moment later he revealed another thought—one that clearly showed his concerns. He declared it was time to bring their son, David, home from where he'd been studying at the Yeshiva in Hebron. Aidel thought this peculiar because David had a few more years of study, but Yosef was insistent.

David returned and some months later he married Chaye, the daughter of religious parents whose names, interestingly enough, were Abraham and Sarah. Then a few months later word spread that a deadly attack had occurred on the Yeshiva in Hebron where David had studied. Terrorists killed many of the students.

For Aidel and Yosef the dream had predicted a happy ending. Their prayers were indeed answered with the sparing of their son whom they had brought home early because of the nightmare.

These perspectives on meaning have considerable validity, yet they do not touch upon deeper issues brought forth in our dreams. Often, nightmares carry messages dealing with complex psychological conflicts. Unraveling your dreams to understand these conflicts can provide significant insights.

In the next chapter, we'll explore the deeper meanings of a variety of bad dreams and we'll be interpreting specific nightmares from our patients. We'll also offer views on common nightmare themes, such as falling or being attacked.

Please keep in mind that personal meanings to nightmares must be arrived at through an understanding of the individual who has had the dream. Ultimately, it is the dreamer who must interpret his or her own dreams. Generalized interpretations may be interesting, but they should almost never be casually attached to your own dreams without careful consideration.

CHAPTER 5

Common Nightmares and Their Meanings

KEEPING THINGS PERSONAL

Life is conflict.

In being human, we can't avoid or escape it though we certainly try to much of the time. We deal with conflict in various ways—sometimes confronting it and sometimes denying it. Often our behavior demonstrates an unresolved conflict—smoking perhaps to temporarily avoid it; drinking to forget it; acting aggressively to squelch it; or overeating to smother it. We use psychological defenses such as suppression, sublimation, intellectualization, or projection, to name a few, to cope with our conflicts.

Nightmares express our conflicts in "dreamatic" fashion, engaging defense mechanisms as well as other psychological ploys to deal with conscious and unconscious material from our minds. Nearly all nightmares reflect conflict. Posttraumatic dreams and some recurrent nightmares may be caused by an undiscovered chemical factor in our brains or they may be caused by "overlearned" responses to stress. Still, the dreams reflect old conflicts from past events.

Conflict arises from incompatible desires and obligations or irreconcilable thoughts and emotions. You love your parents; you hate your parents. You like your job, but your boss frustrates you. Your children are a joy but a real pain sometimes. These are common sources of conflicts—ones we can relate to. Yet, each person's conflicts are distinct, depending upon his or her background and experiences. This manifests in unique ways in each person's dreams.

Jane has a nightmare—a very terrible nightmare. "I dreamed I stabbed my mother to death." If we assume this nightmare offers the dreamer deeper psychological insights about herself, what could it mean?

Does Jane hate her mother and wish her dead? That's an obvious interpretation.

Could Jane be angry with her mom, so she vents her hostility in the dream? That's possible.

Could the dream have nothing to do with Jane's literal mother? Rather, Jane hates being a mother herself and wants to quit being one?

Or, could it be Jane realizes she has the same emotional problems as her mother? Seeing her mother in the dream then serves as an unwelcome reminder of her own troubles and Jane responds by trying to kill her—a way of denying the problems.

Lastly, could Jane actually love her mother—perhaps too much—so that she's become too dependent upon her? The nightmare might reflect her struggle for independence.

Are all these interpretations valid? Certainly. Are they useful ways of looking at the concept of *mother* in your dreams? Most definitely. Do any of these interpretations reveal the message behind Jane's nightmare? Not a one. For us to interpret the meaning of this nightmare we must know more information about Jane—literally hundreds of details about her background and current life situation.

Jane's parents emigrated to the United States from Russia several years before Jane's birth. Her parents had trouble adjusting to American culture. When Jane was born, they wanted her to have an easier time so they selected a common American name for her. But raising a child in America with their traditional conservative values caused much conflict. Things deteriorated rapidly when Jane's mother died and she was raised solely by her father.

Jane's mother had been more the disciplinarian of the two parents. Her father had spoiled her. Now he did an about-face, feeling an obligation to be both a father and a mother. He tried to be strict, but this was out of character; he would waver between his old self and his attempt at disciplining. This confused Jane and in adolescence she rebeled with the common acting-out problems related to sex and drugs. Though Jane loved her father, she saw him as old-fashioned because of his ties to Russia, or we should say—*mother* Russia.

Now you probably sense what the dream meant to Jane. She had this nightmare at a stressful time in her mid-twenties when she worked and supported herself in a town several hundred miles from her father. She'd been thinking about moving in with a man as a prelude to marriage. Her father was enraged. Jane desperately wanted his approval and blessings, and the thought of becoming a wife and perhaps a mother intensified her need for approval from her deceased mother.

Jane and her dad had several shouting matches over the phone. They'd take turns hanging up on each other, leaving them both drained and bitter. After the fifth or sixth fight she had the nightmare.

She quickly focused on the mother from *mother* Russia and the older values it represented, and the mother in *mothering* which her father had attempted. Her attempt to kill off the *mother* was clear to her as an attempt to kill off the old values her father was trying to impose. The nightmare served a positive function by separating out Jane's real love for her father from her disagreements with him over these issues. She was set on maintaining her autonomy, but the next phone call was a happy one with apologies, expressions of love, and an agreement to disagree.

Dream Dictionaries and Dream Symbols

We've shared Jane's nightmare because it highlights the uniqueness of dreams, especially when foraging for deeper psychological meanings. Often people look for quick, snappy interpretations to their dreams and nightmares. They do a disservice to themselves by approaching their dreams this way, and if they are offered some surefire meaning from a so-called dream expert, they are probably being *dis-serviced* by that individual as well.

Looking up an interpretation to a dream in a book or dream dictionary has its origins thousands of years ago. Many books from antiquity have been lost, but the *Oneirocritica* by Artemidorus whom we mentioned in our section on prophetic dreams is the standard from which other dream dictionaries were compiled. Artemidorus had many intriguing ideas about dreams and understood the essential relationship between the dreamer and his or her dreams. Some of his ideas stimulated Sigmund Freud's thinking. In modern times, however, the emphasis has been to simplify things to the point of absurdity. Now you simply look up a dream in the book and find the "answer."

It's true most people have experienced *types* of dreams which other people have also dreamed, and therefore some generalizations may be in order. But to uncover meaning requires looking for the personal nuances in the dream that relate specifically to you.

These dream manuals are too rigid when they make claims, like dreaming about bathing in dirty water means you will become sick. It's not that this particular dream of dirty water—probably an anxiety dream for most of us—doesn't have an important message. Having such a dream might suggest you have unhealthy ideas about how to stay "clean" and therefore you might be heading for the doctor. But to imply that this dream will always mean the same thing to each person is not only ludicrous but potentially harmful.

We'd like to think most people realize this is a form of entertainment at best. Many of the dream dictionaries have introductions mentioning just that—it's not to be taken seriously. Throughout this section, we'll offer some dream dictionary tidbits to show you how misguided they can be and to see where they might be on target.

These "fast-food," ready-made interpretations are more likely to cause you psychological and spiritual indigestion. We prefer the home-cooked variety of dream interpretation. Home cooking means paying particular attention to the individual and his or her personal background. You'll see how much more information can be garnered from your nightmares or your dreams in general by checking out the personal details of the dream and how they relate to you.

In your quest to understand the deeper psychological meanings of nightmares, you'll also begin to appreciate symbols in dreams. Water may appear in your dream as a lake, a river, or the ocean. In these instances, the body of water may represent the unconscious of your mind.

Symbols have universal relevance that can apply to anyone. Working with symbols is a more abstract way of analyzing dreams. The theories of Carl Jung and other dream researchers have focused heavily on symbols. These experts believe certain images show up in our brains just like instincts. For example, if water shows up in your dream and you've recently experienced a boating accident on a lake, then the dream may relate back to the accident. On the other hand, if you don't uncover any personal meaning to water, then considering a body of water as a universal symbol of the unconscious may be helpful in unraveling your dream.

Notice a crucial difference here between symbols and dream dictionaries. "Water = Unconscious" does not provide the complete interpretation of a dream. It is another idea to consider as you review the whole dream.

In looking at common nightmares, we'll see how they fit the so-called "standard interpretations" and how they may be quite different once we take the time to look at the personal elements and the universal symbols in each dream.

ATTACKERS IN THE NIGHT

If you've ever dreamt you were stalked or chased or attacked, you know how terrifyingly real it seems. The common element is the aggressiveness of the attackers. They close in for the kill and you're unable to escape. You're convinced they want to hurt you badly, if not murder you outright.

What do dream dictionaries have to say about dreams of attack? Here are a few samples: You will suffer an insult; dangerous enemies plan to do you in; good fortune is around the corner; and you're running away from responsibility. We give them credit for offering so many possibilities to choose from.

Nightmares of being attacked or chased often include the psychological defense of projection—a defense mechanism which shields you from your own aggressive impulses. Consider Frank, who works as a secretary for Louise. One day she phoned him from outside the office, requesting he redo a letter. There was static on the phone and she raised her voice to make sure Frank understood, but he misinterpreted her action. Frank assumed her raised voice was a sign of anger, but the way he arrived at this wrong conclusion was through projection, that is, he took his own anger and tied it into Louise's voice.

Why would he do this? Frank has been bothered by Louise's authority over him and has built up resentments toward her. So, Frank is the angry one, but he's learned to *project* his own anger falsely onto Louise.

He doesn't have to deal with the anger coming from himself.

Projecting your aggressions and anger onto someone else in your dreams is a safe way of not seeing yourself as the aggressor. We all do this. It reflects our unwillingness to face up to our aggressive feelings, which is certainly no easy task. Let's perform a short experiment to illustrate.

Suppose we ask you to imagine for a moment one of two scenes. In the first, you have a baseball bat in your hand and we want you to imagine bashing somebody over the head with it. In the second, we want you to pretend you're the victim and another person wields the baseball bat against your head. Now pick one scene and briefly imagine it.

Which scene did you choose? We apologize for the ugliness of the example, but it proves an interesting point. Most everybody has a problem with either scenario, but a surprisingly large number of people can never imagine the scene where they are the aggressor. They always pick the role of victim. It is more painful for them to perceive themselves inflicting pain upon others than it is to imagine the pain inflicted upon their own selves.

Inhibiting our aggressions can be healthy. A society in which people constantly unleashed hostilities upon each other would not survive. Whether or not we practice too much repression must be determined individually. If you inhibit all your aggressions, it's possible these strong emotions will return to haunt you in your nightmares.

Mabel is a retired schoolteacher. She's small in stature and reserved in manner. She rarely gets angry at anyone. "I have this recurring dream where a man attacks me with a knife. I always wake up in a sweat." Mabel has had this dream for years and has never come up with a satisfactory interpretation. She was never attacked in real life, nor has she had any problems with knives. In fact, she was quite the mumblety-peg player as a kid. If we want to pursue Freudian symbols—the knife as a phallus—Mabel has told us she's had a healthy sex life with her husband for over forty years.

There are many possible interpretations for such a dream, but we are struck by the fact Mabel admits to having the dream shortly after hostile encounters with other people—encounters where she never expresses her displeasure. Simply put, Mabel has a conflict about expressing her anger. This shows up repeatedly in her dreams in projected form where she turns the aggression onto herself by having herself attacked.

Projection is an interesting psychological defense, but it can be taken too far as an explanation for all aggressive dreams. A woman rightfully rejects this concept when she recounts a dream of an angry man trying to rape her. A projected interpretation would imply the woman wants to be the aggressor to take advantage of the man. In many situations, a woman has this dream because she's been taken advantage of—physically or emotionally—by either an older or physically stronger man. Many women have suffered as children or as adults from sexual abuse. In these cases, the nightmare may be an example of the posttraumatic variety, reflecting real insecurity based on real life experiences.

Projection does exist both in nightmares and in waking life. We ask you to consider it for yourself, but be careful when suggesting someone else is projecting as you may be the perpetrator and not they.

Another way to look at aggressive dreams—and the primary method we espouse—is to analyze who the aggressor is. Ask yourself: What is there about this person that I think is aggressive?

Cassie is a thirty-six-year-old single woman who owns a clothing boutique. She is very concerned about her appearance and originally entered the clothing business as a way of perfecting her image. She is a success at business, but a few years ago she began drinking too much.

She saw the alcohol's effects on her appearance and started to worry. Then she began having nightmares and one in particular drove home the message. "There was a knocking at my door— it was shaking violently—I answered it. There was a man with a beard with a face like mine with big eyes. He could have been drinking. He insisted I was his love. I told him he had the wrong gal. I attempted to force him out, but he turned and attacked. I woke up screaming."

When Cassie was asked to identify this man she said it must have been some drunk. But when she was reminded of the details of her dream, she remembered she'd identified him as looking like her. Although it was an obvious connection in the dream, this took her by surprise. She immediately saw drinking as "threatening" her and leading her to be confused about the problem. So projection is used here—Cassie's drinking problem is projected onto the drunk in the dream. Yet, the attack represents something more specific—not aggression, but the dangers of continued drinking.

In another case, Adeline, a married woman, dreamed of "four dangerous youths standing between Greg (her husband) and me. They are out to get me. One of them stands threateningly before me. He pulls off his wide, black leather belt and snaps it in the air. He has an erection and I know I am in real danger. They intend to attack and beat me."

Adeline's excellent relationship with her husband does not block out her past. She grew up in a tough neighborhood and although she was not sexually abused, she heard about several episodes at school. Once, she witnessed a man dragging a woman by her hair into a house. She also went out with the "tough" guys of the neighborhood and was sexually involved with one.

She felt ashamed of her youthful escapades and put them behind her when she married Greg. She was satisfied financially, emotionally, and sexually in their relationship, but she worried about her previous attractions. This all surfaced when asked to identify her attackers in the dream. What was the real threat posed by the dangerous man with an erection?

She realized she'd been feeling the erotic attractions of a few men at her job. She had tried to ignore this because it brought up memories of her adolescence. The nightmare helped her to accept this aspect of herself. Adeline discovered she could talk with her husband about it and this whole process led to a greater commitment which they shared for each other. Their sexual play also took on a new, more erotic form that was mutually pleasing.

Once again, we see a conflict which comes to light in a very specific dream. In this case, images from the past were incorporated into the nightmare and revealed the nature of the conflict dating back to adolescent sexual affairs.

Dreams of being attacked, threatened, or chased are probably the most common type of nightmare. This may reflect the violent nature of our society. Still, to find the correct meaning of the attack, you must reflect on the personal details of the dream and how they relate to you. You must look to see what specifically is attacking you and what it might represent besides aggression.

THE ANIMAL IN YOU

Animal dreams are common, but our relationships to animals in dreams are varied. Often, in nightmares, they are attacking or chasing you, or they may be biting or clawing at you. Usually animals will relate to either a personal experience or a symbolic message. Animals you are unlikely to have direct contact with, such as monkeys and gorillas, might serve as symbolic figures. These primates often appear in dreams involving oedipal conflicts such as triangular relationships between men and women.

Listen to Kevin's dream. "I emerge from underground into daylight. I see a large structure behind me. It looks like the Sphinx which makes me wonder, 'Is this a riddle to solve?' The structure looks like cardboard, sort of flailing and bending in the wind. It transforms into a sturdier 3-D puzzle sculpture with each piece a different head, making it look like Mount Rushmore.

"I see the heads in the puzzle more clearly as it edges toward me. Some heads are people and some are animals. I do not recognize anyone, but one head is clearly a gorilla's face and it snarls at me, baring its teeth. As it gets closer the gorilla's head grows. Its face becomes more menacing and its jaws open wide. I think I'm going to end up inside the gorilla's stomach. I suddenly 'force' the gorilla backwards by holding up my hand at him. As the gorilla moves backwards, its face continues to snarl, but its jaw and teeth are rapidly decaying. Pieces of stuff—teeth, flesh—fall off its face. I wake up."

Kevin was in therapy during the time of this dream and had been dealing with his problem of being unable to form a committed relationship. Invariably, he found himself attracted to women who were involved with other men. Often these other men would be his own friends and sometimes his best friends. In his real world, Kevin was replaying his early parental love triangle in the form of a triangle with his friends.

When Kevin learned that monkeys and gorillas sometimes represent oedipal themes it made him uneasy. He wondered how healthy it was for him to have forced the gorilla backwards.

He recognized that by pushing it away he might be denying the problem, trying to suppress it. Over many months, Kevin worked through this dream and saw how it related to his real life. He learned to control his "gorilla" nature and avoid unhealthy triangular relationships.

Bears are common figures in dreams and may symbolize the maternal qualities of the mothering bear. Leanne at seventeen was ready to conquer the world. She was self-assured and confident in her abilities at the time she had this nightmare. "I am walking along a path in Stanley Park, Vancouver and come to an opening—a large soccer field. I move onto the field and glance back to see a large bear following me. At first I am frightened, then think, 'I am OK.' The bear swipes at me, cutting me with its nails."

Leanne plays soccer. She does not excel, but plays a good game. She's comfortable with this and has carried her confidence into new situations—some of which she does not have the maturity to cope with. In the nightmare she was on a path that opened onto a large field. An open space provides freedom of movement, but no direction.

When she confronts the bear, instead of heeding the danger, she doesn't give it much thought, reacting like many adolescents. The bear took a swipe at her—a reminder perhaps or a warning to be mindful of her new freedom. In sum, Leanne needs a more mature mother within her to keep her safe and protected. Confidence is good as long as it is tempered with judgment.

There are a number of messages brought to us through animals in our dreams. For example, snakes may symbolize wisdom and knowledge; a feathered serpent may be a symbol of femininity; the bull—sexual prowess; the mouse—introspection; and horses—masculinity or male sexual prowess.

Looking at literature and mythology or other art forms will provide clues to meanings that might relate to your dreams. In movies, animal stories often depict themes related to the symbolism of the animal in the picture. Recent examples include *The Bear*—a story about a young cub searching for a new mother; *The Black Stallion*—the story of a young boy learning his first lessons of adolescence; *Cat People*—a story of a young woman's conflicts with sexuality. And if we look at older movies we may remember such classics as Hitchcock's

The Birds and *Moby Dick* (based on Melville's novel), both of which use animals as important symbols to convey part of the message in the story.

So it's important to recognize that animals may represent a particular theme which will serve as the key to understanding your animal dreams. However, if you're a zookeeper or you've recently visited the zoo, animals might reflect something else, depending upon what encounters you've had. Most of us have contacts with more domesticated animals, such as dogs and cats. Domesticated animals in dreams are more likely to have personal meaning for us based on our daily interactions with them.

Overall, one important way to think of animal dreams is to ask the question: What is the relationship between you and the animal in the dream or, more specifically, who's in control? It usually suggests a healthier mental state if in your dreams an animal is trained and responds to you. Many nightmares depict just the opposite—the animal is in control of events, chasing, attacking, biting, or clawing at you. If an animal is controlling you in a dream, then you might ask whether there is something about what the animal represents which might be controlling you in real life.

Harold had a short nightmare. He dreamed he was bending over, then suddenly he looked up to see a large wolf leaping at him with bared teeth. He awoke before it bit him. When Harold reflected on the dream, he thought about wolf dens and how wolves look after each other and their young. Then he remembered a story about a wolf that had mated with a bitch dog in heat.

These reflections raised all the issues he'd been dealing with in his life. He'd been having an affair which had taken him away from his family, both physically and emotionally; yet, Harold wished to return his devotion to his wife and children. Interestingly, the wolf symbolized both the loss of control he suffered in his affair and his need to regain control to protect his family.

There are many other types of relations to animals in addition to control. Often, in nightmares and in movies, for example, the crow or the raven represents the death of the dreamer or death of a person in the story. However, death can also represent the repression of a conflict or problem.

This idea is exemplified in Debbie's nightmare: "My friend

Linda says something about Little Bo-Peep which she had just been reading and how sexual it seemed. I agreed, saying that when I did a research paper on sexuality, that rhyme was always mentioned as blatantly sexual. . . . then . . .

"I carefully step over the remains of a cat, almost slipping. I'm really grossed out. I can feel the crunch of cat bones under my feet as I get back into the car. Linda and I drive off, and all of a sudden a bunch of ugly crowlike birds rush like an explosion into the car, flopping and pecking—surrounding us in the front seat. I wake with a startle."

Understanding this dream was not difficult for Debbie. She is a student of psychology and mythology. She recited, "Little Bo-Peep had lost her sheep. . . . leave them alone and they'll come home, wagging their tails behind them." Debbie had been exploring her sexuality in relation to passivity and dominance. She was dating a man who was passive and she found herself becoming more aggressive. Although disturbed by this, she also found it sexually exhilarating.

She related her boyfriend's passivity to the sheep. She went on to explore the nature of cats, and saw herself as catlike in her sexuality, but she noticed this image was difficult to accept. She then compared this association to the cats with the crowlike birds. If the birds represented death, they might be signaling Debbie's attempt to kill off her new views towards sexuality.

In other words, the nightmare displayed her new ideas about sexuality and simultaneously attempted to repress these ideas. This dream provides a number of animal figures: the sheep being passive; the cat being aggressive like a jungle cat; and the crowlike or raven-type birds representing death and repression.

So animals in nightmares can be understood by reviewing their symbolism in literature, movies, poetry, and other art forms. And they may also represent their unique biological characteristics. Lastly, they may depict some specific relationship you may have with them, such as with your dog or cat.

KILL OR BE KILLED

Killing someone in your dreams or getting killed yourself is certainly one of the most dramatic nightmares. At first glance this would seem like the worst possible dream, yet to kill or be killed is neither good nor bad until we analyze what else is going on in the dream.

Suppose you dream that you kill Hitler. If you had suffered from PTSD because of a real life experience in a concentration camp and had undergone psychotherapy to deal with the trauma, then such a dream might represent a healthy sign of your successful therapy. Or, suppose you dream of an honest judge rendering a death sentence against you for grievous deeds. Is this an unconscious way of admitting your guilt about something in the past, thus signaling a future transformation?

Jon was a thirty-five-year-old social worker when he had this nightmare. "A young Indian man is standing fifty feet away . . . he raises a bow and arrow and shoots me in the heart." For Jon, American Indian culture represents something positive—a naturalistic religion, a belief in the connection of all things, and a sense of being a part of the whole of nature. Jon's intellectual pursuits in an industrial Northeastern city, however, took him away from these beliefs to the point of creating uncertainty about his future.

Dying by the hands of an Indian was a way of giving in to these ideas and regaining a sense of harmony with himself and his work. Ironically, his dream preceded by five years his move back to the Southwest where he began working on a reservation. So this dream proved somewhat prophetic; yet when Jon first experienced it he was frightened. Only after spending time reflecting on it did he see the positive aspects.

We shared Jon's dream in this section because many people become nervous about dreams of death and dying. They assume the interpretation of such dreams must uncover something horrible or predict something deadly. Clearly, Jon's dream proved to be the opposite. Yours may as well.

On the negative side, killing something in a dream may mean you're trying to suppress or repress it. If you dream of killing a green-eyed monster, could this be an attempt to block out painful feelings of jealousy? And to make things trickier, if you were repressing jealous feelings in your waking life, it might be more difficult to take an honest look at jealous feelings you discover in your dreams.

We all possess a dark side. It comes out in different ways for each of us—greed, envy, jealousy, lust. No one escapes these human desires and feelings and it is usually difficult to

acknowledge these traits within ourselves. After all, who wants
to see themselves as greedy? So like the alcoholic who denies
alcoholism, we likewise try to deny these problems. This may
show up in nightmares of killing something.

Samuel is an honor student. He developed a competitive
personality from his dad who'd done well in business. The
competitiveness also showed up between them in golf and
tennis and other intellectual pursuits. Nearing graduation from
high school, Samuel's father was pressing him about his future,
hoping he would consider a business college. But Samuel was
intrigued with becoming a missionary. His father was perplexed
by this, while Samuel's mother loved it. She and Samuel spent
hours fantasizing about the possibilities. Samuel had found an
area where his father could no longer compete. And in pursuing
the missionary idea, Samuel had bonded more closely with his
mother in a somewhat incestuous manner.

His nightmare's simplicity focuses on the conflict by using a
monkey as the symbol for oedipal relationships. "I am walking
along a dirt road . . . a stand of poplar trees is on my left,
an open field with a few Jersey cows on my right. Suddenly
there is a large male chimpanzee swinging through the trees
making a menacing sound. It's coming at me. I reach for a
stone and throw it, cracking its skull. As it dies, I feel relief
and remorse."

The chimpanzee stands for the oedipal relationship which
has resurfaced in Samuel's real life. Samuel must confront
the natural envy he has for his father's success as well as the
jealousy he feels toward his father's marriage to his mother.
As Samuel bonds more closely to his mother in waking life, his
repressed feelings of jealousy are in danger of emerging more
consciously. Samuel sees himself as a religious person and has
difficulty facing this darker side. To repress those feelings of
jealousy and envy, he kills the chimpanzee in the dream.

On the one hand, some might see this as healthy because
Samuel tries to dispose of negative emotions which are
inappropriate to his relationship with his parents. On
the other hand, we don't usually kill off the emotion
by having such a nightmare—we suppress or repress
it. Commonly, the feelings replay themselves in some
other manner and we are eventually forced to deal
with them.

When exploring nightmares of killing and being killed, try to look at what it is you are killing or what is killing you. If you are killing something "bad," look at it carefully. Is it really negative or are you just perceiving it that way? Ask yourself if it represents something in yourself you don't want to face. Conversely, if you are killed in a dream, consider if you are dying at the hands of something positive.

WATER, WATER, EVERYWHERE

Starting with common dream dictionary ideas about water, we find the following dreams and their interpretations: Emerging from water symbolizes birth of a child or an idea; bathing in clear water means good health; bathing in dirty water means sickness; drinking hot water means you will be molested and persecuted by enemies; spilling a glass of water means death of a child; carrying water into the bedroom means you will be visited by a man with loose morals; water flooding out of your own house means your life is in danger. Once again you have much to choose from if you want to rely on dream dictionaries.

Dreams of being underwater are common. Many people who dream they are underwater describe no discomfort nor difficulty with breathing. Others suddenly realize they're underwater and panic, frantically trying to get to air or to awaken themselves from the dream. With dreams and nightmares of water occurring so commonly, it is especially important to consider your personal beliefs and experiences regarding water. And you might also consider the symbolic ideas associated with water.

The classic interpretation of water, especially a large body like the ocean, is a symbol for the unconscious. This interpretation fits in this next dream. "I am standing chin-deep in the ocean. There is a middle-aged woman with gray-and-white hair in the water too. She is chasing skunks on the ocean floor. I know the skunks are really black-and-white sea slugs. The other woman does not realize she is in the ocean and that she will drown by her misguided behavior. I also know I am she and my fate is tied with hers.

"As she chases the skunks in deeper water, the water goes over her head and I feel it going over my head. I feel like I'm drowning. She then speaks, pointing out to sea. 'Now would you look at that, there's one of those . . .'—She takes after it. I see it is more dangerous, it is coming for me. I anticipate my legs being grabbed and pulled under and drowning and dying . . . I wake up."

Eloise is in a bind. She identifies with the woman with gray-and-white hair who seems oblivious to any danger. This woman is chasing skunks in water. She is something like a skunk herself in having black-and-white fur. What is the relationship between the dreamer and the skunk? If we assume water to be her unconscious, we might wonder if there's something with a "bad smell" lurking about.

In the dream, the woman fails to realize the danger and heads for deeper water to a more dangerous situation. This is puzzling. Is there really something dangerous out there, or is the dreamer perceiving something to be dangerous that really isn't? Which of the two women in the dream has a clear perception of the situation? Is it possible the lady with gray-and-white hair is comfortable because what she is chasing is neither dangerous nor is the water too deep for her?

This nightmare points out many aspects to consider: an animal that becomes something else—skunk to sea slug; the location of the other woman and the animal—underwater; and the relation of the dreamer to the other woman and the animal. Whether the animal is dangerous or merely appears dangerous, the dreamer was afraid, although nothing bad happened to her or the other woman.

As you read this you may have a sense of frustration. If so, you have tapped into what this dreamer felt, too. Eloise was unable to work with the nightmare because she was uncomfortable trying to interpret it. So in this case we are left without a conclusion.

Water dreams in particular highlight the problem of dealing with unconscious conflicts which may arise in our nightmares. In some instances, the material will be too difficult to work with and you may find yourself avoiding any further efforts at interpretation.

Here's another dream of water in a different scenario which still reflects the unconscious mind. Jan had this nightmare during therapy. "I am in my waterbed covered by water though the bed is not broken. I am submerged, I cannot get out. I panic."

Jan came from a broken family; her father had left when she was an infant and she was adopted by her stepfather. Throughout her life she's had unpleasant memories about her early childhood. She could never pinpoint the hardships she'd suffered when she and her mother were abandoned, but the vague memories left her feeling badly.

Jan worked with this dream and thought of the bed as a secure place. She recognized she'd rather "stay in bed" and avoid these memories which therapy had begun bringing up. Being submerged under the water provoked the same feelings she remembered about her difficult childhood. In time, she worked on these painful memories. As expected, both her anxiety and pain increased, but she worked through this stress to gain a better understanding about her current fears of abandonment. Within this context, submerged in water—even a waterbed—can reflect your unconscious conflicts and feelings.

In this next nightmare, water may represent something more mundane. Sally is a full-time housewife and a part-time salesclerk. "I am standing in the bathroom, the toilet starts to overflow, the door is locked, and I cannot get out. The water is rising fast."

Sally cares for two children at home, but receives only limited help from her husband. She relates her nightmare to a sense of being trapped in her role as housewife and mother. This is an obvious interpretation; however, we may want to ask other questions. Why does she have trouble confronting her husband about taking a larger parental role? And why is she resisting mothering? Do the answers to these questions reside in the depths of the unconscious as represented by the water or is the dream a symbol of her burdensome housekeeping chores?

Why not both? Many dreams are layered with meanings. Freud said you could never completely interpret any dream because you could always find new levels of meaning. As this one turned out, Sally was comfortable with her interpretation and it motivated her to make minor changes at home to improve the quality of her life.

Our relationship to water comes in many forms—walking in water, going under a waterfall, sailing, swimming, or engaging in water sports, to name a few. Many of these dreams show a changing relationship to the water and some manifest as nightmares. When you have a water dream or nightmare, understand what the water represents to you, then explore your relationship to the water to see what message emerges.

SEXUAL NIGHTMARES AND ANXIETY DREAMS

We'll describe four sexual dreams of women from four distinct cultural backgrounds. One woman is Canadian, trained as a psychologist. Another is a young Zulu woman of Africa who looks after the family cattle herds. The third is a young Fijian islander from the South Pacific. And the last is a middle-aged Christian Fundamentalist from the southern United States.

It may be easy for you to identify which dream belongs to which woman. But can you identify which dreams are the nightmares? We'll give you a hint—two are dreams and two are nightmares.

Here's the first: "I'm standing someplace. This man comes up behind, or rather it's like a shadow of a man. But then he speaks and he becomes more real. He says, 'I love you.' I say 'I know.' Then a bit later I'm in bed with this person having sex."

The second: "I am taking the cattle over to the watering hole. They are all fine and I lie down under a tree for shade. A young man comes walking along the river. I am surprised and a bit afraid when I see him. As he gets closer, I recognize him as someone I have seen at the neighboring village. He comes and lies beside me. I can feel his erection and I feel myself becoming wet and excited."

The third: "I am on this ledge and I dive into this pool. I'm swimming towards this man. I feel myself getting sexually excited as I swim towards him. The idea of having sex with him is an exciting one."

The fourth: "I am a ways off the trail in the dense forest. I am feeling scared but then look out through an opening and see the path to my home. It is not far and I feel relieved as I run toward my hut. As I get close to the hut, this handsome man beckons me. I feel some excitement but also I'm a bit leery. I find myself going toward him though, and I feel some tingling in my private parts as he holds me tight. I then glance down at his huge penis."

What's your guess? Here are the dreamers' responses upon awakening.

The first dreamer is the Canadian psychologist who feels very comfortable with her sexuality. Her response was simple, "It was wonderful, like a perfect blending"—obviously not a nightmare.

The second dreamer is the Zulu woman. "I've had fantasies of this man since I first saw him in another village. It was a very pleasant dream."

The third dreamer is the woman with the Christian background. She awakened gasping for air as she realized she was sexually attracted to a man other than her husband. She felt shame, guilt, and remorse. It is not surprising she awakened with feelings of panic and anxiety.

And the fourth dreamer is the Fijian islander. "It was a terrible experience. Tutumatua (demon sex god) tricked me to have sex with him."

In analyzing sexual dreams and nightmares it's important to consider the cultural background of the dreamer. Many erotic dreams are pleasurable, but there are also situations which evoke feelings of disgust, revulsion, frustration, and even fear and terror.

Much of your reaction depends on your views towards sexuality. We've learned to repress certain primitive impulses during the day and we may find these impulses seeking expression in our dreams. Having sex with a mother or father could depict repressed incestuous feelings. Having sex with someone of the same sex might suggest repressed homosexual impulses. And, dreaming repeatedly of extramarital encounters may point to dissatisfaction in a current marriage or relationship.

Herb described this sexual dream. "I am walking along a briar patch. My daughter appears and has oral sex with me. I awake stunned and disgusted." Herb had a great deal of difficulty talking about this dream; however, as he worked through it, he was greatly relieved.

The briar patch immediately brought to mind the characters of Brer Rabbit, Brer Fox, and the Tar Baby. He recalled his mother reading the stories to him as a child when he was 4 years old. This thought triggered another memory of the same age when he and a young girl were playing in the backyard. They were exploring each other's genitals when Herb's mother spotted them. They were scolded and felt ashamed.

How did Herb put this together? He remembered feeling good, listening to his mother read the stories, but now he recognized another feeling—one similar to that which he felt with the young girl. It was an attraction. But as a child he had been scolded for having that feeling.

The dream of his daughter brought back memories of his relationship with his mother with the associated sexual feelings. When he awakened he felt the same guilt and shame. Understanding how this dream evolved helped Herb feel more comfortable about what happened in the nightmare. He realized he could be close to his daughter as there was no hidden desire for incest. The problem had been with his mother, not his daughter.

Dreams of this sort might represent nothing more than repressed impulses built up through the centuries-long effects of civilization. Or, they may relate to our own sexual repression which we've experienced in our personal development. Or, to a Freudian, sexual dreams might be considered neurotic fantasies or simple wishes for sexual gratification outside our current life situation.

However, if we look more closely at the content of the dream, we'll find other clues revealing additional insights about our attitudes on sex. For example, if sex is portrayed in a place that is meant for fun, such as a circus or carnival, the dreamer would be seen as fairly free and spontaneous. Or, if the sex dream includes an unpleasant or dirty element, it might be interpreted that the dreamer sees sex in that manner. Sex which involves force used against the dreamer suggests ambivalence—mixed feelings—the desire for sex along with some fear or repulsion.

Sex in dreams and nightmares may represent complex aspects of our personalities, symbolizing more than our attitudes or wishes about sex. This shows up in two dreams of Gretchen which occurred in succession on the same night. "I am in a large commune house, completely encased in glass. Numerous people live there . . . I know one—my sister-in-law. We are cooking in this house for all the people and because of the glass everyone sees everyone else."

Later that night the second dream—a nightmare—unfolds. "I am in a hotel walking down a hallway looking for my room. I cross paths with an attractive blind man. I do not recognize him. He asks me to go to his room where his wife is waiting. This blind man is a singer, performing in the hotel. When his act is over, he will meet us back in his room. In the room, I see his wife wearing a red dress. He returns and next we are all naked and making love. It was extremely pleasant.

"Later, I go to my glass commune house where my brother-in-law is viewing a video which shows exactly my encounter with the blind man and his wife. A lot of my relatives are watching. I am extremely upset and panic. I run to my room, lock myself in and cry myself awake."

The first dream reveals Gretchen's background with issues of privacy and secrecy. She grew up in postwar Germany and lived in a crowded house where everyone knew everyone else's business. When her mother abandoned her and her father, Gretchen was not only crushed by the loss, but humiliated as well because of the constant gossiping in the crowded household.

A few years later when Gretchen began dating, she adopted a secretive attitude about her male friends for fear of her relatives' reactions. When she left home and moved to the United States, she maintained the same private nature. This extended to her marriage and although she felt satisfied with her situation, she could not discuss her sexual feelings with other people, including her husband.

In exploring the nightmare, the idea of having sex with a blind man who couldn't see her was interpreted by Gretchen as highlighting her feelings about privacy and secrecy. The sexual part of the dream—having sex with both a man and a woman was enjoyable to her, but once she was discovered, that is, on videotape, the dream became a nightmare. She felt humiliated and shamed.

This dream was sexual, but the focus was really on the problem with her family. She could not be open with them without fear of recrimination. By exploring this nightmare, she learned how she had fallen into this pattern not only with her family but also with her husband regarding issues of sex and other matters.

Another way to look at this nightmare is to examine the relationship Gretchen has with the blind man and his wife. There is no suggestion in the dream that the man or wife have any problems. They accept Gretchen without reservation. So for the moment, let's remove the aspect of physical sex from the dream and think of it as a symbol for a *union*. In this case, sex symbolizes a *union of ideas*, suggesting that Gretchen desires a more intimate and expressive marriage. While the dream reflects on the surface the wish for infidelity or a *ménage à trois,* in reality, as Gretchen continued her therapy, she recognized her desire to have a committed, monogamous, and honest relationship with her husband.

You may look at some sexual dreams literally to see if they provide insights into your sexuality. If it's a nightmare, perhaps you're trying to repress something. But along with this straightforward approach, we suggest you look at sexual relations as a symbol for the union of ideas. The sexual theme may be secondary. If you dream of sleeping with a woman, perhaps you are trying to integrate some feminine aspect of your personality. Or, if you dream of having sex with a man perhaps you are attempting to unite with the masculine side of yourself.

Sex as a symbol for the union of ideas will show up in a variety of ways in dreams and nightmares. Angie was a very good singer and had performed in small bands in her late teens and early twenties, but after marrying Chuck, she kept the books and ran the office for his automotive repair business. Her dream/nightmare returns to her past.

"I am at a concert with Chuck. An English group is performing and a guitarist is eyeing me throughout the show. Next, I'm in a room with the band and other guests. The guitarist approaches me and says he's in love with me. He reaches up from behind me, touches me, then kisses me passionately. I tell him I am married and that my husband is here.

"Then we're in another place. I am sitting on the floor with lots of records, travel bags, and the guitar owned by this guy in the band. On top of the guitar is a picture of him, smiling, and inscribed underneath 'I love you, Angie.' I go to a room by myself, and the next thing, someone is touching my shoulders. It's him. I suddenly feel dizzy, like I'm going to faint. We kneel down on the floor together. We kiss for a long time and make love. Suddenly, my husband walks in and I look up and feel awful and confused."

As far as Angie knew on the conscious level, she had no strong love or sexual feelings for any other men except her husband. She explored this idea openly and there was little to suggest she was lying to herself. She recalled having a passionate relationship with another musician prior to her marriage, but she felt her husband to be equally passionate, if not more so.

When exploring who this musician might be, and what he might symbolize, she blurted out "music, of course." With this, the dream made sense. She loved music passionately but because of her work and marriage, she let her musical side fade. The nightmare was a reminder to return to what she loved so dearly. She also recognized that her husband, although trying to be open-minded, did have jealous feelings about her love of music.

Sex is one of the most powerful experiences we enjoy as humans. At its highest pinnacle we think of it as making love, that is, blending or merging with another human being. On a more physiological level, we might view sex as a need that must be satisfied in its own right or as an instinct to produce offspring.

In our culture, as in all other cultures, many of our conscious thoughts—whether in the form of active thinking and feeling or just plain daydreaming—wander into areas with sexual themes. It should come as no surprise then to frequently encounter sexual themes and actions in our dreams and nightmares as well. To get the most understanding from these particular nightmares, remember to consider sex as a symbol for merging or uniting, and not just as a need to be fulfilled.

"FALLING" DREAMS

"Falling" dreams are common. Most people have experienced them at least once in their lives. Calvin Hall suggests these are punishment dreams for something the dreamer has done against his or her conscience—the price paid for doing the misdeed. One dream dictionary breaks falling dreams into several categories. Falling from a high place indicates misfortune. Falling from a medium height indicates a loss of honor. Still another dream dictionary equates falling with: high anxiety, yielding, loss of self-control, helplessness, or a lack of support.

We have seen some truth in the above; however, our suggestion is to look at the "falling" in the nightmare to see *what* and *how* you are falling away from something. Looking at the dream situation will be more revealing than simply saying you're out of control. You need to know *what* is out of control.

Katherine is a widow who works part-time. She is comfortable financially, living on her salary, her inheritance from her parents, and her husband's life insurance. She has good friends, no serious illnesses, and no significant mental symptoms. In short, she functions well in life. She has had a problem, though, with chronic nightmares—forty-four years' worth.

Katherine had two "falling" dreams. "I am floating on a little boat—floating away. There is music in the air. I'm happy. Suddenly the boat tips over, but there is no water—just a deep void. I'm falling . . . falling down into nothingness. There is nothing to hold onto. I'm screaming and reaching out to someone. I wake up sweating with my heart beating rapidly." The first part of the dream reads like a child's fantasy. She is deeply involved in the dreamworld and unaware of any danger—like a child who can't swim, yet walks playfully out onto a diving board. When the little boat tips over, Katherine falls into an abyss—there is nothing to grab onto, creating a sense of isolation.

Let's put this together with her next falling dream six days later: "I am walking down a path. It's like a jungle. I walk for miles—the path is never-ending. Then I see vapors and steam rising below me. I see a light far away. It's an opening above me, but I can't reach it. Suddenly, I see hands reaching out from the opening, trying to help me up. I see my mother and father. I shout, 'Mom, Mom, help me!' I reach out to them, jumping up in midair, but I slip and tumble down into nothingness."

Again, note the childlike quality. It reads a bit like *Alice in Wonderland*. The road is unending, much as a child would perceive it. She sees a mysterious light coming from an opening, then her parents' hands. She calls for help and reaches for security, to no avail, as she falls.

Katherine has an insecure child inside her. Her parents and husband have died. She feels abandoned like a child, which leaves her clinging and panic-stricken. This does not mean Katherine is immature like a child. On the outside, she appears mature, competent, and professional. But there remains a lonely child inside that she fails to acknowledge and nurture. This child emerges at night in her dreams. She feels helpless, lonely, and without any control over her sense of security. So, in this case, we can apply the standard interpretation referring to loss of control.

Let's look at Jake's story. He's a forty-three-year-old mechanic. At age five, Jake's father went to Korea to fight in the war. His dad returned safely, but his absence left an indelible impact on Jake—he grew up too fast. He remained serious, perhaps too serious, about everything. As he got older, Jake worried about his father's health. His dad smoked too much and was having leg cramps from poor circulation. They would often squabble over his health. Jake's dad would chide him for his serious manner.

After one such squabble, Jake had a nightmare. "I am in Richmond, British Columbia to attend a berry festival. The landscape is rocky. The resort hotel is on a steep cliff. There are many people roaming about, but I only recognize my father. The people are murmuring and staring at me. I realize something is wrong. All of a sudden I am sitting on a tall rock with my foot over the edge. A fellow whom I never saw before is sitting by me. He offers to tell me what is happening. It seems I intruded on something that was going on and the people want to get rid of me. They start pelting me with rocks and I am losing my balance and falling over the edge of the cliff—I wake up scared."

Jake is falling from a resort where there are a number of people, including his father. A resort is a place to have fun, something Jake is not especially skilled at. Jake's father represents that carefree attitude—to the point of not taking *care* of himself. Much of the dream suggests this aspect of Jake. For him, the need to feel *in control*, to be in charge, to feel safe, has never allowed him to have fun or to feel carefree like his dad. So he feels *out of control* in a place where he could relax. Falling, for Jake, shows he is really too much in control and needs to learn how to relax.

Here's a third falling dream to consider. Allan was contemplating a move back to Colorado to spend more time with his teenage son. "I am with my ex-wife in Colorado looking across the valley. The other side looks manicured, with poplar trees and patches of open meadow. We drive across the meadow in a four-wheel-drive jeep, and I see large strips of indoor/outdoor carpet laid across the ground. It's nice to drive upon, but looks very out of place. We cross the valley and drive up a large hill

to the top of a small mountain. Suddenly, we drive to the edge
of a cliff. We brake in time, but we're halfway over the edge.
Then my ex-wife leans forward and this tips us. We fall to the
rocks below and I wake up."

Allan divorced years earlier and moved east. His career kept
him from the mountains he loved and left him little time for
maintaining family contact. In thinking about moving back, he
wondered if Colorado would provide the job opportunities he
needed. He also wondered if he was expecting too much to
think he could become close to his estranged family again.

The nightmare depicted the problem graphically. Though the
mountains were a source of comfort and familiarity to him,
Allan could easily see where the dream led. Falling, in this
case, suggested a very real danger in trying to fix his past.

As you've seen from these examples, the key to falling
dreams may center on the other elements in your dream story
and how you are falling away from them or what you are falling
towards. While staying with the general theme of out-of-control
is useful, looking over the dream relationships will yield more
insight for you.

NATURAL DISASTERS

Tidal waves are rare events. Most people have never experienced one. However, they are common in nightmares. They
often represent the dreamer feeling out of control relative to
the events highlighted in the dream—be it Mother Nature or
some other situation.

Consider Geoffrey's nightmare: "I am in a condo similar to
the one we use in Hawaii. I am with my wife and brother and
sister-in-law on the balcony. A tidal wave is pushing the water
as high as the balcony. I hear a noise and look up to see the
balcony cracking and falling apart. We go inside and close the
doors and windows, but the water keeps coming until it breaks
the windows and rushes in."

The condo in the dream was bought during a peak business
period. It was all paid for; however, a drop in the market
made finances extremely tight. Geoffrey was in jeopardy of
having to sell the condo to maintain his home. The business
reversal brought on some anxiety which was expressed in the
nightmare.

Earthquake dreams are also common. People who've suffered one may be reliving a real-life trauma in their dreams. Or, if you've never experienced a quake, the nightmare could represent your feminine side because the earth is generally considered a feminine symbol, as in Mother Earth. So, we might speculate that a feminine power or energy is unleashed in a destructive manner in an earthquake dream.

Lynne is very conservative and prides herself on her classic, expensive taste in clothes. This mirrors her fairly rigid approach to life. Right out of high school she went to junior college, then to college, and then on to her master's degree in business. At thirty-one, she was a successful businesswoman, but she remained single and childless. Lynne's mother took pride in her accomplishments, but Lynne questioned whether she'd missed out on something.

She described this nightmare after entering therapy. "I am in a jewelry store with my mother. She's complaining because they always put the earrings behind the counter. I point out they're right in front of her nose. I browsed over some earrings when suddenly an earthquake shook the shop. I pushed my mother to the floor to protect her. Through the windows, I could see other buildings shaking—they looked like they'd collapse on top of us. We ran to a vehicle outside and raced to get away."

After exploring the nightmare on her own, Lynne could see that her mother in the dream might be an extension of herself. This frequently occurs with dreams that include your family members. Then, she considered what the earth symbolized to her. She immediately responded with the phrase "Mother Earth," and then put the dream together as a conflict between her professional life versus her personal concerns. The earthquake highlighted the ambivalence of her feelings regarding career goals and motherhood.

Next time you have a natural disaster nightmare, look to see what is being shaken up, disrupted, or overwhelmed in the dream. Perhaps that will reflect something affecting your real life.

DRILLING, EXTRACTING, OR LOSING TEETH

Teeth are one of the most universal dream objects and often they are experienced in nightmares as falling out, pulled, or drilled upon. In ancient times, dreams of losing a tooth predicted a death of someone close, perhaps the dreamer. In Navajo culture, losing a tooth is seen as a bad omen and the dreamer may seek out a medicine man for advice. Some additional interpretations of teeth dreams include: symbol of death, concerns with aging, loss of powers or money, impotence, embarrassment, or passivity. Once again, the dream dictionaries are loaded with possibilities.

Do any of these notions apply to Rosita's nightmare? "I am in a powder room in a disco looking in a mirror to fix my makeup. I notice a bunch of teeth have fallen out. They're attached to a silver chain. I try to put them back in, but it doesn't work. I spit them out and some fall into the sink. I am so worried because I have to go to work and I can't go like that. I wake up and grab my mouth, relieved it's a dream."

Rosita is an Hispanic woman who operates a successful restaurant in Santa Fe. She's done well over the last ten years because of the hard work she and her family have put into the operation. Recently, she's wanted to spend more time with her two children. Having neglected her own schooling as an adolescent, Rosita also wanted to be involved with her kids in their school activities. Her eldest was in the second grade and the other was in kindergarten. There was an opportunity to assist the teacher in some outings and to do remedial reading with her children; however, she was unable to do either because of work at the restaurant.

In the restaurant Rosita does everything. When there's a time-crunch she even washes dishes. She tastes the food to insure superior quality and her main focus during business hours is to ensure the customers are properly taken care of, the food is served promptly, and everything runs smoothly.

She quickly made the connection of how important it is to have her teeth, so she can smile at her customers, taste food, and speak effectively to manage the restaurant. Without her teeth, she couldn't do the job. Thinking about this, Rosita broke out laughing and said, "Now wouldn't that really be wonderful if I couldn't go to work and had to stay home with my kids?"

In this nightmare we have a straightforward scenario in which Rosita wished her teeth fell out so she could quit work to be with her kids. So, the "loss of powers" interpretation from the dream dictionaries might apply; however, we think the dream is simply a direct extension of Rosita's reality. It is like dreaming about animals if you are a zookeeper. Animals could be extensions of the zookeeper's daily reality without having special symbolism. In the same way, Rosita's teeth symbolize her connection to the restaurant.

There are more complex and symbolic ways of looking at teeth. We use our teeth to chew and bite and they are nearly essential for eating and helping us to *integrate* food and sustenance into our bodies. If your teeth fall out in a nightmare, you might focus on the inability to "chew" on something and integrate it into yourself. Think about what's going on in the rest of the dream. What is it that you're having trouble digesting? That's where you might find the key.

"My teeth were loose and falling out of my mouth by the handfuls. I needed help. I needed to find a dental record that would clarify the last job the dentist did on me, proving he owed me or there had been some fault. I was becoming impatient and really worried about all my teeth falling out. I tried to find Dr. G.'s phone number, but it was unlisted. Someone said there was a security registry, which I found. I phoned him. He was not pleased I phoned and said if I was not in pain, in his opinion it was not an emergency. Someone said to glue them back in and I started to do that, but I lost some and the glue was not sticking and I began to panic."

This is a dream from a 38-year-old woman, Melissa, who was unhappy with her job for the past two years. There is an attempt in the dream to blame the dentist for not having done a good job. This could be the defense mechanism of projection whereby the blame for something is put on somebody else. The dreamer attempts to correct the problem by gluing her teeth in, but this fails. The dream also contains a conflict between her and her dentist or, as it turned out, what the dentist symbolized to her.

In this case, Melissa saw the dentist as a career professional and this triggered some new thoughts she had about her own career aspirations. She was a professional woman and had recently been passed over for a position in the company. She felt she'd done an excellent job and deserved the promotion and was blaming the company for its male selection policies. When questioned about this, she believed her opinion was accurate, but she also admitted that the branch of the company she would be transferred to was outside her area of training. In fact, if offered the job, she would have turned it down because she was interested in another division of the company and knew there would be an opening soon. In spite of this, she felt rejected for not having been selected.

So this dream symbolized the difficulties Melissa was having in making the right career move and in dealing with her prideful feelings over the rejection. She was unable initially to integrate the feelings, so she ended up projecting them onto the senior management who had refused her promotion.

Dreams of teeth often represent this inability to take in and use something or to integrate something in a positive way. This theme of integration is an important one and we suspect it may account for why so many people report dreams about losing teeth.

Incidentally, in all of the teeth dreams we've related, not one person reported a death of a close family member and none of these dreamers themselves died. These cases were of patients seen more than five years ago. So the widely held myth about teeth loss and death didn't apply in these instances, nor have we had other encounters with dreamers who met untimely ends after such nightmares. One woman dreamed of losing her teeth nearly every week while she was in college. She's alive and well several years after these recurrent nightmares ceased.

In real life, teeth can fall out with age or in various diseases and their loss may indicate something important. Dreaming about teeth loss may yield important insights as well, but you must review the entire dream to uncover its meaning.

KICKING THE HABIT

Earlier, we mentioned Jordan, who developed bad dreams after becoming addicted to a narcotic painkiller following dental surgery. It took him nearly a year to deal successfully with his dependency to drugs. During that time, while he was working to stay clean, he would occasionally have a recurrent nightmare.

"I'm shaving in front of the bathroom mirror. I'm very tired, I have a headache, and I don't want to go to work. I open the medicine cabinet to see if there's anything I can take to make me feel better. Right in front of me is a bottle of oxycodone. I grab the bottle and open it, then take two pills. For a split second I feel tremendous relief. Then I realize what I've done. I start to cry. I can't believe I gave in so easily. I start pounding my fists on the wall and then I wake up."

This kind of dream with infinite variations has been played out by innumerable people who have quit using drugs, alcohol, or cigarettes.

Mel had at least a dozen dreams of smoking cigarettes for several months after he'd quit. Each time he felt tremendous anxiety for having "broken" his oath to quit and each time he felt a wave of relief when he awakened to realize it was only a dream. "I had grown to hate myself for smoking and to actually start smoking again—in the dreams—recreated those disgusting feelings. I can't describe how good it felt to realize I hadn't smoked again."

What do these kinds of anxiety dreams reflect?

There has been at least one study which looked at dreams of people recovering from drug addiction. People who more frequently had these kinds of dreams did better in dealing with their addictions. Although the findings of the study were not conclusive, you may find this type of dream helps you build confidence in yourself if you've had a problem with drugs or alcohol.

You may ask how would you build confidence from giving in to the addiction in your dreams. Wouldn't that mean you're still really addicted? Perhaps. However, most people who have these dreams usually wake up feeling very upset at first, only to feel much better later as they realize they didn't break their commitment to abstinence. This process, while no doubt painful, may actually serve to strengthen their resolve to stay clean and sober.

These kicking-the-habit dreams are similar to examination or test dreams. Matt, an art gallery manager, had given up smoking marijuana for several months before he had this dream. "I am at a party. It's a lot of fun. Everybody's dancing all over the place. Some guy hands me a joint. Without thinking, I take a couple of hits. I suddenly cringe, realizing I have betrayed myself. When I woke up I felt badly at first because even though it was a dream, it seemed like I had failed a test."

Later, Matt worked through the dream and realized that the bigger test was still before him. Since then, he's done very well and has remained off marijuana for three years.

It's important to remember that drug problems are usually lifelong problems. An addict who attends an A.A. meeting will usually begin his talk with the words, "Hello, I'm Bill and I am an alcoholic," or "I'm an addict." Many of these people have been in recovery—clean and sober—for years, but they still refer to themselves in this way. Some use the term "recovering alcoholic" or "recovering addict." So, from the people who know the problem best—drug addicts and alcoholics themselves—we know they must be vigilant for the rest of their lives.

Dreaming about using drugs may serve as an important reminder or an appropriate warning that will help the addict to remain clean and sober.

EXAMINATION DREAMS

Max was thirty years old when he graduated from medical school. He achieved above-average marks on his exams, but did especially well in biochemistry. When he began his residency in family medicine he occasionally would have nightmares where he'd be back in medical school trying to pass a biochemistry test. "I'd be sitting at my desk and the clock would show less than five minutes to go and I hadn't even begun the test."

Max noted that residency was more stressful than medical school because the time-demands were greater. This dream would occur after an unusually busy day when he felt unable to spend as much time with his patients as he would have liked.

Freud wrote about examination dreams and also mentioned the views of one of his colleagues, Wilhelm Stekel. They both noticed that these types of dreams invariably depicted a test the dreamer had already passed, and often it was a test in which the dreamer had performed exceptionally well. Freud had recurring dreams of retaking his history exams in which he had achieved high marks.

Stekel and Freud noticed these dreams often occurred when a new "test" is about to face the dreamer. It doesn't have to be a school exam; rather, it could be some new challenge at work—a paper to present, a speech to give, or an appointment with a demanding colleague or mentor. The dream, despite being filled with anxiety, is actually a way of reassuring the dreamer once he has awakened. As Freud noted, "Don't be afraid of tomorrow! Just think how anxious you were before your matriculation, and yet nothing happened to you." The reminder that you've already succeeded is clear enough—once you've awakened from the dream.

Julie had done well throughout the semester, but her English professor required a passing grade on the final or else the panel of instructors would automatically fail her. The night before the exam she had two dreams. "I dreamt I went to the panel of instructors to take the test and they started asking me questions. My mind went completely blank. Then later that night I dreamed I was to carry my test papers to the panel, but I lost them along the way." She woke up both times very anxious, but that morning she passed the test with flying colors.

The same thing occurred when she took her certification exam to become a teacher. Twice she awakened from her sleep having dreamt she missed the exam because she forgot to set her alarm clock and then later because she set it wrong. Again she passed her test, though her troubled sleep the night before added to her anxieties.

Perhaps the dream dictionaries have finally got it right when they say good news will follow on the heels of dreaming of failing a test.

In the following section we'll teach you a method to interpret your own nightmares, but first we wish to devote the next chapter to the people who made this book possible—the chronic nightmare sufferers and other patients we've worked with whose cases contributed enormously to the content of the stories you've been reading.

CHAPTER 6

The Chronic Nightmare Disorder

CHRONIC NIGHTMARE SUFFERERS

Although there are no useful statistics available, it's safe to say the average person experiences some type of distressing dream every month or so. Most of the time this will not awaken the person from sleep.

There are, however, a number of people who experience bad dreams more frequently. Some have had nightmares since childhood, while others developed a chronic nightmare problem as an adult. Considering that we spend five years of our lives dreaming, we can easily sympathize with those who suffer from chronic nightmares.

The most widely used statistics on chronic nightmare sufferers refer only to people who are awakened by their bad dreams. If you suffer from nightmares once per week for six months or longer, then you are considered to have chronic nightmares. However, this view neglects many individuals who suffer frequent anxiety dreams which don't awaken them, yet still cause much distress. We think the current statistics woefully underestimate the true incidence of distressing dreams as a chronic problem. Even so, sticking with the criterion of awakening from the dream, more than 5 percent of adults suffer from chronic nightmares in the United States.

That's over ten million individuals, or one in twenty people!

While the percentage of children and adolescents with frequent bad dreams is unknown, it is estimated to be higher than that of adults. So the problem of chronic nightmares is widespread, but what's truly extraordinary is that chronic nightmare sufferers have the problem for years, perhaps decades, before seeking professional help, if they seek help at all.

Barbara is a forty-five-year-old hairdresser. She's had nightmares for forty years at a rate of one every night or more. She could not recall ever having gone even one week of her adult life without bad dreams.

In one typical five-day span she had these dreams:

Monday: "I'm in my bedroom at my mother's house. Flying bugs and black-and-yellow butterflies jump at my sister and me. We kill the bugs, but then a whole bunch fly above the door—they're all over the walls and ceiling. They're getting on us and we can't kill them fast enough. We run from the bedroom."

Tuesday: "I'm in Don's apartment. He has no shirt on. I have a big knife with a long pointed edge. I insert the knife into Don's abdomen and continue pushing it up towards his neck. His skin peels back easily."

Wednesday: "I am standing on a terrace. I see two babies falling from above me. They fall headfirst and I watch as their little heads smash against the concrete. Only they start bouncing and continue down a series of steps, bouncing against each step, headfirst. I turn away before their tiny heads break open."

Thursday: "I am standing in a driveway of a beautiful white mansion. I have a gun in my hand and I'm waiting for a man to come out. I am supposed to protect him. He comes out, accompanied by two guards. I fire a warning shot and the man and one of the guards rush to a car and drive away to safety, but one guard is left—I know he is the bad guy. I aim the gun at him. He is terrified, but I fire the gun and nothing happens. I fire again, still nothing. Now he comes towards me and I keep firing my empty gun. He's closer now, right next to me and he pulls out this little thing which squirts me with water, then he pulls out another tiny gun and puts it up to my neck. He shoots me and it hurts a lot."

Friday: "I'm at high school. Someone is shooting and everyone is trying to catch the person. I run to a corner and hide. People rush by me. I see the guy point the gun at someone else, then there is lots of gunfire."

Barbara woke up from every one of these nightmares. And her awakenings were invariably accompanied by severe emotional and physical reactions, including a racing heart, shortness of breath, and intense fear. The dramatic nature of Barbara's dreams and the frequency with which she experienced them for so many years are common for many chronic nightmare sufferers.

More than half the cases of chronic nightmares start before the age of ten, and almost two-thirds of the total number begin before the age of twenty. Some of those afflicted while young somehow manage to "grow out" of it. But if the nightmares begin in adulthood, the problem is more likely to continue for ten or twenty or as much as thirty years.

A major stressful event may precede about 60 percent of cases. For example, in our discussion of traumatically induced nightmares, we described Vietnam veterans, accident victims, and others who have suffered through emotionally or physically traumatic events. These unfortunate individuals may experience a high number of disturbing dreams. And, it is routine for the content of their nightmares to be directly related to the prior event.

Stressful events may act only as a catalyst for the problem. That is, the incident may not cause the nightmare; rather, it serves as a trigger for a person who might be predisposed towards having bad dreams. In many cases, however, no specific incident can be targeted as a trigger or a cause.

The largest subgroup with chronic nightmares is women. Why women have more nightmares than men is not known, but several surveys consistently demonstrate this finding. The problem with relying on these surveys, though, is that many people are embarrassed about the disorder, and simply do not seek medical or psychiatric treatment. It is also speculated that men are reluctant to admit the problem, and therefore their numbers are underestimated.

These data are merely demographic—they tell us statistics on a superficial level about nightmare sufferers. If we're going to understand the nature of chronic nightmare sufferers, we need to explore the psychological traits and characteristics of these people.

PERSONALITY TRAITS AND CHARACTERISTICS

A fair amount of research has been conducted on chronic nightmare sufferers in the last few years. Two comprehensive books on the subject appeared in the 1980s. The first, entitled *The Nightmare: The Psychology and Biology of*

Terrifying Dreams, was written by the psychiatrist we've mentioned earlier, Ernest Hartmann. The second, entitled *The Nightmare: Psychological and Biological Foundations*, was written by a group of psychologists, including its editor, Henry Kellerman.

These researchers studied a variety of individuals with chronic nightmares and attempted to discover patterns that might underlie their personalities. They wondered if there are specific traits or characteristics that set chronic nightmare sufferers apart from other individuals.

Specific traits might account for why some people experience nightmares and others do not. Unfortunately, much of the data is inconclusive. They mostly point to the theory that there are specific groups of people—best called *subgroups*—who seem prone to nightmares. These subgroups are not fixed in stone and may need revising as we learn more about the disorder. Furthermore, some groups will overlap.

Combining the research information from other experts with our own experience in treating chronic nightmare sufferers, we would suggest there are at least five major subgroups:

1. Normal individuals who do not fit into any special subgroup;
2. People who possess a quality described as "thin boundaries," which describes a way of relating to things in an overly sensitive manner, commonly seen in, though not limited to, certain types of creative individuals like artists or writers;
3. Individuals who have suffered trauma as adults, including emotional and/or physical trauma;
4. Individuals who suffered abuse as children, especially sexual abuse; and
5. Individuals with schizophrenia.

Schizophrenics account for the smallest subgroup. Most of the people in the other four groups would be considered relatively normal by most researchers; however, there are experts who believe some nightmare sufferers are more vulnerable to other mental health problems, such as depression, insomnia, and anxiety, as well as the posttraumatic stress disorder. This notion of vulnerability is controversial. Some believe in it strongly, while others feel there is no definite link between nightmares and psychopathology, that is, mental illness or mental health problems.

Why do some experts believe nightmares are mostly found in individuals with mental health problems?

The answer has a lot to do with interpreting the research data of the studies performed on chronic nightmare sufferers. Two important studies were performed by Hartmann. In the two studies, he worked with approximately fifty people. These nightmare sufferers were recruited through an advertisement in a Boston newspaper. Hartmann questioned them extensively about their nightmares and backgrounds. He conducted elaborate and extensive psychological testing, using recognized and respected formats for analyzing psychological traits and characteristics. His data showed that some people with chronic nightmares were previously undiagnosed schizophrenics.

This raises another question: Do people suffering from chronic nightmares have schizophrenia lurking somewhere in their background?

We think not. There are many other studies which have examined chronic nightmare sufferers, including our own work, which do not show this pattern. In fact, 50 percent of Hartmann's group did not fit any abnormal patterns whatsoever and would be classified as completely normal. At present, there is no evidence to show that nightmare sufferers are at a greater risk for schizophrenia than anyone else. We believe schizophrenics represent a definite subgroup of individuals who may experience frequent bad dreams, but the overwhelming majority of chronic nightmare sufferers do not have this serious mental health disorder.

The second subgroup are those with thin boundaries—a term used by Hartmann to explain the personalities of some chronic nightmare sufferers. When someone criticizes us with a cutting remark about the clothes we're wearing or the style of our hair, most of us develop a healthy defense system to let these thoughtless comments roll off our backs. Some nightmare sufferers haven't developed such defenses. They take the criticism to heart instead of mentally standing up for themselves.

Their sensitivity doesn't necessarily stop with themselves. When another individual experiences pain or suffering, these individuals with "thin boundaries" may have greater empathy, as if they were able to share the person's experience and feel their pain and suffering. Furthermore, their sensitivity also includes the element of perception, that is, they are more sensitive to noting things about other people, especially feelings.

Patricia is such a person; she was a sensitive child. She thought her older brother a bore and a bully and her mother too socially self-conscious and uninvolved with her. Her father lavished too much attention on her, calling her "sweetheart" in a way that made her feel uncomfortable.

Patricia dealt with her family by withdrawing into a fantasy world where reality and fantasy merged. She liked other kids, but her fantasies surpassed anything they offered. This pattern continued through puberty where Patricia remained undeveloped with a thin, anorexic physique. Although attractive, she wore plain clothes and no makeup. At fifteen she fell in love, gained ten pounds and started socializing. Her boyfriend on the junior varsity basketball team was not too popular, but the next summer he grew four inches and that winter made the varsity team. Then he dumped Patricia.

She was devastated, lost weight, and didn't come out of her shell for a year. As a high school senior she got involved in the class play. She drew upon her ability to fantasize by immersing herself in the roles of the characters. She loved the theater, but she had too much anxiety onstage. She dated sporadically and upon meeting a man, she would open up too soon, scaring him away with too much candor.

In college, Patricia protected herself by keeping friends to a minimum, yet whenever she became involved, she worried about all their problems. She even worried about the problems of the characters she portrayed in her theater activities. She finished her master's degree in theater and took a job teaching theater at a junior college.

She knew her life was a paradox, loving theater and fantasy, yet feeling too self-conscious to perform onstage. She could never focus on her own feelings or the feelings of a character. It was as if the feelings of everyone around her, stagehands, other actors and actresses, and the audience all kept merging with her own feelings.

The only way she coped with the intensity was to seek solitude. Her dreams, however, failed to protect her. She had nightmares about her love rejections, about being late for exams, about not finishing her work. Then, as a teacher, she had nightmares about her students. Any student who had the least bit of trouble suddenly became Patricia's personal problem.

Marriage put stability into her life and she felt better. At the age of 29 she had her first child which was fortunate for two reasons. Having a child was a joy and proved to be a very educational experience for Patricia. Good fortune shone on her with the selection of a woman pediatrician with a strong background in psychology. The doctor immediately picked up the clues about Patricia's problems with ego boundaries. Raising the baby turned out to be an extraordinarily useful way for Patricia to learn about boundaries as she watched them evolve in her own child.

Although her nightmares had increased before delivery, within three years after the birth of her child, they were nearly gone. Five years later, she was back teaching and her daughter was in kindergarten. Now she kept her students' problems at bay. She even failed a student and felt she had done the right thing without tearing herself up inside.

Patricia, like some others with the chronic nightmare disorder, suffered all those years because she was too open and defenseless. Instead of developing an impenetrable armor, these individuals allow things inside. Referring back to schizophrenics, we find people with this illness also have problems with ego boundaries. But this is a more serious problem for schizophrenics because they may lose sight of their own identity.

How do chronic nightmare sufferers acquire these thin boundaries?

One possible answer is heredity. In Hartmann's study he paid special attention to the patients' relatives. He discovered that some patients who did not suffer from schizophrenia had at least one close relative who did suffer from this serious mental health disorder. On the other hand, many of the patients we've encountered have experienced child abuse. We suspect child abuse could play a significant role in acquiring this sensitivity.

We've looked at two subgroups: schizophrenics and those with thin boundaries. Two other groups relate to traumatic experiences, either as an adult or a child or in some cases both. In our discussion of traumatic causes in Chapter 3, we pointed out the unpredictability of who will and who won't develop nightmares. Furthermore, we can't even predict which types of nightmares they will experience. Some trauma victims will develop specific nightmares which replay the incident. Others may develop night terrors. Most will show a pattern of symbolic dreaming where the nightmare may or may not mirror the original trauma.

Our research indicates that child abuse, especially sexual abuse, is more common than previously thought as a cause of nightmares. One reason for this finding may be our society's recent attempts at dealing with this pervasive problem. For a long time we have lived in virtual denial regarding sexual abuse of children. Only in the last ten to twenty years, if that long, have people begun communicating, openly or in therapy, about the sexual abuse they suffered as children. This is a major problem our society faces which we are only beginning to address.

The last and largest category described is normals. Does this mean all the other subgroups are abnormal? We do not think so. As we said, the subgroups overlap. Many people in the other subgroups, with the exception of the schizophrenics, often function at healthy levels in society.

This brings us to controversial points discussed in the scientific literature. While several studies support the notion of greater vulnerability to mental health problems in nightmare sufferers, there are many experts who take issue with these conclusions. They point to the large number of subjects who turn out to be normal in many of these same research studies. And, they describe their own clinical experiences in dealing with frequent nightmare sufferers where they have also found a high percentage of normal people.

Many of these experts look at chronic nightmares as a particular *process* that some people experience, while others do not. The nightmares may serve an adaptive or therapeutic function for certain types of individuals. These notions come from the experience of psychiatrists and psychologists who feel it is unwise to categorize nightmare sufferers on the basis of objective psychological testing. Instead, it's more important to take into account the whole picture of the individual's life.

Of course the problem we are struggling with here is: What does *normal* mean?

In our work, we've seen evidence that supports both views. The great majority of individuals who we've studied have led prosperous and functional lives in terms of marriages, jobs, and family relations, despite having suffered for years, if not decades, from chronic nightmares. However, at times their suffering manifested with more symptoms such as anxiety, depression, and insomnia, as well as psychosomatic complaints such as bodily aches and pains.

These theories certainly seem to be at odds with each other. How can you function well with all these distressing symptoms? Again, what does it mean to be normal?

Do we look at psychological tests and pin a diagnosis on someone or do we observe their level of functioning in society and the community? We hold more to the latter view. In support of that view is the fact that the overwhelming majority of chronic nightmare sufferers do not appear to suffer significant impairment of daytime functioning.

Some of these individuals might benefit from psychotherapy. A few might require extended counseling with a mental health professional. Still, most people with chronic bad dreams can benefit from treating their nightmares with the technique we'll be describing in Part III of our book.

WHAT IS A CHRONIC NIGHTMARE DISORDER?

As we noted, the American Psychiatric Association has designated the term *Dream Anxiety Attacks* for those suffering from nightmares. The essential feature is: "repeated awakenings from sleep with detailed recall of frightening dreams. These dreams are typically vivid and quite extended and usually include threats to survival, security or self-esteem."

For many individuals with chronic nightmares, however, this pattern doesn't fit. Many report a vagueness to their bad dreams and are unable to recall much detail. Yet a dreadful or frightening response is evoked which awakens them from sleep.

Bert, a seventy-two-year-old military retiree, had nightmares once a week for forty-five years. Here's one of his typically vague dreams. "My son is involved somehow, but he's not visible so I don't know which son. A highway appears, but I can't make out where because the terrain is fuzzy. I am walking down the center stripe. The traffic is fairly busy, but it's more like I feel the cars coming at me. I don't see them that well. I try to dodge them on instinct."

Jeff, a thirty-two-year-old cartoonist, suffered nightmares a few times each week. "I am mad, but I don't know why. There's a feeling of betrayal and resentment. I feel fragments of things . . . yelling out in anger and my wife saying, 'I don't want to hear that.' "

And as we've mentioned repeatedly, some may not awaken from the actual dream, but instead remember the nightmare upon awakening in the morning and, in so doing, produce a new round of anxiety and dread. Sally is a clerk in a department store. She's suffered from nightmares once a week for twenty years, but seldom is she awakened by them. "I am at work. I start arguing with a clerk. She slaps me across the face, cutting me with her fingernail. I hit her back, then go to look at myself in the mirror. I'm extremely worried about my face."

In another dream Sally describes these images. "My husband and I are asleep on a park bench. We're homeless and dressed in rags and covered with newspapers. An old man flicks a lit cigarette on us, setting the papers ablaze. We jump up and put out the fire, then move to another bench, only the bench has one end dangling off the edge of a cliff. I'm yelling, 'No, no.' Suddenly two planes collide above us and explode in midair."

It's difficult to imagine more intense dreams, but Sally was awakened by neither one, although in the morning she recalled the nightmares and felt anxious and sick to her stomach.

Also, what is scary or threatening is defined by how the dreamer feels about it. Miguel is an artist who's had nightmares every other night for the past 30 years. Often he has violent and graphic events occurring in his dreams, but there are other times where he notices feelings of deep depression and fear in dreams he's unable to interpret.

"I am hunting seashells on the ocean floor near Greenland. I'm under huge icebergs. As I bring up the shells, I feel clumsy. The shells fall out of my hands. Some drift under the icebergs. I'll never be able to retrieve them. Other shells hit bottom and break. I wake feeling depressed."

It is important to realize the nightmare sufferer's imagination may produce a range of images from the vivid to the vague where the content *might* explain feelings of fear or dread or terror. Or, in other cases, unless the content is thoroughly analyzed, we may never find an explanation for why the dreamer experienced a distressing emotional response.

Because there is such a wide range of experience among people with frequent bad dreams, it is our belief that the criteria for the chronic nightmare disorder should be expanded to include those people who don't fit the narrow psychiatric definition.

HOW DO YOU SUFFER?

Let us return to our story of Emily—our first case history in Chapter 1. Before she got rid of her bad dreams, she had developed a lengthy bedtime ritual.

"When I went to sleep at night, I spent a lot of time preparing my bed. I knew this was silly, I mean, I knew it never stopped my nightmares, but for some reason I thought it might. Besides, I felt more comfortable doing it. I would pull each cover, one at a time, halfway down the bed. I knew I was stalling, but I'd gotten into the routine of doing it this way. After I hopped into bed, I flipped on the radio and glanced through a few fashion magazines, then I started a crossword. Usually that was it, but if I still felt anxious and it wasn't too late, I'd call a friend or my brother and try to talk about nothing for a while. At some point I'd get so bored or exhausted I'd fall right to sleep."

Does any of this sound familiar?

If you're a chronic nightmare suffer or an insomniac you can probably relate to Emily's ritual. In our studies, nearly everyone complained of difficulties with sleep. For most people it was the impossibility of returning to sleep after their nightmares. Many reported taking hours to go back to sleep, if they could at all. Others have developed chronic insomnia because of their fear of what awaits them in sleep.

While sleep deprivation causes untold stress on the nightmare sufferer, the stress of the nightmare itself causes a strain on the individual which may have an even greater impact. Think about this for a moment: Suppose you dreamt once a week you murdered your mother or your father or your spouse. Trying to write off these horrible images with pat phrases like, "It's only a dream," just doesn't work. It may only be a dream, but to have these horror stories played out over and over again causes most nightmare sufferers to feel badly about themselves.

Whether the person's dreams are even more revolting and disgusting than murdering a family member or whether they're the more subtle type which nonetheless provoke their own brands of dread and fear, the effects of chronic nightmares can be quite devastating to your self-esteem.

WHEN TO SEEK HELP

Many psychiatrists use the figure of six months' duration to make the diagnosis of chronic nightmares. This is probably a reasonable guideline, although we must point out nearly every patient we've seen has had the problem for five years or longer. The average chronic nightmare sufferer usually has the problem for more than ten years.

Why is this so? Another way to ask this question is: When you don't feel well, how long do you wait to see the doctor? Usually not too long if you're suffering a physical illness and you want relief from pain or fever or some other symptom.

With chronic nightmares there is a huge obstacle to overcome—people assume nothing will change. In fact, people with chronic nightmares rarely ask for help for the specific problem of nightmares. Generally, a patient will seek counseling for depression or anxiety and mention a problem with nightmares as well. Although many people responded to our ads about our research studies on nightmares, we know of few cases where patients came on their own to our clinics asking for help to treat just their bad dreams.

This raises the question again of which came first—your nightmares or your symptoms? Do feelings of anxiety and depression cause nightmares? Or, do nightmares cause feelings of anxiety and depression? If you got rid of the nightmares, would the bad feelings resolve? Much of our research indicates your mental health may improve if you eliminate your bad dreams. We will continue to discuss this crucial issue in various places throughout the remainder of the book.

So when should you seek help, and what kind of help should you be looking for?

We certainly recommend that you *not* wait years before trying to treat your nightmares. If you suffer from chronic nightmares, chances are you've done so for a long time. In the next sections of the book, you'll find the tools you need to work on and conquer your bad dreams.

Most earlier theories on the treatment of nightmares promoted extended psychotherapy to eliminate bad dreams. Bad dreams were looked upon as the symptom of another problem which needed to be addressed. By treating the other problem, the nightmares should vanish.

We will be outlining a simpler approach to dealing with your bad dreams. In this approach we will concentrate on the nightmare as its own problem with its specific effects upon you, the nightmare sufferer, regardless of the dream's so-called underlying cause and meaning.

Perhaps nightmares yield valuable clues towards a better understanding of yourself, but is it possible that bad dreams might only represent a nightly annoyance which can be eliminated easily?

Actually, we think both views are correct. That is, nightmares do have meaning, but for many people with chronic bad dreams, nightmares can also be approached as a distinct and treatable problem. In our next two sections we'll give you the opportunity to look at both perspectives. We'll teach you how to interpret your own troubling dreams and then we'll teach you, step by step, how to banish your nightmares.

PART II

How to Interpret Your Bad Dreams and Nightmares

CHAPTER 7

Recording Nightmares and Identifying the Dream Elements

THE NIGHTMARE: A BEST FRIEND IN DISGUISE?

Interpreting nightmares is not easy.

Though many books have been written about dream interpretation, no book can ease the difficult process of working through the emotional conflicts highlighted in your nightmares. Analyzing bad dreams is likely to raise some issue, memory, or feeling you might otherwise prefer to leave sleeping.

We cannot suggest an easy way of dealing with these conflicts. In fact, it's not supposed to be easy. But like your best friends who are willing to tell you what they really think when you really need to hear it, there may come a time when you'll be ready to listen to what your nightmares have to say to you.

When that time comes, we want you to be ready.

We'll teach you an organized way of looking at your troubling dreams. The guidelines and steps we provide in the next four chapters will help you begin the delicate process of looking at your nightmares in a more constructive way. Using these steps will also help you build the confidence you need to forge ahead.

Why forge ahead? What can you gain by interpreting your nightmares? Very simply, your disturbing dreams may disappear if you interpret them. And, you'll gain new insights and understanding of yourself. This process will help you resolve emotional conflicts that have troubled you, which in turn will allow you to redirect your energies in more positive ways.

Whether you are an occasional or a chronic nightmare sufferer, you know your dreamworld contains a mixture of good and bad dreams. The steps we outline can be used on your good dreams as well as the bad ones. But this book is really about nightmares, not just ordinary dreams. For some people, these next chapters may prove very difficult to work on.

If you're nervous about interpreting your nightmares, we suggest you consider this quote from Fritz Perls: "Don't push the river; it flows by itself." If you've had chronic nightmares and you've thought about them—and thought about them again and again—don't push yourself trying to interpret them if it makes you feel like you're beating yourself over the head with a cast iron skillet.

We recommend you begin working on this section of the book because we believe you'll find our method an excellent one for analyzing your nightmares. But if you find it too difficult, there's no reason why you can't skip on to the third section and return to this part of the book at another time.

In the third section, *Turning Nightmares into Dreams*, we'll show you how to get rid of your troubling dreams. And to conquer your nightmares, we're *not* going to ask you to interpret them. If the time comes when you're ready to look more closely at your dreams or the rare nightmare you have after successfully using the treatment, then please refer back to this section.

If you're familiar with the works of Freud and other pioneers and experts such as Hall, Jung, Perls, Faraday, and Delaney, you may recognize variations on their techniques in the following pages. We are especially indebted to one man, Rolf Loehrich, a psychoanalyst-philosopher who spent the major portion of his life developing a unified dream theory.

Still, we must realize science has never proven one method of dream interpretation superior to another. You may find certain styles of dream interpretation more appealing to you. Though we hope you'll take time to learn our method, we encourage you to explore the techniques of other dream investigators as well.

Now here's a quick outline of the steps we'll go through in Chapters 7, 8, 9, and 10:

1. *Recording* your nightmare and learning to achieve some *distance* and *perspective* from the bad dream;
2. Picking out the *dream elements* (people, animals, etc.) in your nightmare by underlining them in your record of the dream;

3. *Associating* to these dream elements to see what comes to mind about the figures in your dream;
4. Putting yourself back in the nightmare to explore the *relationships* between yourself and the various dream elements to uncover the meaning of the dream;
5. Relating the *meaning* of the dream to *current or previous situations* in your life;
6. Consider what *actions* or *responses* you'll make with the knowledge gained by your interpretation of the nightmare.

Let's look at two examples—one simple and one complex— as a brief preview to working through these six steps.

We'll italicize the dream elements for you in David's dream. "I am *playing football*. I have the *ball* and I'm *running* in the clear. I see several *tacklers* out of the corner of my eye. I try to get away, but they're gaining. I suddenly notice I have no football pads on to protect me. I panic as I feel them nearly on top of me. I wake up in a sweat."

David is 28 and stopped playing high school football ten years ago. He has two kids and a wife, a large mortgage on his house and other financial pressures. When associating to football players, he recalled his skill as a running back but also remembered his fear of the bigger players on the defensive line. Some of them outweighed him by fifty pounds.

In David's work, he has a middle-management position where he routinely takes orders from senior executives. He sees the senior executives as "the big guys who carry more weight." He made the connection that the intimidation he felt from football was similar to how he felt toward his bosses. The dream helped him to recognize his real life concerns and face up to them in an honest way.

In this next example, there are numerous dream elements, but we'll only italicize a few. Carol had a nightmare that her boyfriend, Ted, was a dolphin stuck out of water. "I am in bed. Ted is next to me, but he's a *dolphin*. He makes squeaky noises like *Flipper*. I realize he'll die if I don't get him into water. I run to the bathroom and turn on the water to the tub. Then I soak a bunch of towels and wrap him up. I'm so upset I want to cry, but I'm so frantic I can't. All of a sudden Ted is alive and *human* again. I am so happy. He shows me his hands which are now webbed. He looks sad and apologizes for his condition. He's worried I'll be angry. I decide *I can accept him* even if he has webbed hands."

Carol had this dream three months into her relationship with Ted. Her associations drew her to Flipper the TV dolphin—a show she watched religiously as a child. She thought of Flipper as heroic and telepathic—a perfect creature she could depend upon and one that could guess her every need. This was the cornerstone to understanding the dream because in the story the dolphin was the opposite—weak and helpless. Was there anything in Carol's real life to explain the paradox?

Her relationship with Ted had evolved in a similar way. Carol had quickly become infatuated with Ted in the first month. She had idolized him, making him out to be a strong and decisive hero-type. But soon Ted started acting inappropriately—at the oddest times he would make comments about himself that seemed like he was cutting himself down.

Ted's behavior seemed sort of—*fishy*—to Carol. She wondered if he was the strong, decisive type, or were his own putdowns more on target? Was he fishing for reassurance in their relationship? Was he really a weak and helpless creature whom she would be stuck with? These inconsistencies had Carol wondering what to do about the relationship.

Though this particular dream did not consciously prompt Carol to sit down with Ted to talk about their relationship, it was a week or so after the dream that Ted openly expressed his discomfort with his role as the perfect creature. He wanted Carol to see him as a real person with his own imperfections. He wanted her to accept him.

When Carol thought more about the dream she recalled worrying about being stuck with a fish out of water and how much better it would be if he were human again. Once he was human again, she felt tremendous relief and was eager to accept him in his present condition. In real life, their relationship evolved more maturely in the ensuing months.

So Carol quickly found the cornerstone of the dream in her beliefs about dolphins—a symbol from her childhood memories. It represented the perfect mate, yet her dream showed her how it wasn't so perfect after all. In the end, selecting someone more "human" would prove more fulfilling.

Carol's dream is a complex one and we have only uncovered one of its many layers. There are many other questions raised which we haven't answered and there are many more dream elements to explore. This would take time and work. As you explore your own dreams, you'll see how much more elaborate they can get. Much will depend not only on how much time you can devote to exploring your dreams, but of greater importance will be how honest you can be with yourself as you uncover the various layers of meaning within your nightmares.

Now, if you're ready to continue, we want you to select a nightmare you can work with as we go through the steps.

STEP ONE: RECORDING NIGHTMARES AND GAINING PERSPECTIVE

Recording is the first step. Please grab a pen and paper. Write down your nightmare in the first person, present tense, that is, use verbs that descibe the action as if it is occurring right now. "I *see* the claw coming closer. It *is* big, red, and sharp. It *snaps* at me." Avoid I "saw" or it "was" or it "snapped." Using the present tense usually helps you remember more details about the dream. So jot down the nightmare now in as much detail as you can recall. Things which seem minor at first blush may lead to significant discoveries. After you've recorded the nightmare, you'll be ready to continue.

To analyze nightmares, we have some huge obstacles to overcome. Namely, these bad dreams disturb us, therefore we are understandably worried about dwelling on them, especially if all it's going to do is make us relive the bad feelings.

This is where ordinary dream interpretation diverges from nightmare analysis. So-called normal dreaming allows us the luxury of sitting back and dwelling on our dreams to our heart's content. The idea of dwelling on a nightmare sounds like a dreadful idea. "So tell me, Mrs. Smith, about that dream last night, what do you think of when you recall that man stabbing you in the chest with a pickax?"

Just asking the question makes our mythical Mrs. Smith cringe at having to replay the episode. We don't want you to torture yourself with this stuff. You know better than anyone how painful it can be. So the next thing to accomplish after recording is finding a way to put distance between yourself and the bad dream. You'll have plenty of opportunity to get into the raw feelings of the dream, but now we want you to learn how to take a step back so you can ease your way in.

There are many ways to achieve this distance. We'll briefly describe three roles you can assume that will get you over this first hurdle: the Recorder, the Scientist, and the Hollywood Producer.

You're already familiar with the *recording* method if you've been able to write down your dreams. This usually externalizes the nightmare, that is, it makes you see it outside of yourself. By writing it down, you've taken it out of your head and put it on paper. This can be comforting in the "It's only a dream" kind of way that begins the process of distancing. This approach works for most people, but there are some who cannot write down their bad dreams. Even so, a few notes can help and will prove invaluable for the other steps of dream interpretation.

The scientific model asks you to look at your nightmares *objectively* without attaching judgments. So if Mrs. Smith describes the gory details of her attack, she would not ignore the frightening emotions she felt; rather, she would focus on that fear for a bit. She might ask herself, "When did I have this fear before and what were the circumstances?" She might draw further associations to that fear without making herself uncomfortable thinking about the pickax.

This approach is geared for people who can detach themselves a bit from their feelings, so they can look at things objectively. But even if you're very sensitive and emotional, you can still gain a more objective perspective with practice.

The showbiz approach asks you to look at your nightmare as a *movie* or a *play* you might see in a theater. Though you usually find yourself in the starring role, focus on the nightmare as a whole. You'll come back to analyze yourself and the other characters later. Ask yourself, "What is this story about?" There's a plot happening here, so take a look at it. This will take you away from being *in* the action and allow you to be an observer *of* the action.

Most people use a combination of these methods, for example, writing down the dreams *and* looking at the dream in a different light. Get yourself comfortable with whatever combination works, or create one yourself. We'll assume you record your dreams. And we'll stick with the Hollywood analogy because we'll use examples from the world of movies to help you understand many things about your dreams.

STEP TWO: IDENTIFYING THE DREAM ELEMENTS

Dream elements refer to the "things" in our dreams—people, animals, objects, places, and, most importantly, the action taking place in the nightmare.

Looking Over Your Cast of Characters

If you were a Hollywood producer, you'd be mulling over all kinds of issues in deciding who to star as the villain in your movie. Who's available to play the part? How much are they going to cost? And of prime importance, who's really the best person for the part of the bad guy?

Producing your nightmare seems to ask similar questions. Who's available from your day residue to be brought into your dreamworld? How much are they going to "make you pay" by their presence in your nightmare? And why are they the best person to get the point across which your unconscious has been struggling with?

Now let's take a closer look at those whom you've selected to star in your nightmare story.

Dream figures is the general term we give to people, creatures, and things found in your dreams. Most of the time you will be the central figure in the story, but often there will be other people playing roles, too. For example, *friends* and *family* regularly appear in people's dreams. Sometimes this follows from your daytime experiences and conflicts with them.

Other times, because you are so close to your friends and family, they may appear in the dream as an extension of yourself. Bill dreams about his father driving a car wildly out of control near the edge of an embankment. When Bill was young, his dad injured himself in a single-car accident due to his own negligence. When Bill dreams about his dad driving recklessly, he knows it's really about his own negligence in dealing with stressful aspects of his life.

Sometimes characters will show up that don't have a personal relationship to you—*unknown figures*. You may have to work harder to sort them out. They are there for a purpose. Remember, you produced this movie and you selected the cast. You'll have to ask yourself a series of questions to get ideas. Are they young or old? What kind of clothes are they wearing? What are they doing—standing around, letting you take the fall, or are they engaged in some activity with you or against you?

A further way of looking at unknown people in your dreams is to ask the question: If the camera were focused on this unknown individual in a movie, what would the director want me to see? In the same way, ask yourself what your unconscious might want you to see.

The most important question to be asking yourself is whether the unknown person reminds you in any way of yourself. Your unconscious mind may have developed the habit of casting you in roles of unknown figures.

Evelyn grew up in a small town in Alberta. Her parents were Ukranian. They had been very strict. She graduated from high school and married at eighteen. Three years later she had two children. At twenty-five, she was working while her husband went to college. At thirty, she started her own business and several years later she had a successful culinary shop. Then the restlessness set in. Everything her husband said to her seemed to annoy her.

This was her nightmare. "There is an attractive woman with sparkling eyes following me. At first I think she might be a friend because she smiles. I begin to sense an evilness about her. For some reason she wants to hurt me. She wants to destroy me and my marriage. She doesn't want my husband for herself. Her purpose seems to be to destroy my whole life. I try to run away but she always finds me. The harder I try to lose her, the more determined she becomes. I am frightened and don't know how to deal with her."

In therapy, Evelyn was not ready to find meaning in her bad dream, yet six months later, the unknown woman turned out to be herself. She discovered her annoyance with her husband was the unexpressed resentments she had built up over the years. She wanted to decrease her remaining household obligations and concentrate on business. Her years of working had given her much confidence, but her husband reacted with fear to her independence and tried to hold on tighter. This increased Evelyn's frustrations. So the unknown dream figure was really Evelyn trying to be free within her own marriage.

In the common nightmare of being attacked, people describe an assault, yet they can't identify the attacker. Usually a man is the assailant in men's dreams, while women usually have dreams where either a man or a woman is the attacker. Men apparently see men as aggressors and women see both men and women as such. In our society, most people have encountered situations involving violence or aggression. What's your personal experience with these types of conflicts, and how do you see men and women in these roles? Answering these questions may yield important clues to how you see your dream figures.

It will also be useful to take a closer look at your attacker. If it's a man attacking, is he big or small? Does he carry a weapon? Do you remember anything about his face? Does any characteristic of this person, even if it's a vague one, remind you of someone else? If it's a woman attacker, ask yourself the same questions.

Allasandra is a Portuguese woman who speaks three languages and reads prolifically. She is a single parent who has many good friendships with men. But because she considers herself of high moral character, she has trouble meeting her sexual needs.

"I am standing next to a park bench. Three people are there—a prison guard, a criminal, and a woman. The criminal is somewhat spastic, but very nondescript. Suddenly he reaches over and puts his hands up the dress of the woman. He is very uncoordinated, but he puts his fingers into her vagina. I am aghast as he removes his moistened hands covered with her secretions."

She thought of the guard as controlled and nonsexual. She thought of the prisoner as possessing two sides—one good, in trying to be free, and one bad, as he was guilty of a crime. She related this to her own situation of trying to be freer with her sexuality, yet feeling constrained as she felt it would be "criminal" to do so.

Special people are last on the list of dream characters. These are individuals with special attributes such as extraordinary skills, training, insight, and power. A classic example is dreaming of a judge who passes a sentence upon you, condemning you to death for a crime you have supposedly committed. Another example would be doctors. Physicians are figures of authority in our society and their power allows them to delve into the lives of their patients, both physically and mentally. It is not uncommon for people to dream about doctors invading their person or privacy in some nightmarish manner. On other occasions you may dream of important historic figures.

Howard's nightmare centers on the late president, John Kennedy. "President Kennedy just passed us going the other way. I call out and run after him. He runs down a dirty dark alley and soon there are guys following us with guns. I wake up scared."

Notice how Howard initially is going in the opposite direction of Kennedy and then tries to run after him. When exploring his associations to this special figure, Howard mentioned he didn't care for JFK; he thought JFK was an intellectual elitist. Yet in the dream Howard runs after him.

The same pattern fits closely with Howard's real-life experiences. At work, he's overly sensitive to intellectual authority figures, distrusting them, getting angry at their bossiness. Ironically, Howard finds himself trying to beat these people at their own game, that is, he tests and challenges other people's positions through his own intellectual skills. So, on the one hand, Howard claims to abhor the qualities of a man like JFK, yet he goes right on using his own intellect in that very same way.

For the special people in your dreams you have to determine what's special about them and ask yourself what they might be representing. The judge could be passing judgment. The doctor could be raising issues of death and dying. Other figures such as kings, queens, politicians, or religious figures may have special meaning for you.

Before we move on, make a list, or underline the dream people in your nightmares. Separate them into three groups—family and friends; unknown people; and special people. As you do this you may find you start associating without further prompting. If so, make notes by each person.

As we continue exploring the other dream elements, you may have other flashes of insight about one of these people. If so, go back and jot it down.

Two other important dream figures are *animals* and *objects*. Many people have nightmares about animals. Dogs, snakes, insects, and spiders are common. The most important question to ask yourself is whether or not the animal represents something in your personal world or whether it is symbolic. If you dream about dogs and cats, chances are you've had personal encounters with these domestic animals. On the other hand, if you dream about lions and elephants, this might reflect something more symbolic.

Begin with some basic questions. Were you ever bitten by a dog or a spider? Do snakes or rodents roam your neighborhood? Or, if you're thinking the animal represents something symbolic, what do you know about this animal? Have you heard about the protectiveness of a mother bear, the sexual prowess of a bull, or the courage of a lion? These specific attributes of different animals may be relevant.

Consider this nightmare about monkeys. "I'm sitting on a bar stool. The room is dark, all blackness, except for a spotlight from above. I start to climb down from the stool and I hear this awful growl. I see a large monkey with a mean face with large pointed teeth bared at me. I am so terrified I can't scream. I know *the monkey will not let me move* from the stool as I stare back at it."

Monkeys are not household pets and therefore if you had such a dream you might begin with the symbolic meanings of monkeys as a likelier source of information. Monkeys may represent conflicts around jealousy, in which case we might interpret this by saying the dreamer was paralyzed by her jealousy. Sometimes your animal figures will fit into a clear-cut symbol from some universal mold, but often they will not. Before gravitating towards a standard meaning, be sure to explore what personal experiences or knowledge you have of the animals in your dreams.

"I open the door and crush Couver, my beloved spaniel. He lays there terribly wounded and I think he is dying." Katherine is a spiritual person and was struggling with her allegiance to two different Christian faiths. At the same time, her dog was aging and she suspected a serious illness. When exploring this dream, Katherine's reaction was to express her fear of losing her dog, but she also made the connection that dogs symbolized spiritual guides in various religious writings, such as Goethe's *Faust*. So the nightmare took on two distinct meanings for her, both representing important concerns—the dog as a symbol of her spiritual quests and a dying dog which aroused anxiety about her aging pet.

Objects could be anything in the universe, not to mention the fantastic things we conjure up in our dreams. Cars, planes, buildings, houses, fences, and roads are common objects, but the list goes on forever. A key here is to note who possesses the object. If it's your car, then whatever happens to that car may represent something happening to you. If it's not your car, then you're back to asking why is this car in your dream? Again, if a movie camera focused on the car for a few moments, what is it your unconscious might be depicting?

Lisa is a 35-year-old bookkeeper who dreams about her computer. "I have a deadline to meet. I hear a noise, someone laughing in a weird sarcastic way. I turn to my file cabinet, but instead I see a computer with flashing eyes and a wide-open mouth . . . laughing. The keys start clicking on their own, then suddenly the keys are spitting out a green, slimy liquid. The liquid falls to the floor and turns into snakes."

So we have a common object—a computer—acting on its own. It takes on animal-like properties by spurting out fluid which turns into snakes. It is no longer the dreamer controlling the machine, but the machine dominating the dreamer. Who's in charge here—the computer or Lisa?

This nightmare reflects Lisa's current job. She feels dominated by work. The computer has become her enemy instead of her tool. Every morning when she arrives at the office, she sees the day's schedule glaring at her on the green screen. She feels as if it controls everything she does. She expects one day it will take control of her or attack her. The color green here may also reflect envy as in "green with envy" because Lisa finds herself envious of the computer's powers. She feels she can never compete with it. So in evaluating objects, keep in mind your personal relationship to them.

Before we move on to the next dream element, we'll say a few words about colors in dreams because these often refer to colored objects. Some people are more aware of color in their dreams, while others dream in vague colorless tones. Some dream researchers think specific colors symbolize specific qualities or themes, while other experts do not. Though this point is controversial we'll list a few of the standard themes to give you some ideas to mull over:

Orange: relating to triangular relationships, oedipal
Yellow: money, integration, taking in knowledge
Purple: magical, intellect
White: mother, purity, creation
Red: love, passion, Christ
Blue: father, law, intuition
Green: envy, jealousy, rivalry

These are a few ideas relating to color in dreams. We won't mention more because it's important to consider your personal meaning for the color. Color in dreams may show up in a favorite piece of clothing you or a loved one wears. Or some other object will possess a color, reminding you of a prior personal event. After you've searched for your personal connection, then consider color as a universal symbol.

Take a moment to look over the animals and objects in your nightmare. Record them or underline them, then take a few minutes to make notes of any thoughts or feelings that have arisen about these dream elements.

Settings, Locales, and Scenes

The *setting* for your dream is an area commonly overlooked. There are a lot of insights to be gained by spending a few moments thinking about where your dream has unfolded. Is the setting mundane—is it where you work every day or is it your own home? If you were to dream repeatedly of your house collapsing, would this be saying something about your homelife? Or what if your dream depicts a horrible situation at work?

Donald is a building contractor who dreams at least twice a year about collapsing buildings. He is never injured or harmed in the dreams even though he is in the building that collapses. Donald's view is that the dream reflects his fears related to his line of work in building skyscrapers and about the inherent insecurity of his profession where job offerings suddenly collapse in midair when a bidding war is lost.

The same reasoning might explain the dreams of a trauma nurse in our emergency room. "I am shot in the chest and I walk into the trauma room, but nobody will help me. I attach myself to the heart monitor and notice my heart is beating wildly out of control. I cry out for help and hear someone say, 'We'll be with you in a minute.' I collapse on the stretcher, then I wake up."

If not your home or work, what about *locales* highlighting your personal background? A place in your past where you played ball or a park outside of town where you took walks with your first love—are these backdrops for some terrifying occurrence in your dreams? Always look for the personal angle.

David changed his name and embarked upon a spiritual quest, but his past nagged at him. "A redheaded boy from my childhood is delivering a load of scrap metal to a lot next to the swimming pool from my old neighborhood. He delivers the scrap to a house next to the pool. Now we're in the basement of the house and we're trying to get out through a hole under the porch. Once I get into the hole, I get stuck. I can't get out or come back inside."

The home was his family's of years ago. David had considered himself normal, but by the age of twenty-five after being dissatisfied with his work and life in general, he found himself aimlessly searching. So he began his spiritual quest. He was raised Catholic, but did not feel connected to that religion. He discovered a small, eclectic religious sect in Vancouver and gave up drinking alcohol and eating meat. He lived communally with these people which gave him a new sense of commitment.

But he still had doubts. He would often dream about having a beer with one of his buddies from his adolescence, then awaken feeling guilty. This anxiety dream of his old house reminded him of his mixed feelings about wanting to be part of the mainstream—the way things were in his past. The "stuck" feeling in the dream corresponded to the stuck feelings he had about moving on from the past into his new world.

What about fantasy places or other *scenes* that don't ring a bell? Now you're back to the same kind of thinking you have to do for any unknown dream elements. In a previous case, we described Jake as a man incapable of letting go and having fun. In his nightmare, he found himself at a resort—a place for fun—yet he seemed to be spoiling the party for everybody. Near the end of the dream he falls—wildly out of control— off a cliff away from the resort. Even though the resort didn't have personal meaning to him, it showed up as an excellent symbol for his problem of feeling out of control whenever he has to relax.

There are other things to look at in the setting if you don't find the meaning popping out at you. Is it day or night? What kind of weather? Hot or cold? Is it raining, snowing, or sunny? Are you inside or outside? Is this a quiet place or a noisy one? These details create powerful images for you when you're watching a movie, even though you may think of them as the backdrop. In your nightmares, they serve equally dramatic functions, so try to note them.

Energy in Dreams

Sometimes a form of energy or power will show up in your dream. How this power is directed in the dream may reflect on how constructively or destructively you may be using your own energy or how you perceive other people or things using their energy against you.

Joanne is a part-time interior designer. She was hired to do layout at the World's Fair in Vancouver. It was a one-time job, but it put her back in her trade after a layoff of several years. Her success at the Fair gave her confidence, but it was short-lived. Three months later she was doing part-time child-care work making minimal wages again.

Joanne's dream: "While waiting in line at the World's Fair, I was looking around the area and noticed an electrical transformer station. It was fenced in and a lot of young boys were around it. It was the power source for the French Pavilion. I had a feeling these kids were going to blow up the transformers. Suddenly, the electricity went off and the transformer blew and a large fire erupted. A man tried to stomp out the fire. The kids had their clothes on fire and everyone was trying to put it out."

Her nightmare represents her struggle to gain energy and momentum to get back into her craft. In other words, she needed to find the motivation to push herself into full-time work with interior design. The children's clothes on fire represented her relation to the children she looked after at work. She loved her own daughter and was comfortable being a mother, but looking after other children extended her beyond her limits and was pointing her in the wrong direction. She needed to get over her lack of confidence and find the energy to redirect herself.

Martha's waterfall nightmare shows energy threatening to go out of control. "We walk down a steep embankment. As we reach the bottom we spot a small stream running into a larger creek. I jump across the stream, jumping on stones and splashing freely in small pools of water. It feels exhilarating and I continue up the creek to where a sheet of clear water pours down from a waterfall. I walk through the water which is only ankle-deep, but then some man behind me yells that I cannot go that way because I would be swept away. I turn around to go back, but I panic as I see the precariousness of my situation."

The waterfall in Martha's dream suggested a sense of freedom and joy. The water represents freedom of movement like the waterfall itself, which is a form of power and energy. For Martha this showed her desire to be free to enjoy herself and have fun. On the other hand, the dream suggests she must keep in mind the power which lies behind these actions. The energy must be directed and not out of control.

This is a common theme in young adults or children in their late adolescence as their desire for freedom can end up in dangerous rebellious behavior. Martha is twenty-four and she appropriately took the dream as a warning and explored ways of enjoying her freedom without putting herself in jeopardy.

Directed energy enhances our intellectual, creative, and emotional lives and provides the human power to accomplish our goals and aspirations. Undirected energy can be a source of destruction. Observing the flow of energy in your dreams will provide valuable clues to the interpretation.

Lights, Camera . . . ACTION!

This is usually the heart of your dream, especially so in nightmares. You're running away from something. You're being attacked; you're falling; you're injured or dying. Judging by the box office hits of the last several years, we know action draws people into movie theaters. *Batman* and *Indiana Jones* movies are loaded with action and adventure. Our nightmares compete all too well with these blockbuster hits—too bad we don't get paid any money for them!

What is the action in your dream? Are you being chased? If so, can you escape or are you hunted down? Do you ever fight back? Does your attacker possess a weapon you couldn't possibly overcome? Is it a knife or a gun? If you're falling, what are you falling from—a building, a cliff, or into nothingness? If you're injured, how did it happen? Were you pushed? Was it an accident? And what part of your body was injured—your legs, your head, or your heart?

Actions form the core of your dream story. If what you experience is too powerful and intense, jot down a few key *verbs* and *nouns* that allow you to focus on the action without dwelling on the horrible effects. If you're being stabbed with a knife you could write "stabbing knife."

Details are important, however, so if you can write, "He twisted the large blade into my heart, ripping open my chest," you'll have more information to work with in your analysis. On the other hand, if it's too gruesome, just make a note that you're being attacked by someone with a knife. Later, if your interpretation is coming into focus, you may find you're able to reevaluate the gory parts to gain further understanding.

What if you are running away? Could running away from something in the dream suggest you are running away from something in real life? Look at the other elements around you—the other people, the setting, or perhaps the animals, if they're chasing you. What are you running from? Or what are you trying to reach?

Ed was stuck in his job. He felt dissatisfied and depressed as he continued looking for another line of work to enter into. His pursuit of new work had isolated him from his friends, both at work and otherwise, as he was spending all his time in the search.

Four months into his quest, he had this anxiety dream. "I am moving all my possessions in a large truck. When I arrive at my destination I can't unload my things because no one will help me. I see many people I know from the place I work, but they will not help me. I am anxious because the rental is costing me money."

Here "moving" is the main action of the dream and for Ed that easily translated into moving to a new job. But as the dream suggested, this transition was costing him, both in money and in his lack of support from his friends. He realized he needed to be more patient, and, above all, maintain contact with his friends to feel supported in his search.

Sometimes the action will be less direct and more symbolic. Phil had been working diligently in his therapy group for two years. He had successfully dealt with a number of issues and was reaching a point where he was ready to end his relationship with the group. Just prior to that he had the following nightmare. "I am swimming with a friend in a clear lake. I panic and nearly drown but manage to get across the lake to the shore."

Swimming is an activity where you have control over water. Swimming also provides a means of movement, allowing you to traverse something. In Phil's case, he traveled across the lake. This related to his past years in therapy. Swimming represented the therapeutic work he'd done. Drowning symbolized two things—the overwhelming feelings he experienced as he did his therapy and his concerns about leaving therapy. The positive thing about the nightmare was that instead of awakening from it with the sensation of drowning, Phil found the strength to swim to safety.

So by looking over the actions, you've taken a big step toward getting to the core meaning of your dreams. You're ready for the next phase—associating. Here, we'll have you review the same dream elements—the people, animals, objects, settings, energies, and actions—but now we want you to *direct* your associations in more specific ways.

CHAPTER 8

Directing Your Associations and Finding the Right Relationships

STEP THREE: ASSOCIATE, ASSOCIATE, ASSOCIATE!

Associating to dreams is the key to unlocking the meaning. You've already done this as you've reviewed your dream elements. Thoughts and feelings have popped into your mind yielding clues to the nightmare's message. This is known as *free-associating* and is an effective technique if you let your mind relax and observe the ideas flowing through your consciousness. Freud established this technique, and since then there have been a slew of other methods used by other dream investigators to draw associations out of dreams. Even Fritz Perls, who claimed *not* to interpret dreams, had people come up with associations as they acted out the characters in their dreams.

In our method, we want you to *direct your associations*; that is, we want you to focus on two areas:

• How the nightmare relates to your personal experience;
• How the story in your dream relates to universal stories and symbols that are seen in movies, books, fairy tales, or other art forms.

By directing your associations towards the personal and the universal, you'll discover enough information to fully interpret your nightmares.

How Your Nightmare Relates to Your Personal Experiences
Look at your personal history and experiences, and ask if there's anything in the nightmare that seems similar to or somehow reminds you of an event in your life. Focus on your

personal experiences. These may be recent or may be from an earlier time. An interesting thing about dream analysis during therapy is that your dreams will often mirror current experiences if you're dealing with lots of stress in your life. If things settle down in your current life, your dreams may bring up older experiences. Your aim is to see if a similar story from your recent or distant past is replayed in the nightmare.

Jim had a bitter argument with his dad concerning Jim's business dealings. Jim messed up a stock investment and his father's attitude made him feel small, as if he'd regressed to boyhood stature. Shortly thereafter he had a bizarre nightmare of a giant frog hopping toward him. When Jim associated to this dream animal, he recalled catching frogs as a kid.

At first, that's all he remembered. Then he focused on past personal events and suddenly recalled what had happened to the frogs. He stored them in an aquarium, but forgot to feed them. They died, then decomposed, creating an awful smell, for which Jim's father was unforgiving. Jim got a spanking and had to clean up the mess.

Jim saw the connection to what had happened to him as a kid and how it was replayed in his argument with his dad— make a mess of something, and you get yelled at. This was an appropriate warning to Jim, who has not been responsible in money matters.

Jim might have come to this insight when he listed his dream animals. Sometimes you'll get it right away, but many times you won't. That's why it's important to direct your associations toward your *personal history*. Memories will return in time. These memories will help you relate your associations from some meaningful events in your past to the current nightmare.

Nightmares, like most dreams, have a story quality to them. Often, they have beginnings, middle parts, and endings. Sometimes you'll wake up before the "ending." In any event, the nightmare story has to come from somewhere. What better place than a "story" you've already lived in your own life?

The story can occur very recently, as in Neil's case. He'd been working to establish closer ties with his brother and had thought things were better. When Neil was hospitalized after a car accident, he phoned his brother to ask if he would go to his apartment to water the plants. His brother's refusal seems to have prompted a nightmare.

"Suspecting a burglar, I quietly get out of bed and reach for my gun. Entering the front room, it is a mass of green foliage, but behind the plants I see vicious black panthers lurking, waiting to jump me. I aim my gun to kill them only to realize it has turned into a poison sprayer. As I begin spraying, I realize I am killing my plants."

Neil was angry with his brother for not helping, yet he had trouble with that anger because he considered himself a pacifist. He saw the jungle cats as powerful, aggressive animals, while the plants symbolized his docile, passive side. It was terrifying for him to kill the plants and lose that side of himself. He would have preferred to have killed the aggressive panther side.

Whether the personal story replayed is old or new or—as often happens—a combination of past and present, looking over these events in your life will usually turn out to be the most fertile way of harvesting the meaning from your dreams.

How Your Nightmare Relates to Universal Symbols and Stories

This next part is a tricky one, but it's a lot of fun if you get the hang of it. Here, you'll try to find a universal story or a symbol corresponding to your nightmare. You'll be looking for something which at first glance seems outside your personal experiences.

Consider this dream from Arthur, a man with assorted conflicts revolving around too little time spent at home and too much time spent at work. "I have forgotten to buy Christmas presents for my wife and children. I come home to a dark house and the roof is leaking. I wake up very depressed."

Does anything come to mind?

Arthur drew an immediate association to the movie he'd seen on television the weekend before—Dickens's *Christmas Carol*. That made everything snap into place. The message was loud and clear that Arthur ought to weigh more carefully the balance between his work and family life.

In Arthur's example, you can see an immediate association fitting neatly into the scheme of the nightmare. It may not come that easily. Your nightmare may not be so direct and you'll need to do more associating before you successfully find a universal perspective.

Consider Katie, a soft-spoken physical therapist, who has suffered nightmares for nearly twenty years. As a child, Katie lived a sheltered life, mostly because of an experience from which her father had suffered. As a child, Katie's dad spent two years in a concentration camp in Poland during World War II. Because of her father's strong reaction to this horrible experience, he vowed to make the world more perfect for his daughter. Not only would he not talk to her about the camp, but he sheltered her from any negative experiences. He tried building an unrealistic world for her without strife or conflict.

From her adolescence onward, Katie suffered this recurrent nightmare: "I am sitting in my *huge, comfortable bed*, but I am frightened as I look past the footboard. *Three wicked fairies* are coming toward me in the dark. I cannot see them clearly, but I know they're wicked. They intend to do me evil. As they get closer, I *feel trapped*. I can't take it anymore and awake screaming."

In this dream we have a few elements: a large bed and some special people—the fairies and, of course, the dreamer, Katie. The setting is her own home and the actions are that she feels trapped and afraid of evil people coming after her. Katie went through her associations and the prime clue she came up with was that her mother used to read her fairy tales at bedtime. She was asked if there were any fairy tales she recalled. She mentioned "Sleeping Beauty"—the Dutch version. She was encouraged to go through the tale to see if she would find more connections.

"The king and queen planned a party for their daughter. All the kingdom was invited except the bad fairies. One bad fairy escaped and made it to the castle. A good fairy spotted the bad one casting an evil spell on the daughter. The good fairy quickly cast another spell to protect the daughter.

"The bad fairy's spell would have killed the daughter; the good fairy's spell allowed her to live, though she would remain asleep until she was brought back to wakefulness by the kiss of a prince. The good fairy also cast a spell on the whole court and put them all to sleep, so when the daughter awoke, the whole court would be the same. This was to help her avoid being shocked by any changes that had occurred in the world around her while she slept."

That was as far as Katie needed to go in telling the tale. A number of new connections came into focus. In a certain way, Katie had been asleep much of her life, sheltered and protected from seeing the world as it really is. She recalled her parents saying she shouldn't worry about things. They would tell her to wait until she was an adult to consider certain issues. She admitted to a fairy-tale quality to her childhood.

The tale of "Sleeping Beauty" also made the connection to her problem with men. Katie had expected some ideal man to solve her problems. The large, almost royal bed fit in nicely with this idea as Katie saw it befitting a princess.

Katie then returned to the three bad fairies in her nightmare and decided they might be like the one bad fairy in the tale of "Sleeping Beauty." The question arose whether these dream fairies were truly evil, or just seen as evil? Could they represent the real world with all its "evils" from which she had been sheltered? These were not easy questions to answer. Katie realized she'd lived in a fantasy world much of her life, but felt she was making progress learning to deal with reality. Interpreting the nightmare reinforced her desire to face the tougher issues of the real world which she'd been avoiding for so long.

As you can see, it might take a bit of time and effort to uncover clues from universal stories, but you can expect large rewards for your efforts.

Throughout the book we've described people who've had bad dreams after viewing a movie. This is another fertile ground to explore as you match up universal stories to your own nightmare's story. Plays and television shows should be considered as well. As best they can, each media attempts to tell a story, many of which on closer inspection reveal themselves as takeoffs on older stories. These older stories clearly reflect some of the myths and universal themes we want you to be comparing to your nightmare, such as the story of Oedipus and the issues of incest and rivalry or the story of Cain and Abel and the issue of responsibility to our fellow human beings.

These stories are well known to most people and represent universal themes, but you don't have to use the older stories if the newer versions in plays, on television, or in the movie theaters make more sense to you. According to Freud, Hamlet retells the oedipal tale quite well, and we would add that TV soap operas do so as well with their constant supply of love triangles.

This may be the reason it is so common for people to dream about the events in a movie or TV show after watching it. As the story unfolds, your unconscious probably picks up a lot of messages to incorporate into your dreams. So don't hesitate to consider movies, television, and other art forms as you look for comparisons to your dreams.

Universal symbols serve the same purpose as stories, fairy tales, or myths. If I mention the crucifix to a Christian or the star of David to a Jew, they would have no difficulty drawing meaning from these symbols.

Sometimes the symbol will be obvious, even if the dreamer has difficulty accepting its meaning. Such was the case with Gail. "My young daughter is attacked by a bull with large horns and it leaves a huge scrape on her forehead. We are shocked. I feel tremendous anxiety as I think of her being hurt." Just a few days prior to this anxiety dream, Gail had another dream. "I am having therapy with my doctor, but my eyes are closed and I can't get them open."

Not being able "to see" was a common occurrence for Gail. She often blocked out her own insights. When exploring the bull, she became anxious and could not deal with it. When finally getting to the meaning of the bull in the next therapy session, she accepted it as a symbol for sexual energy.

Why was this dream of the bull coming up now?

Gail's mother was visiting soon. Her mother is a restrictive person who stifled much of Gail's freedom, creativity, and sexuality. So dealing with the bull also meant facing her own anger about the restrictive cloaks she'd lived with for years. In the dream, her daughter was the same age Gail was when she had so much difficulty with her mother. Exploring this led to her memories of the conflicts with her mother and her subsequent anger. It also helped her to resolve the anger.

Another way to interpret symbols is to find a way to view them from a universal perspective. For example, suppose an eagle appeared in your dream. Try thinking about the eagle as the title of a poem by a master poet, then imagine how that poet would express the universal attributes of the eagle.

Some attributes which come to mind include the eagle as a symbol of justice in the courts; as a patriarchal symbol, such as the fatherland in the United States and Germany; and as a symbol of freedom. You still need to put these ideas together with your dream of an eagle, but now you have these new concepts to work with which might reveal the theme played out in your nightmare.

"I am with my friend, my mentor. He is ill and I watch him as he breathes his last breath. I look up and I see an eagle passing overhead. I wake up grief-stricken."

This dream was very moving for the dreamer, as his real-life mentor had died several months earlier. The mentor had been a strong father figure to the man for several years and thus the eagle served as an appropriate symbol to their relationship, guiding him toward just actions.

Many of the concepts regarding symbols and myths in dreams come from Freud and Jung. Freud noted that recurring objects show up in dreams, often suggesting sexual themes. Jung was interested in the universal nature of symbols and believed certain dream images were common to all mankind. Both men strongly believed that translating dream symbols is an integral step in dream interpretation; however, they clearly and *repeatedly* emphasized that symbols require a personal perspective.

Neither man dictated that you take the symbol *first* and apply some strict definition to it, as is done in dream dictionaries. The *individual* must connect with the meaning of universal symbols and see how these meanings relate within his or her dreams. Directing associations towards universal stories and symbols may be difficult for some people. Personal associations come more easily. If you're not clear yet on associating to universal themes, we'll be showing you other examples in the dreams we analyze in the later sections.

What if You Feel Blocked in Trying to Associate?

You may find yourself unable to associate to your dream elements because the images are too disturbing, or you have unconscious resistances blanking your mind. Consider help from friends, relatives, or a therapist. Talking about your dreams with other people whom you trust may open you up more in your attempts to associate. Having an additional ear to listen to your story may give you the support you need to continue.

If you're blocking, a helpful technique is exploring the resistances themselves as they happen. As you attempt to associate to your dream figures and you find yourself blanking, a closer look may reveal certain feelings cropping up. The feelings generated may reflect similar feelings from a time in your past.

Toby blanked when she associated to a *deck of cards* appearing in her dream. Though nothing came to mind, she noticed she was suddenly angry about something. She explored the anger for a moment and recalled an episode as a kid when her parents were playing bridge and wouldn't let her stay up to watch a TV program. So if you spot a feeling and then think about *when* you felt the same way in the past, you'll often discover a similar conflict in your nightmare.

The problem here is we've developed defenses or defense mechanisms to protect ourselves against pain caused by a previous emotional trauma. When we explore the problems or the conflicts in the nightmares, we must try to go beyond our defenses so we can reexperience the emotions to gain insight into ourselves.

As soon as we reexperience the feelings, however, we get gun-shy. We try to defend ourselves again. If we had few conflicts and few defenses, then exploring our nightmares would be easy. Getting past our defenses requires skill, imagination, creativity, patience, honesty, and time.

STEP FOUR: PUT YOURSELF BACK IN THE DREAM TO FIND THE RIGHT RELATIONSHIPS

In the first three steps we've spent a lot of time outside of the dream. You've recorded the dream, dissected it into its various parts, and then associated to all of your dream elements and figures to determine what they symbolize.

Now you've come to the most difficult step, where you must put yourself back into the nightmare: difficult because you will have to look closely at your *feelings* which cropped up during the dream when you first experienced it.

The key idea to think about in this step is *relationships*. Finding the right relationships is a simple concept, but one which may confuse you in the setting of dreams. What you want to do is define the relationship between yourself—the dreamer—and the other elements or figures *in your dreams*.

Suppose you are chased by a huge frog in your nightmare and you feel threatened. You could define this as a *threatening* relationship *in the dream*. The confusion stems from trying to think about how you might feel about frogs outside of the dream in your waking world. That's what you did in steps two and three when you listed your dream figures and made associations.

If frogs don't scare you in your waking world, you might decide that the frog *in your dream* isn't really a threat. That would be a mistake. Frogs may not be a threat to you while awake, but whatever the frog represents or symbolizes in the dream probably is a threat. And that's what we're trying to uncover. So it's important to keep your waking feelings and your dreaming feelings separate. In this step, you're exploring the feelings you have *in* the dream.

To reinforce this point, let's look at the exact opposite situation. Jan dreamed of a vicious man who said, "I'm going to kill you." But in the dream, instead of feeling threatened, Jan was angry at the man. Even though the man in the dream is violent and threatening, Jan's relationship to him is an *angry* one because those were *her feelings in the dream*.

We are reminded of a nightmare which Freud encountered in a young woman. She had a very disturbing dream about her small nephew. The woman's sister had already lost one son, Otto, at an early age. "I saw Karl lying before me dead. He was lying in his little coffin with his hands folded and with candles all around—in fact, just like little Otto, whose death was such a blow to me."

Freud then quotes her reaction to this morbid dream: "Now tell me, what can that mean? You know me. Am I such a wicked person that I can wish my sister to lose the one child she has? Or does the dream mean that I would rather Karl were dead than Otto, whom I was so much fonder of?"

One of the keys to unraveling this dream for Freud was in getting the patient to describe her feelings *during* the dream. We've heard her reaction *after* the dream. It reveals her shame and disgust. Yet, during the dream, the young woman recalled she felt neither pain nor grief at seeing the dead boy.

Now Freud knew there was a literary professor in town whom the young woman had been infatuated with for years. However, because of a falling-out with her family, this professor rarely visited them anymore—except in extraordinary circumstances, such as . . . a death in the family. Freud asked the young woman if she recalled anything special occurring at the funeral of Otto, and she quickly mentioned how the professor had visited them at their home.

This then was the real emotion of the dream. The young woman wanted to see the professor again and knew that the very last time she had seen him was after Otto's funeral. If the other nephew were to die, then this man whom she carried a torch for would surely visit again. Obviously, the young woman didn't wish the child to die. Rather, she simply wanted to find some excuse to see "the man of her dreams" once again.

The key is to look at the feelings you experience *during* the nightmare and see what the relationships are that you experience in the dream. This is crucial to understanding the deeper meanings of your dreams. Your reaction to the dream is also important, but sometimes you'll have to be careful not to let that reaction confuse you in your search for the meaning.

Lydia's Baby

Lydia is a thirty-four-year-old housewife who came to therapy for one reason—ulcers. Since the birth of her son two years ago, she has suffered chronic stomach problems. Eventually she was diagnosed with peptic ulcer disease, requiring medication on a daily basis to control the problem. But the medicine didn't always work and sometimes it made her nauseated, so she'd skip it for a few weeks until she couldn't stand the burning and pain.

Her doctors suggested stress reduction to improve her condition. Shortly after entering therapy she had this nightmare: "I am sitting down for dinner but feel queasy in my stomach. I can't understand what is wrong. I can't think of anything I have eaten that would make me sick. I feel I am going to vomit. On my way to the bathroom, I start vomiting up something. I look down and I am shocked to see parts of a baby lying in my pool of vomit."

This dream ultimately showed a connection between Lydia's

stress and her interactions with children. Lydia's own childhood was fraught with neglect and problems, primarily because she was adopted. This produced a great deal of resentment, part of which also stemmed from Lydia's unachievable expectation that her parents be perfect. When she had her own child and discovered the demanding nature of child-rearing as a single parent, all that resentment surfaced again. And yet she knew she couldn't achieve the perfection she herself had demanded from her own parents. Still, she expected no less if she was going to feel good about herself.

Now let's look at this nightmare in light of putting yourself back in the dream to find the right relationships. As the dream starts, the baby parts are in the stomach. The relationship initially is that the stomach and the baby parts are bound together.

Then, the dreamer vomits up the baby parts, signifying a change in the relationship. What the stomach held is now released. The parts are now freed from the stomach and the two are separate.

Finally, the dreamer sees the baby parts and feels revulsion. If the baby parts represent her own repressed feelings over a difficult childhood, then *in the dream* the dreamer is reexperiencing that revulsion.

Lydia's childhood was difficult "to stomach." And when she first looked at the dream, she couldn't deal with it either. She was stuck at the grossness of the baby parts. However, when we asked her to think about the relationships, instead of fixating on the grossness, she was able to see the important connection from her past which was still eating up her insides.

Those baby parts bound into her stomach symbolized the conflicts that were aggravating and possibly causing her ulcer. Throwing up the baby felt like a replay of Lydia's own rejection by her biologic mother who "threw her up" for adoption. And it symbolized her own turmoil in trying to throw off her stressful role as single parent.

The whole picture drawn by the nightmare's story graphically depicted several important conflicts stirring up trouble in Lydia's life, but to ferret them out, she had to put herself back into the dream to see the relationships between herself and the other dream elements.

Nathan and His Boss

Nathan, a junior accountant at a large accounting firm, had this common nightmare: "I am running down an *alley, chased* by a *man* with a *knife*. He's catching up to me. He thrusts the knife towards me. He tries to *cut* me . . . I wake up."

Nathan's initial associations were as follows: *alley*—reminded him of a place behind the office building where he'd heard someone had gotten mugged a week earlier; *chased*—he blocked here and could think of nothing; *man*—the man was somehow mean and very intent on hurting him; *knife* and *cut*—he thought of the knife as a weapon to cut or injure or dissect.

Now we'll walk you through Nathan's therapy session to show you how he found the right relationships. Keep in mind that this conversation transpired two months into Nathan's treatment for depression, and that some rapport had been achieved between doctor and patient. Here's an abridgement of the conversation:

Doctor: You say this man is intent on hurting you.

Nathan: I just had a strong feeling about that.

Doctor: Does that feeling remind you of anything?

Nathan: Remind me?

Doctor: Does it make you think of a time when you felt someone else might have been trying to hurt you?

Nathan: (blurts out) I feel that way all the time about my boss.

Doctor: Uh-huh.

Nathan: He's a real bastard. I've been there a year and he still tries to put me down in front of the senior accountants.

Doctor: And you feel ashamed and stupid.

Nathan: Real stupid. It's like he's proven I'm incompetent (suddenly looking uncomfortable).

Doctor: You appear nervous.

Nathan: Yeah, it makes me angry to think about it. I don't know why I let him do it. I'd really like to get back at him.

Doctor: Get even?

Nathan: Yes, reverse the tables.

Nathan unloads a bit on his boss and seems to feel relieved, at which point the doctor brings up the dream again.

Doctor: You've come up with some ideas in your associations about your boss. Now let's go back and look at things inside the dream. You said you were running down the alley?

Nathan: Yeah, the alley was a way I could get away from this guy.

Doctor: And you mentioned the alley was a place where somebody was mugged?

Nathan: It's a scary place. Dark corners. Occasionally I park my car where I have to walk through the alley to get to it. It makes me feel uncomfortable. And that mugging seemed awfully violent.

Doctor: So you were escaping down the alley.

Nathan: Hmmm. Escape and violence are connected somehow? That doesn't make sense to me.

Doctor: Well, we've got a relationship between you and the alley. It's seen as an escape and there's something about violence related to it.

Nathan: Well, the guy is easy—really threatening and he frightened me.

Doctor: So your relationship to him is threatening. What about the knife?

Nathan: Well that's a way of killing people. I guess my relationship to it is that I'm scared of it.

Doctor: You also mentioned the knife is used for dissecting.

Nathan: (suddenly looking very uncomfortable; he pauses for a full minute.) Going through this stuff isn't easy. It's painful. (nervous laugh) I feel like I'm being dissected.

Doctor: Yes, and it feels like I'm dissecting you.

Nathan: I know you're here to help me, but sometimes it feels like the pain is more than it's worth.

Doctor: And that feels threatening. Like the knife?

Nathan: (pauses) Yes.

They explore their therapeutic relationship for several minutes and the difficulties inherent in opening up and the potentially threatening nature of such a relationship. Then they return to the dream.

Doctor: If you explore the feelings you've brought up, can you put this together to form a whole picture?

Nathan: Like I said, maybe that man [in the dream] is supposed to be my boss and I'm just reliving my fears about working with him.

Doctor: Reliving your fears?

Nathan: Yes . . . him and others.

Doctor: Others?

Nathan: (thinking) Not a lot of others, but I have had problems like that with bosses before and a few other people.

Doctor: (remains silent)

Nathan: I used to feel that way toward my dad . . . especially golfing. I was pretty good when I was thirteen, but he was always better. We would play for a quarter a hole. I could win a few, but he always came out ahead. I tried being a good sport, but I didn't like losing all the time. I remember getting nervous and tense whenever I had to make a putt . . . I'd get a tight feeling in my gut. It's the same feeling I get when my boss puts me down . . .

I never connected these two things before. Do you suppose I've been replaying these golf games all these years with my bosses? And maybe it explains what I was feeling about you.

Putting these all together, Nathan sees himself chased by a man with a knife in his dream and that man and knife represent the threat of his boss, his father, and his therapist. In the nightmare, Nathan is unwilling to deal with this in any way, so he wakes up to avoid dealing with it at all. In real life, he didn't relate well to authority figures. He was unable to express his anger or accept constructive criticisms. Instead, he turned sheepish and eventually resentful and in time suffered depression.

Where would Nathan go from here in analyzing his dream? Because he was in therapy, a lot of questions came up around this central issue expressed in the nightmare. What is his real fear of authority figures? Is his boss cutting him down all the time or is he trying to make valid suggestions which might improve Nathan's work performance? When does he feel it's okay to express anger? And, how does he express his anger— violently, or with some appropriate thought behind it?

When Nathan worked on these questions, the nightmare again proved helpful, because he could look at his response in the dream as another indicator of his problem. He recognized that he'd never dealt with his anger toward his dad for setting him up to lose, or his boss for putting him down. He realized he hadn't even been able to confront his own therapist about his overly analytical style which Nathan felt was too unsupportive.

As he explored these issues further in therapy he began to differentiate the putdowns from valid criticisms. He also recollected that his boss started criticizing him after Nathan had failed to respond to earlier positive suggestions on how to improve his performance. This didn't justify the putdowns; however, Nathan noticed that the putdowns diminished significantly when he welcomed his boss's advice rather than opposing it. He never told his boss what had happened in therapy; he just noticed they started getting along better. Working on his feelings with the therapist, including his valid criticism of the therapist, set the stage for dealing with the other issues.

For Nathan, a typical nightmare turned out to have a specific meaning concerning his attitude towards authority figures. Suppose you had a similar dream, would this same interpretation apply to you? It might; but we want you to work with your own associations to see what feelings come up, and then put yourself back in the dream to find the right relationships for you.

Now that you've looked at your dream as a whole again, you've come through the hardest, and certainly most rewarding part of dream interpretation. Invariably, your nightmares will portray relationships of a serious nature—your life is at stake; injury is threatened; or your security or self-esteem is endangered.

To get to the core meaning of your nightmare, you've got to work through these dream relationships to uncover the root conflicts or problems that may have instigated your bad dreams. The key to putting yourself back in the dream to find the right relationships is learning to ask yourself a lot of questions and eventually learning to ask the *right* questions.

Looking over the action in the nightmare ought to suggest a basic conflict. Say you're running away from something in your dream. Perhaps the conflict reflects on *what* you're running away from, and *why*. If so, what questions can you ask?

What is my relationship to the person(s) I'm running from? Are they known or unknown? Do they represent a specific threat to me in my real life, or are they a symbol for something I am afraid of? Are there figures in the dream that can help me? If so, who are they, and do they help? Do the figures who oppose me always win out? Do I fight back? How do I fight back? If I'm running away from one thing, is there something else I'm running towards? Is there a safe haven I see up ahead? If so, what is that safe haven, and do I ever get there?

Learning to ask these questions is like asking the questions you raise about your relationships in daily life. Your friends, family, and work colleagues all interact with you in assorted ways. Use the same thinking about a conflict you have in real life to help you find questions to ask about the relationships in your dream.

Why is my boss angry at me? Is she overreacting or do I have a problem? Why is my husband acting coldly towards me? Did I offend him? Is he in a bad mood because he had a bad day at work? Why is my friend too busy to talk to me? Is she going through a rough time? Did I say the wrong thing to her? We ask ourselves these questions every day of our lives.

Consider the old saying: "A wise man's question is half the answer." We can all learn to find wisdom in our dreams and nightmares if we are willing to ask the right questions.

You've made your associations to your dream elements—the people, objects, animals, settings, powers, and actions. And you've explored your personal history and universal stories and symbols to direct your associations. Finally, you've begun exploring the relationships in the dream to uncover the meaning of the nightmare. Now you're in a position to take that meaning and apply it to your real life.

CHAPTER 9

Relating the Nightmare to Your Life, and Taking Action

STEP FIVE: HOW DOES THE DREAM RELATE TO YOUR EVERYDAY LIFE?

Let's quickly review the four previous steps. Number one is recording your nightmares and learning to achieve some distance. Two is picking out the dream elements. Associating to these dream elements is number three, and putting yourself back in the dream to explore the relationships between yourself and the various dream elements is number four.

Now you are ready to relate the story of the nightmare to your waking life to find the relevance. As you do this, more meaning from the nightmare will emerge, and the message it is conveying to you will become clearer.

We have already done this step with Nathan's dream. He was fearful of a man in an alley who turned out to be a symbol for several real people—his boss, his father, and his therapist. All of these people have threatened Nathan's self-esteem in real life, just as the man in the alley threatened him in the dream. By putting himself back in the dream and reliving these feelings, Nathan was able to find the meaning of the nightmare.

Using the dream, Nathan was able to get in touch with some old feelings relating to his father. He discovered that these same feelings were projected onto his boss as well as other authority figures, such as the therapist. Gaining this insight into these old conflicts inspired him to change the way he viewed his work as well as his therapy.

Terry's Poisonous Green Apples

Terry and Clayton's friendship had been strained on several occasions. Terry recognized he had been the initiator all too often to keep the friendship going. They had talked about this one-sidedness, then decided to keep in touch. Subsequently, Terry's marriage began to falter, leading to a difficult separation that was tearing apart his family.

Clayton was well aware of Terry's dilemma. When Terry unexpectedly received a letter from Clayton, he assumed it was going to be a good will gesture. The letter, however, turned out to be a long exposé on the joys of Clayton's family life. Clayton also included a slew of family photos. Perhaps unintended, but this seemed to twist the knife a bit deeper.

Terry recognized the obvious hostility, but still had doubts about giving up their friendship until he had this anxiety dream. "I am playing catch with Clayton with a green apple from one of his trees. After several throws, I decide to take a bite of the apple. While chewing it, I suddenly realize the tree was sprayed with insecticide. I worry that I might be poisoned. But then I realize I've only taken a small bite and that rain may have washed away the spray."

When Terry wrote down the dream he saw the obvious connection to the "poison" that had seeped into his friendship with Clayton. With the help of friends in a dream group, he also saw how the green apple related to some of his own envious feelings. So on many levels, Terry was able to relate the interpreted dream back to his everyday life.

Louie's Dinosaurs

"There are two dinosaurs fighting. One is a bit larger than the other. I'm in between and being thrashed about. I'm not sure I'm going to live."

Louie started off saying it was kind of a funny dream and it didn't mean much. He didn't know why the dinosaurs were fighting. They weren't attacking him. He was then asked to associate to the dinosaur and he immediately said "Mother." This was unusual, because Louie usually pondered questions. This time his response was immediate. He associated his sister to the smaller dinosaur.

Louie attempted suicide several months before this dream. He'd gone through some difficult times, including the loss of his job. He also drained his savings account, then, several months later, he had to move back home with his mother because of a physical handicap he developed. His mother didn't really want him home because she was afraid he would make another suicide attempt. His sister and mother had been arguing about what he should do—whether he could drive a car or not, and whether they should give him any money.

Louie still couldn't relate to the dinosaurs fighting, despite these fairly obvious connections. Then, he was asked to put himself back in the dream to look at his relationship to the dinosaurs. He then said, "They're fighting over something. I'm so close—it's dangerous. They may kill me."

He was asked to think more about what was going on in the dream as it related to him. "They scare me. If I can't get away they'll crush me." Did he see this relating to his mother and sister fighting over him? Yes, he got the point. "I feel powerless to do anything. I feel like a pawn in their little chess game." So by going back into the nightmare, Louie not only saw the relationships in the dream, but he made the connection to his real-world relationships as well.

Once you've made that connection, it's time to consider the action you want to take in light of your new knowledge.

STEP SIX: TAKING ACTION

Ultimately, you must make the connection to your real life, or else the nightmare will have little value. Only then will you be able to respond accordingly.

With Terry, there was a decision to be made regarding a friendship, which although somewhat enlightening, ultimately required too much of his energy. Severing ties with Clayton was not easy, but the dream guided Terry in his decision.

In Louie's case, after several individual and family sessions he was able to express his need to make his own decisions. He also gave reassurances about avoiding suicide and, over time, he regained some independence from both his mother and sister.

In previous examples, we've mentioned how other dreamers reconsidered their real-life situations based on new knowledge from interpreting a dream. We've spoken of Nathan, who learned how to use constructive criticisms to his benefit, instead of thinking someone was stabbing him in the back. We told you about Lydia, who learned how her emotions were eating her up on the inside, aggravating her ulcers. She attempted to make some changes in her life to deal more realistically with her unrealistic attitudes about parenting.

We would all like to learn something from our dreams to help us understand ourselves better and eventually promote healthy changes. Let us offer a few suggestions regarding taking action to change your life.

Making changes is often difficult because it's much easier to fall back into our own particular patterns of behavior. If we're used to yelling at people when we get angry, then, for whatever reasons, it may be difficult to alter that pattern.

Oddly enough, one of the reasons for staying fixated in a pattern is that we're afraid people will respond to us differently if we change. And, changing brings on new feelings which we may find more difficult to deal with—even more difficult than our current feelings.

Anger is a good example—we can use it to keep people away. Softening makes us feel more vulnerable, and getting closer to people can feel risky. Some men fear this softening. They feel they are losing their independence or becoming less masculine. Women, of course, have similar feelings, and we all fear rejection on one level or another.

Mostly, these fears are unfounded. But people must go through periods to see what kind of responses they'll get from their changed behavior. This testing-out or trial run can be a time when the changes slip away, so we suggest:

1. Decide on the changes;
2. Make a firm decision to try them out for a period of time;
3. Don't give up if at first things backfire or don't work out perfectly; and
4. Be prepared to work on any new problems that come up because of the change.

With this attitude, you'll be able to stay with it and be successful over time. This is where friends or a therapist can help because they can provide support during periods where you're feeling unsure of your new direction.

We've now gone through the six steps. Let's look at some additional factors you may wish to consider in the course of your efforts at nightmare interpretation.

What if You Get Stuck?

The early analysts, including Freud, conducted a great deal of self-analysis, and based much of their theories on self-discovery. So, it's possible to analyze your own nightmares; however, you need to watch for pitfalls.

The major reason for getting stuck is that, in exploring your nightmares, you're going to be confronted with some strong emotions. Clearly, the conflict that caused you to repress your feelings may now prove unpleasant as it resurfaces through dream interpretation. No one wishes to subject themselves to pain. But the hope is that the insights you gain will be ample reward for the discomfort you must feel in getting there. And often it's really the *fear* of painful emotions that turns out to be more distressing than the real emotions you uncover from your nightmares.

How can you keep on a steady course and go through the nightmare to find a meaningful interpretation?

First, you may have noticed the difficulty some of our patients had in getting to the crux of their dreams. In the actual therapy setting, sometimes they had to be brought back to the tense spot in the nightmare. If you are working on your own, this process may be more difficult. And, because of the complexity of some dreams, keep in mind that it may appear to take more time to interpret your nightmares compared to those you've just read about in condensed excerpts.

For some, this will always be a delicate and fragile process which may, at best, be encountered with a therapist or a friend or in the setting of group therapy. For others, you may have to use the time-honored and, in this case, ironic approach of "sleeping" on it. Your efforts could turn up too much material and too much emotion for you to deal with at once. Another night's sleep might bring a new dream, relating back to an older one you've been struggling over. Also, waiting to review the nightmare and your notes at a later date is a reasonable approach.

A therapist can also help if you get stuck. The therapist is a person trained to help you through these difficult conflicts. For people with serious mental health problems, a therapist can be invaluable both for working through these matters and also for determining the best treatment approach.

Another option is to work with a friend or a group. If you do this, there are some things you will want to consider. In working with a friend, trust is very important. You will want to know that the person will not use the information against you.

On the other hand, just as the intimacy of friendship can be helpful, it can also get in the way. A friend who is too close to you may be reluctant to share something for fear it will hurt you. Such a friend may also feel you could take things the wrong way, and thus damage your friendship.

Another problem in working with friends is that you will spend too much time exploring what each of you knows of the other's life instead of trying to explore what the nightmare is truly saying. In other words, you'll get off on tangents and fail to come to an understanding of the nightmare.

Working in a group has many advantages, especially a dream group where each person is intent on exploring dreams and nightmares. Groups have more potential for objectivity because you most likely don't know each other outside the group setting. Groups also have the advantage of different people to provide different perspectives which can lead to more accurate interpretations.

Whether you work with a friend or in a group, giving and receiving feedback is an important aspect of your activities. Some guidelines to giving feedback include:

- Make your comments specific and relevant to the part of the nightmare you're addressing;
- Give your ideas directly to the person and not through a third party;
- Give your feedback caringly without being judgmental;
- Avoid giving advice; and
- Give the person a chance to respond to what you have said.

If you are on the receiving end of the feedback, you can get more out of it by receiving openly. Do not make excuses or be defensive, but instead acknowledge the value of the feedback you've been given. Look for the truth in what is said, rather than what might be inaccurate about what has been said.

Thank the person for the feedback and discuss it further rather than letting it drop. If you are puzzled by someone's comments, ask for clarification and continue to explore. If you find yourself becoming emotional or sensitive, stay with those feelings to understand them better.

The most important guideline in analyzing nightmares, whether you do it by yourself, with another person, a group, or a therapist, is to explore nonjudgmentally. Judging whether something is right or wrong can present a huge obstacle to understanding the nightmare and how the nightmare relates to your life.

How Will You Know if You Interpret a Nightmare Correctly?

You may discover many possible interpretations to your nightmare—perhaps more than you want. If you have a wide selection of ideas to choose from, the hope is that a whole picture will form, giving you a gestalt and an "aha!" experience—the whole nightmare's meaning suddenly reveals itself to you. Now you can take action with your new insights.

At other times questions will remain. And you may need more time to discover the meaning of the dream.

Whether it comes quickly or with more work, eventually you'll ask yourself: How do I know if I've got it right?

This is an easy question to answer. You will know because you will know. Let us explain.

When you've worked with your nightmares, either alone, or in a group, or with a therapist, you develop a sense about whether you have hit the mark. As all dream experts have repeatedly said, the only person who can tell if you have the right interpretation is *you*.

There will be times when someone else will see the meaning behind the nightmare before you do; however, for the most part you will have a strong feeling if it is right—when it is right! People have described this as a sense of "resonating," or "clicking," or "hitting the mark," or "seeing the light."

Whatever you choose to call it, do not feel you are mistaken if you reject the interpretation because it does not feel right. On the other hand, be prepared to accept it if it *does* feel right! As you interpret more dreams and nightmares, you will learn to trust your feelings in sensing this.

One word of caution must be offered. This sense of knowing is *not* the same as the feelings you may have uncovered by interpreting your dream. If you feel badly about what you discover, that is, you are emotionally upset about what you've unraveled in your interpretation, this could be correct or incorrect. Likewise, if you feel good about what you've discovered, it does not automatically mean you have the right interpretation.

These feelings of good and bad suggest you are *judging* rather than *exploring* the nightmare. This can lead you astray. Feelings are important to help you understand your dreams, but *the feeling* we are talking about here is one of "knowing." It produces a sense of inner calm or inner quiet without other associated feelings. It is a sense of being aware with nothing else intruding.

This concept of knowing is a difficult one because it cannot be described adequately on intellectual levels. For example, if you are looking at a sunset, you can experience the sunset without having other thoughts. In a way, it is like being there and being a part of the sunset. You may have thoughts such as, "Isn't this a beautiful sunset," or "It's so good to be here," or "Why couldn't my day have been like this moment." But these thoughts are just that—thoughts *about* the experience, *not* the experience itself.

As you feel the sunset—at least for one brief awestruck moment—none of these thoughts exist. You just experience the sunset.

This is similar to the experience of knowing something "is" without any other thoughts. There is no need to defend it, support it, or explain it. You can just be with the knowing without any drive to go further. You're with it, you know it, it's there, and it's okay.

Not okay in a sense of judgment, but it's okay to be there with it and not need to do anything further. If you've never had this sense of knowing in the past, you will recognize it the next time you have it and you will understand what we've said here. If you've had that sense of knowing in the past, then most of what we've just said is unnecessary. You already knew what we were talking about.

We encourage you to apply these steps and guidelines to come up with your own sense of what your nightmares are saying to you. In time you will probably add a few more steps to satisfy your own needs when interpreting dreams and nightmares.

In our last chapter on interpreting, we'll look at more complex situations so you will gain some understanding of the difficulties that can arise. We trust this will help you feel less frustrated when you explore a nightmare that seems complicated.

CHAPTER 10

Nightmare Interpretation with a Therapist

Each person will follow the six steps in his or her own way. Many of you will leap past some steps and get right to the heart of the nightmare. With other dreams, you'll find you have to plod along for a while before you get anywhere.

Don't be discouraged if the going is slow. Remember, in real life, people in therapy may spend hours, days, or even weeks thinking over a particular dream or nightmare before they uncover the pearls of wisdom hidden inside.

To give you a more realistic idea of what it's like to work on a dream with a therapist and to show you how complex dreams may appear, we're going to share the experiences of three patients. In each case, we've provided an abridged version of real dialogues that took place between the patient and therapist.

EILEEN'S MISSING STAIRCASE

Eileen is a fifty-one-year-old nurse working for a health care organization. She travels to various isolated locations to evaluate programs in public health.

Eileen recounted her anxiety dream. "I walk into this old house. It has a nice old piano, oak floors, Victorian-type furniture. No one is there, just me. I go out to the back porch and look out at the grounds. There are trees, but they appear windblown and have unusual shapes which make it seem like they're from another place.

"I look for the *back staircase* leading down to the backyard, but it's not finished. Whoever built the house did not complete the *steps*. I feel anxious in my attempt to leave and don't fully understand why."

Therapist: You mentioned the old house?

Eileen: Well, it was a nice old house. It reminds me of the one I grew up in. We had oak floors and a piano.

Therapist: Tell me about it.

Eileen: I get a good feeling thinking about it. It was a good time in my life. We had strong family ties, and I had lots of friends.

Therapist: And the house in your dream?

Eileen: It felt the same way. Sort of comfortable.

Therapist: There's no one there.

Eileen: It still felt welcoming.

Therapist: The oak floors, furnishings?

Eileen: Nothing unusual. Not really prominent in the dream . . . just reminded me of the furniture in the house I grew up in.

Therapist: As you describe the dream, it seemed like the house was out of place in the surroundings.

Eileen: Well, it is, kind of. The trees are ones like you might see in Australia. In fact, I went to Australia just after this dream. I even looked for this house. I thought the dream was a premonition. I didn't find it, though, and the trees weren't the same.

Therapist: The setting . . . what does it remind you of?

Eileen: I don't know. Just a different place.

(Eileen becomes slightly agitated and tense and her voice changes slightly at this point.)

Therapist: If a movie director was shooting a scene in a place like this, what would the scene be about?

Eileen: I don't know. It's just maybe like a place in Africa.

Therapist: You mentioned Australia. Where in Australia?

Eileen: The southern part of Australia. Out in the country. I didn't really see any place that looked like it.

Therapist: I noticed when you talked of the setting, you seemed to get stuck and your posture and voice changed.

Eileen: I don't know.

Therapist: You said you looked out the back door to the scenery?

Eileen: Yes.

Therapist: And there was no staircase and you felt anxious.

Eileen: Well, I don't understand why they didn't finish those steps.

Therapist: And where do the steps lead?

Eileen: Out to the back, where the trees are.

Therapist: It sounds like the feeling about the house is different from the feelings outside the house.

Eileen: Yes, the house is comfortable. The outside is foreign.

Therapist: And your present work? Coming out here? Being in this place? [Somewhat isolated community on the Navajo Reservation.]

Eileen: Well, my job takes me to different places. It is hard. I'm not as close to my family and friends. It's certainly not like when I grew up. I do miss it, and I do get lonely and feel disconnected.

Therapist: Disconnected? And in your dream, the stairs are missing. How do you get from the house to the outside?

Eileen: Well, I came into the house through the front door, but the way to the back is sort of through the back staircase, but it's not completed.

Therapist: (silence)

Eileen: It's hard . . . (she pauses). I think I'm getting it. But you know, this dream took place a while ago. I was in a similar situation and, in fact, it was just before going to Australia. I was leaving my family behind. It's difficult having a sense of home and belonging with the kind of job I have and all the travel. I love new and unusual places. But also family and friends . . . it's sometimes impossible to combine.

At this point, Eileen discovered the meaning of her dream. You may have noticed that she was having trouble associating and relating to the unusual trees and landscape. When you have difficulty associating, more than likely you're blocking out certain feelings. In Eileen's case this really was near the focal point of her conflict. In terms of the dream story, the conflict is revealed in the contrast between the comfortable house on the inside and the foreign landscape on the outside and the fact that the two could not be bridged because of the absence of the staircase.

In this brief story of Eileen, we have gone through each of the steps. The therapist asked her to give her story in the first-person present tense and so, as she recited the anxiety dream, she was externalizing it to achieve some distance. She did not write it down; however, telling it to someone else can function in a similar manner.

Then she looked at the various figures and made some associations. Notice how she related the home, the piano, and the oak floors to her childhood home. Since all these figures related directly to her childhood home, they were not pursued further as individual elements.

Then she looked at her relationship to these figures. She felt comfortable in the house, but found the outside foreign. This gave her the contrast between the two spaces. Even when the therapist asked her about the house being empty, she was still able to see the home as a comfortable place.

The main conflict, then, revolves around the comfort of the home and the foreignness of the outside. There appeared to be no way to bridge these two because the staircase had not been built. In putting this all together and relating it to her present life, she was able to see her love of travel and her work taking her away from another need—love from her family.

Eileen recognized the problem in satisfying these two needs and wanted to make a special effort to maintain her contacts with her friends and family while continuing in her present job. In Eileen's situation, she chose not to give up either, but to make both a possibility in her life.

HARVEY'S WAKE-UP CALL

Some nightmares are more complex. Going through the steps can be complicated and confusing. Often, dreams and nightmares have various levels of meaning. Each can provide insights that can be valuable. We all have so many more dreams and nightmares than we could possibly work with, it's important to know your limits in what you're going to work on. Unless you're extremely compulsive, it's okay if you simply want to look at one part of the dream and understand that one part.

Harvey was laboring under financial pressures due to a lost client. He was depressed about not having money to send his kids to the best university. And, at the same time, his wife had undergone a serious operation on her pancreas to remove a cyst. She was having a difficult recovery.

Here's how Harvey recounted his complex nightmare to the

therapist. "I am asleep in a large bed with my wife, a child, and, I think, my sister. The bedroom is adjacent to a large room where mass is being said. I awaken in the dream by hearing a sermon. I get up and, just as I finish dressing, a priest comes in with a young Japanese man. I tell the priest I heard his sermon.

"Next, I am in the parking lot at St. John's parish church, picking up my wife and sisters. Then, I am in the church sitting in the front pew.

"My pastor is very sickly. His hair is white and he has a crewcut. He is having a difficult time officiating at mass. During the sermon he needs help to stand. I get up to help him and someone else is there. The priest tells me to go away. Suddenly, I feel anxious, stupid, and out of place, and wake up feeling panicky."

In discussing this dream with Harvey, the first part did not reveal much. Harvey had no understanding of why the Japanese man would be there. The main aspect of the dream that emerged was that a sermon woke him up out of the bed. He saw his wife, child, and sister as representing family ties.

In real life, he also felt he was "asleep" relative to his family. The setbacks they'd all suffered had been difficult and he found himself not wanting to think about them.

Therapist: You said you were at the parking lot next to the church, picking up your wife and sisters?

Harvey: Yes. I was. And the next thing I knew, I was in the church with my family, sitting in the front pew. You know, I never do sit in the front pew, so that's strange for me.

Therapist: You never sit in the front pew?

Harvey: No, I feel uncomfortable there. You know, I am active in the church and partake in a lot of pastoral duties. I feel comfortable up on the podium, for example, reading to the congregation. But somehow, I just don't feel comfortable in the front pew. (He laughs.) Maybe I'm feeling that the priest is too close . . . he's looking at me or judging me.

Therapist: You sound a bit guilty about that?

Harvey: (nods)

Therapist: And you mentioned you were there with your family.

Harvey: Yes. I was. And maybe there's something there,

because, you know, I have been somewhat neglectful. My wife has been having problems and I guess I just haven't felt strong enough to provide her much support. It's been going on for so long I guess I'm feeling burned out.

Therapist: And you feel you should do more?

Harvey: Yes, it seems like I never do enough. I'm always getting down on myself. Sometimes I lie awake worrying at night and don't get much sleep. But then I find myself not doing some small things that could help.

Therapist: Well, this might fit with your guilt about sitting in the front row. And then you mentioned the pastor.

Harvey: Yes. You know, it's interesting, because in real life he has black hair and has sort of an Afro cut and he's really quite a strong and robust person.

Therapist: But in the dream you said he was sickly, had white hair, and wore a crewcut.

Harvey: It was like the way the priests used to wear their hair in the fifties.

Therapist: And you said he needed help with the sermon?

Harvey: Yes, I was supposed to help him, but when I did, they just told me I was stupid and I felt out of place and got really anxious. You know, I've stopped going to mass recently, and I have taken a leave of absence from my pastoral duties.

Therapist: Yes.

Harvey: Well, you know, my excuse was I had to help out my wife and the family. I guess what's happened is I haven't been going to church and I don't really feel I've been doing a good job with my family either.

Therapist: In the first part of the dream, it was the sermon that woke you up and your family was there in bed with you.

Harvey: Yes, when I was going to church, I guess it made me think more about what I was doing and, more recently, I've been able to pretend like there's no problems.

Therapist: So, what happens when you put all of this together . . . what you have so far?

Harvey: Well, I guess if you look at the sermon as waking me up, you could say I need to be awakened. I need to attend to my family, and . . .

. . . you know, usually my guilt isn't justified. I get guilty over the smallest things. I know I've had a hard time recently, but what my wife has been going through, and the kids, is really much more difficult. Even though it's hard, I guess I'm going to have to get back into paying attention. And I think I can do that, because the end is in sight. I told you my wife's surgery went fairly well, and, well, she's been in bed at home all week, getting up somewhat. The doctor told us that she can expect a fairly fast recuperation over the next eight weeks, and after that she should be all right.

As Harvey explored his connection with the church, he discovered he had done exactly the wrong thing. The church had been a source of strength for him. He also knew it forced him to take a close look at himself to help him make the right decisions. To feel good about himself he knew he was going to have to refocus his energy to provide for himself and for his family.

Harvey was only able to work through one part of the dream, and yet he still uncovered more than enough meaning to find valuable insights. In turn, he used this new information to move himself in a positive direction.

DENISE'S ENCOUNTER WITH THREE MEDICINE WOMEN

Denise, is a young professional Native American woman. The night before she had this anxiety dream she saw the film, *Running On Empty*. The movie is about a young man coming to terms with his parents who have been on the run for twenty years because of a crime committed in the 1960s.

"In the dream, I am coming from Port Orchard to Gig Harbor. I am with my brother and his wife, another close friend, Jim, and the mother and father and two boys in the movie *Running On Empty*. We are together until we reach the intersection and I go ahead on past the intersection.

"I am on my bike holding a small black object the size of a hockey puck. It is a container that holds all my emotions. It is dark because they are packed in there so tight. Suddenly, the container slips out of my hand. I panic as I watch it roll across four lanes of traffic.

"There are some men across the road who work in a garage. Seeing my plight and hearing me yell, they grab the container and give it to three medicine women who smile and say they will get it back to me safely.

"These medicine women have herbs for sale along the roadway. I am relieved knowing they have the power to give me back the container. Then they throw it. It makes a high, arcing trajectory like a rainbow. I caught it, relieved."

The dream setting involved the road between Port Orchard and Gig Harbor. This was important to Denise, as her father had grown up in the Seattle area and had gone there in the summer to camp and fish. She had also gone to this place with her parents as well as with her previous boyfriend. So, this setting also had the significant association of a previous love relationship.

There are several dream persons in the dream who can be put into the three categories: friends and family, including her brother, his wife, and Jim, a close friend; the unknown persons, including the family from the movie and the men working in the garage; and the special persons—the three Indian medicine women who wield special powers.

Therapist: You are on the road to Gig Harbor?

Denise: Yes, it's a place I have been many times, as I told you.

Therapist: The other people you were traveling with?

Denise: Well, there is the family from *Running On Empty*.

Therapist: Uh-huh.

Denise: Well, you know the movie.

Therapist: Tell me about it.

Denise: Well, these people had done something wrong a long time ago and they were trying to escape from being punished for what they had done. It was a real struggle trying to keep the family together.

Therapist: Struggle?

Denise: Yes, especially as the boy got older . . . he became more attached to his music and a young woman.

Therapist: (silence)

Denise: And the other problem was the children had friends but always had to leave them behind.

Therapist: And your brother and sister-in-law.

Denise: Well, he has just finished architectural school and he started working for a large Vancouver firm. She is an accountant. They are both really busy but trying to have a baby.

Therapist: And your friend Jim?

Denise: Well, he has been a close friend for the last couple of years and we have helped each other get through medical school. He is married, so there have been limitations to our relationship. I'm going to miss him when he goes away for his internship in Montreal.

Therapist: You're going ahead of the group on your bicycle.

Denise: Yes, that is strange because I just got a new mountain bike and I'm not a good bike rider.

Therapist: So what happens between you and the other people on bikes?

Denise: Well, as I head down this road to Gig Harbor the others are left behind. That's where I begin having trouble.

Therapist: Leaving them behind leads to trouble?

Denise: That's when the container slipped out.

Therapist: The container . . .

Denise: Yes, it's shaped like a hockey puck.

Therapist: Can you tell me more about the hockey puck?

Denise: Well, my emotions were so tightly packed that it looked kind of dark like a hockey puck.

Therapist: A real hockey puck?

Denise: Well, you know, it gets knocked about on the ice.

Therapist: And your emotions?

Denise: Well (pause); I have been finding it harder to be close to Jim and my brother and sister-in-law while I am single and they are all happy in their marriages.

Therapist: And where do you stand in all of that?

Denise: Well, when I look at what I just said about the children always having to leave their friends I guess I am feeling that way too. I am leaving medical school. I am having to say goodbye to Jim over the next few months and that is really hard. (Pause.) I guess my emotions do feel like a hockey puck, knocked around a bit.

Therapist: Before we go on to the last part of the dream, is there anything more about the setting, the road to Gig Harbor?

Denise: Well, not too much. I guess as I explore the other people in my dream . . . it relates to the same thing. I think of it as a summer place. A place where we are together as a family.

Therapist: So the road then is special to you because it leads to your summer place and the idea of family.

Denise: Yes. But, the real road is not four-laned. So I don't know why this one in the dream is.

Therapist: Is there anything special about the number to you?

Denise: Four lanes? The first thing that comes to my mind is the four directions, north, south, east, and west. The directions are important in my traditional beliefs.

Therapist: And this relates to the medicine women?

Denise: Well, the medicine women are very special to me as guides and healers, physically, mentally, and spiritually. (Pause.) I guess I am feeling a little bit uncomfortable with this. I've always been interested in our culture and native beliefs, but I've been so involved with Western medicine I'm feeling disconnected from traditional healing practices.

Therapist: In the dream, how did you feel about these medicine women?

Denise: I was relieved when the young man gave my emotions to them. I forgot to mention when I first dropped my emotions across the road, I felt grief-stricken. I was so anxious that I would not get them back. So when the medicine women got them I was still tense, but somewhat relieved. When they threw them back to me I knew things would be okay.

Therapist: We have gone through most of your dream. Have you noticed anything we have missed?

Denise: I do not think so.

Therapist: (Silence.)

Denise: I have not really said much about the young men at the garage.

Therapist: (Silence.)

Denise: Well, they were just men working at the garage . . . nothing special.

Therapist: Is there anyone you know who works at a garage, or is there anything special about this garage?

Denise: Well, my ex-boyfriend worked as a mechanic at a garage before he went back to the university. Although he supported my traditional beliefs, we had planned to work somewhere other than for Indian people, and that bothered me.

Therapist: This young man in your dream gave your emotions to the medicine woman?

Denise: Yes, when we broke up I started thinking more about working with my people. And for a few months I spent more time with other native students.

Therapist: And your feelings about this?

Denise: I have been fairly good at keeping my emotions at a distance. Medical school, the breakup with my boyfriend, saying good-bye to Jim have all been really hard, and it's been a struggle. (She is very emotional at this point, then several moments later laughs a little.) I guess I am not so good at keeping them away.

Therapist: You also mentioned your emotions were thrown in an unusual arc like a rainbow.

Denise: The rainbow has always carried special significance for my people. (Pause.) And last summer I was driving north with Jim to one of the rural clinics. It was a stormy day, but clearing. There were really black clouds to the east. And as we rounded a corner, there was a huge double rainbow. We stopped and watched it. It was so beautiful.

I was driving alone past that same place last week and felt sad, thinking of saying good-bye to all this.

Denise continued with her therapist. She discovered she had been keeping her emotions at too much of a distance. By getting in touch with her feelings and her spiritual connections of her own culture, she was able to see more clearly what she needed to do in terms of her career as a physician, and she also recognized her desire to make her own family.

As we can see, there were numerous parts to this dream—a movie, in-laws, a close friend, native women healers, and, of course, the hockey puck type object with her emotions. Yet, this seemingly complex array of figures all fit rather neatly together to create a relevant story for Denise.

In some ways, these complex cases will be more the norm for people attempting to work on their own nightmares. That's why we've spent the time going over them. You may find the number of characters seems unwieldy or the dream itself seems long and convoluted. Most dreams are manageable; however, using the steps will help you organize them more clearly.

These steps are intended to be the basics to get you started. They are not meant to be exhaustive. In fact, we do not feel we are at a stage of understanding with dreams or nightmares that we could give a complete list of steps.

We would also repeat that this is only one method of interpretation. There are many others that are equally valid—each with its own advantages and disadvantages. We believe, however, this simple, direct method will serve as a good foundation for those unfamiliar with dream interpretation. And, it will help those who've attempted unsuccessfully to interpret their dreams with a more complicated technique.

This would be a good time to ask yourself how you're feeling about your nightmares. What insights have you gained? What aspects do you find difficult to confront? And we hope that as you learn something about yourself, you'll be able to move from that awareness towards a new and positive direction. And, likewise, if you see progress in your dreams, accept the compliment your unconscious is providing you and let yourself feel good about it.

Depending on what you've achieved so far in your efforts at nightmare interpretation, you may want to continue exploring your bad dreams to see what impact that has on them. For some, it will make your nightmares go away. For others, though your new insights may be rewarding, the nightmares persist.

If so, stick with us. In the next section, we'll show you how to abolish your bad dreams.

PART III

**Turning Nightmares
Into Dreams**

CHAPTER 11

Treating Your Nightmares and Bad Dreams

OLDER AND SOMETIMES WISER APPROACHES

In the not-so-distant past, many cultures approached their bad dreams as if they were real. If you were a Cherokee Indian and you dreamed a snake bit you, you'd treat yourself for a snakebite. If you were from Morocco and you dreamed of a dead family member, you would make an offering at the grave. And if you were an Ashanti from Africa and you dreamed of committing adultery, you would pay an adultery fine—the fine-collector no doubt achieving early financial retirement. In these instances, people took their dreams literally.

If you were a member of the Senoi tribe of the Malay peninsula, you might have used a technique called *face and conquer*. This method was attributed to the Senoi in the 1930s, when their tribes were researched. Since then the accuracy of the claims by the initial explorers have been challenged, but the alleged technique is so intriguing we'll share it with you.

While you are dreaming, you confront whatever attacks you and defeat it. As the theory goes, the dream images represent different parts of your personality. To become a whole person, you must attend to all psychic forces emanating from within, including the hostile ones. The Senoi children were supposedly directed to kill their dream enemies in their sleep. The spirit of the defeated enemy would rise up; only this time it would be friendly to the dreamer.

In our own country, Navajo Indians with posttraumatic nightmares have used a special ritual known as the Enemy Way Ceremony. This involves three nights of dancing, prayers, chanting, and sand-painting, involving the individual, his family and friends, and the community.

The Navajos developed an early understanding of the Post-traumatic Stress Disorder. They recognized that warriors had problems after waging battle and needed to expunge memories and "spirits" to bring the man back into harmony with the Navajo way of life. We know of two patients who served in World War II and suffered from PTSD. Both their nightmares and other symptoms were diminished by engaging in this traditional approach.

Each culture's techniques have their own validity. Our Western culture emphasizes intellectual approaches. Sometimes, we look for a simple solution, such as "It's only a dream." These words often allay children's fears about their bad dreams, especially as they learn the distinction between the dream and waking worlds.

Adults may need more information to ease their fears about nightmares. Saying "It's only a dream" may not erase the traumatic images or the bad feelings. We want greater understanding. What are bad dreams? What causes them? What do they mean?

We trust we've answered these questions in the preceding sections of the book. General information and personal dream interpretation are two important approaches that can help you understand your nightmares. Just by learning important facts, you may have erased your fears about bad dreams and thus disposed of them. Or, perhaps you've unlocked a significant conflict mirrored in your bad dreams through dream interpretation. This too may have ended your nightmares.

While these methods work for some people, unfortunately they do not work for the majority of chronic nightmare sufferers. Even traditional psychoanalytic or psychotherapeutic methods which delve into the heart of your emotional conflicts do not have such a good track record.

So how are you going to get rid of your nightmares?

COGNITIVE/BEHAVIORAL THERAPY

In the 1960s, a new perspective was gained on the problem of troublesome dreams. Reports appeared in the scientific literature showing that nightmares could be successfully and rather easily treated with behavioral methods. These methods did not focus on the cause of the nightmare;

instead, the researchers treated the bad dreams as the problem.

What do we mean, "treat the bad dream as the problem?"

An analogy to quitting smoking or losing weight proves useful here. Cigarette-smoking and overeating are habits which many people would like to overcome. In psychological terms, we could analyze people with these problems and speculate on various technical diagnoses to explain why they continue to smoke and overindulge in food despite their desire to stop. Would these psychological diagnoses help them quit smoking and overeating? For some, yes; but for many, as in the case of nightmares, this focus on the underlying cause usually does not result in a cure.

With cognitive/behavioral methods we focus on how to change the thinking and the behavior of the individual so he or she can stop smoking or lose weight. That's why the methods are called *cognitive*, referring to your *thinking*, and *behavioral*, referring to your *behavior*. Often the methods are combined, as will be done with the technique we'll be teaching you to abolish your nightmares.

In the simplest terms, nightmares are viewed as a bad habit which you somehow learned and now wish to eliminate. The nightmare is the specific problem we'll be treating. If you're so inclined, you can look for causes behind the nightmare, and you can explore the emotional conflicts reflected in your bad dreams. However, in the cognitive/behavioral approach we don't focus on cause and meaning.

Cognitive/behavioral methods can reduce the frequency of nightmares very effectively. Let's begin with a question we expect you to be asking right about now.

WHY PUT YOUR TRUST IN THIS BEHAVIORAL METHOD?

The best answer is because it works!

And to inspire even more confidence, let us inform you that similar techniques have successfully combated nightmares over the past fifty years.

As early as 1936, a report appeared in *Parents Magazine* describing a technique for preventing nightmares in adults and children. Based on the concept of suggestion, a series of phrases is repeated to a child in order to get her thinking about new and less threatening images which she might "include" in her dreams.

In 1945, *The Military Surgeon*—a medical journal—reported a single case describing a desensitizing technique in which a soldier was instructed to consciously repeat his nightmares aloud until he was at ease with the troubling aspects of the dream. The author called the technique "psychiatric first aid," and used it frequently in the treatment of "combat dreams" or recurrent nightmares relating to war.

There have been many others who've used similar methods, probably as far back as classical times. But with the advent of modern behavioral methods in the 1960s, there has been a steady increase in the cases treated in this manner.

In 1964, one report described hypnosis for the treatment of nightmares associated with test anxiety. In the same year, a report described a woman with a recurrent dream of being chased. She was advised to stand her ground in the dream and this proved effective. Notice the similarity to the alleged Senoi method of face and conquer.

Many research articles have appeared over the last three decades detailing variations in technique, including those by Bishay, Fleming, Geer, Haynes, Marks, Mooney, Moss, Schindler, Silverman, and Stampfl, to name a few. Most of these studies describe single cases of chronic nightmare sufferers treated with assorted behavioral methods, such as desensitization and imagery rehearsal.

Desensitization is a method of recalling the bad dream and reviewing it until it no longer affects you. This is combined with a relaxation technique to master any anxiety arising as the dream is recalled.

Desensitization was applied to a variety of nightmare problems, including a man dreaming of killing his mother, a woman dreaming of being attacked at knifepoint, a three-year-old leukemia patient suffering separation anxiety, a Vietnam vet whose buddy was blown up by a mine, and one patient who believed he was persecuted by the devil in his dreams. All nightmares were successfully eliminated.

The only two scientifically controlled studies on nightmares prior to our own work used desensitization and relaxation methods. Cellucci and Lawrence performed the first study in

1978 and reduced nightmare frequency by 79 percent in patients using desensitization only. In 1983, Miller and DiPilato did the second controlled study using desensitization and relaxation. Their subjects' nightmare frequency was reduced by just over 75 percent.

It was particularly interesting to us that these researchers elected to work with the patients over several weeks. Each technique required the subjects to have weekly sessions for one to two months.

Not long after these studies, our colleague and mentor Robert Kellner, Professor and Vice Chairman of the Department of Psychiatry at the University of New Mexico School of Medicine, chose a different approach. He worked with psychiatry residents to treat four chronic nightmare sufferers, but used only *one* short treatment session. The method he used is known as rehearsal, or imagery rehearsal, where the nightmare sufferer visualizes the dream in a changed form. Three of the four people eradicated their nightmares entirely.

This led to our research in collaboration with Dr. Kellner. We wanted to compare the rehearsal and desensitization methods. And we wondered if we could treat people for chronic nightmares in just one session.

Our first study compared the two techniques—rehearsal and desensitization. We reduced nightmare frequency by 70 percent with both desensitization and rehearsal; however, we also discovered imagery rehearsal was much easier and less time-consuming for the average person.

So we performed a second study, using only the rehearsal technique. We also used an untreated control group to compare the effects of treatment and no treatment. This is a standard method in research studies. The treatment group receives the treatment and the control group does not. We did, however, have the control group record their nightmares.

On the average, the people entering our study from both groups had suffered chronic nightmares for fifteen years. They had bad dreams which almost always awakened them two to three times a week.

After one session, those treated practiced the rehearsal method on their own for the next three months. There was virtually no contact with this group until three months later when they filled in their follow-up sheets. By then, the frequency of nightmares had dropped to an average of one bad dream every three weeks. Again, this was greater than a 70 percent reduction. In fact, 90 percent of the treated group reduced their nightmares to an average of less than one per month, within six months of learning imagery rehearsal.

Two other interesting findings emerged. The control group that merely recorded their bad dreams had a 45 percent reduction in nightmares. And both groups reported that the intensity of their nightmares had decreased. With further follow-up from selected patients, we've also discovered that the frequency of nightmares continues to decrease as far out as twelve to eighteen months from the beginning of treatment.

Perhaps the most intriguing finding from both studies involved the use of symptom checklists to evaluate our patients before and after treatment. These checklists produce a score which measures the degree of anxiety or depression you may be feeling. At the outset, several of the people had high scores, indicating moderate degrees of anxiety and depression. Three and six months after treatment our patients filled in the same symptom checklists. Many of the subjects' symptoms had changed dramatically. In fact, most of the scores demonstrated a significant reduction of anxiety and depression.

This was an intriguing finding because it suggested nightmares caused the symptoms. Once the nightmares improved or were eliminated, the symptoms improved or were eliminated. It's possible the single treatment itself reduced the symptoms, but this is unlikely because it is rare in the fields of psychology and psychiatry to have such a pronounced treatment effect with just one session.

Although many of these theories need further study and investigation before they can be considered scientifically proven, we can categorically state that nightmares can be significantly reduced and, in many cases, eliminated by behavioral methods such as imagery rehearsal and desensitization.

WILL BEHAVIORAL THERAPY WORK FOR YOU?

This three-step method is designed in a self-help format so that you can teach yourself how to banish your nightmares without having to work extensively with a professional therapist.

Some people reading this book, however, may have significant psychological problems that are causing the bad dreams. For those, it's important to consider psychotherapy in addition to using the behavioral technique. Of course, when you think of all the things that might be causing nightmares—child abuse, drugs and alcohol, medications, major life stressors, past traumatic events, physical illnesses, depression, acute psychosis, and so on—you might ask, "How do I know if I should do this on my own, or with professional help?"

In actuality it isn't hard to decide. The first question to ask is, "If I didn't have these nightmares, would I consider my life to be reasonably normal?" If you answer yes, you've excluded a number of causes.

If you're on medications, simply ask your physician if the pills might be the culprit. Try to recall if the bad dreams started before or after the medications.

If you're having a psychotic break, you're unlikely to be reading this book, but if you're worried about the possibility, there's nothing unusual about asking close friends or people with whom you work if they think something is seriously wrong with you. This might seem like an odd thing to do, but we assure you everybody at one time or another wonders about their sanity.

If you suffer from schizophrenia and you're doing well either with medications or therapy, we see no reason why you can't consider this behavioral treatment. We do, however, advise you to work with your doctor if you're going to proceed.

If nightmares are a recent experience in your life, there may be an obvious stressful cause which may require other considerations in addition to the behavioral treatment.

If you choose to get professional help for whatever reason, you can work on your nightmares as well. It would be helpful to you and your therapist to discuss the treatment.

The bottom line is that most people know if there's another stressor or problem they need to address in addition to the nightmare problem. If you use the technique and you're dissatisfied with the results, talk it over with a therapist trained in behavioral methods.

One small caution must be delivered here. In our studies, no individual got worse using the techniques we taught. However, in other studies a rare patient has described worsening nightmares. Those people who got worse, though, were patients suffering from severe mental health problems including schizophrenia and personality disorders. Therefore we don't really know why they got worse. It may have had nothing to do with their treatment. However, we must repeat, if you suffer from a serious mental health problem, we advise you to discuss this technique with your therapist before proceeding.

DO YOU REALLY WANT TO GET RID OF YOUR NIGHTMARES?

Please don't think we're asking the question to suggest you shouldn't get rid of your bad dreams. It's just that in our research we've discovered that a tiny percentage of people with chronic nightmares are attached to their bad dreams. They have difficulty giving up the nightmares because they've developed what might be called a "need" to have them.

This probably sounds a bit peculiar and certainly won't apply to most of you because you really want to abolish your bad dreams. But we've treated a handful of people who were actually upset with how quickly their nightmares vanished. One man was so confused about his feelings that within a week of completely eliminating his nightmares, he intentionally stopped his treatment because he just couldn't accept that his bad dreams had disappeared so easily.

His nightmares returned, though not as frequently, and he quickly decided enough was enough. He returned to his treatment and has achieved success again.

We'll talk more about this later, but please take the time to think clearly about this question: Do you want to get rid of your nightmares?

Just one more question, then we'll get started.

IS THERE A PLACE FOR DRUG THERAPY?

Occasionally, there are patients who will benefit from drug-induced changes in the sleep cycle to reduce their nightmares. There are three types of drugs which are most commonly used: sedatives or sleeping pills, tranquilizers which reduce anxiety, and antidepressants which treat depression.

Sedatives should be avoided, if possible, because they frequently lead to dependency on the drugs. People become hooked on sedatives rather easily and cannot sleep without them.

Tranquilizers and antidepressants may be useful if a person suffers a significant life crisis which causes nightmares, anxiety, and depression. A death in the family may cause severe symptoms that usually respond in time to psychotherapy; but, if symptoms and nightmares persist, tranquilizers and/or antidepressants may reduce the frequency of nightmares as well as improve the problems with anxiety and depression.

These drugs may work by affecting the REM stage of the sleep cycle. A problem can arise, however, if the drugs are discontinued too abruptly. Not only does REM sleep return, but it may return with a vengeance. It's as if REM is making up for lost dreams, giving the dreamer fits by lengthening the dreaming periods and intensifying the images. This is known as *REM rebound*. If the drugs are gradually reduced over a few weeks as is recommended, then REM rebound is mostly avoided.

A variation of REM rebound is seen among alcoholics who self-medicate themselves with alcohol. They do this primarily to avoid the unpleasant symptoms of alcohol withdrawal. The alcoholic, having gone without a drink for one or several days, finds him-or herself anxious and agitated, suffering from all kinds of aches and pains. Taking a drink will usually eliminate these symptoms until the next period of abstinence.

But alcoholics often talk about other reasons for dimming their consciousness with alcohol. Sometimes, this relates to disturbing dreams. After drinking for a period of time, it's clear to the alcoholic the bad dreams seemed to have disappeared. This is the same effect seen with the other drugs, that is, REM suppression. By altering the sleep cycle, alcohol can banish nightmares.

REM rebound will occur when the alcoholic stops drinking. Alcoholics who become clean and sober often suffer horrible, painful, and vivid nightmares. Also, they can suffer hallucinations—veritable waking nightmares—if they develop delirium tremens, or DTs.

People suffering from nightmares and psychotic disorders, such as schizophrenia, may find relief of their symptoms and reduction of their bad dreams with appropriate medications.

Other indications for drugs occur when an individual suffers from a different type of sleep disorder, such as night terrors, or the REM behavior disorder. We'll talk about treating other sleep disturbances in the last section of the book.

So there are a few situations in which frequent nightmares can be treated with drugs; however, if your doctor seems too quick to treat your bad dreams with medications, then we would respectfully suggest you seek a second opinion.

CHAPTER 12

Guided Self-Management

WE GUIDE, YOU DRIVE!

These chapters are designed in a specific way to maximize your efforts in getting rid of your nightmares. The method you'll learn has been used successfully by other nightmare sufferers. They followed the step-by-step approach we will teach you. We are confident you will have an excellent chance of eliminating your nightmares by following this same step-by-step process.

The instructions are not difficult. Much of the program will be enjoyable and will teach you how to relax. It will take some time, however, to go through the steps properly. We're not talking about a lot of time, but you'll need to practice the lessons each day for several days in a row. The total time you take each day will be no more than an hour, and probably half that. Setting aside a particular week when you know you'll be able to practice the lessons will go a long way towards getting the most from your efforts.

We'll start with the principle known as *guided self-management*, or, more simply put: We guide, you drive!

Let's take a closer look at this concept in an area you're probably familiar with—health and medicine. Suppose you develop a fever and some belly pain, and your doctor says you need your appendix removed. You're taken to the operating room and the doctor administers anesthetic to put you to sleep. Then the appendectomy is performed, and the next thing you know, you wake up in the recovery room.

In this case you entrusted yourself to the care and judgment of your surgeon. And once you did that, you really didn't have any conscious control over the surgery. This kind of treatment is almost totally *passive*. Sure, you made the decision to go ahead with the operation once your doctor advised you, but then it was all in the surgeon's hands.

Let's look at the opposite example, that is, totally *active*. Again you develop belly pain, now with some diarrhea, but no fever. The pain is crampy and it comes and goes with your visits to the bathroom. You think it's something you ate, so you give it some time, sticking with clear liquids like tea and juice. A day later it's resolved. This time you had decided you could handle the problem on your own, independent of a doctor or anyone else's advice. You managed everything without other guidance.

Guided self-management incorporates concepts from both the active and the passive. You'll start out following our directions, but you will end up mastering the technique so you can manage the problem yourself.

If you can stand one more round of belly pain, let's suppose this time you have an ulcer. You go to the doctor who recommends three things: antacids, relaxation exercises for stress, and a realistic plan for you to deal with those problems that are causing the stress.

You take the antacids and practice the relaxation techniques, both of which give you relief. But, more importantly, you carefully review the problems in your life that are causing the stress; then you develop new goals and expectations to cope with this stress in a healthier way. The ulcer heals, but several months later a relapse threatens. This time you're prepared. You restart the antacids, practice your relaxation techniques, and look honestly at the new problems that are causing the stress, working out a new plan to deal with them.

In guided self-management we want you to take more responsibility for the things you'll need to do to get rid of your nightmares. And, to improve your chances of success, we also wish to guide you along the right road.

Guided self-management has been used in a variety of newer forms of treatment. For example, people with tension headaches have been taught techniques of relaxation to try to relieve the problem. After a few lessons with their doctor or therapist, they practice these techniques on their own. Eventually they learn the skills well enough to go it alone. Then, if a headache threatens, they are equipped to deal with the problem independent of their therapist.

Guided self-management has been used on many other health problems, including insomnia, phobias, pain control, and cigarette smoking. People respond to this kind of treatment because it gives them greater control and power over their problem. Along those lines, there are several important ideas about the process that will help you get the most out of it.

The following specific points all relate to your personal attitude about how you're going to approach your own treatment.

WHAT'S IN AN ATTITUDE?

Everything!

Right now, you're reading this book. What does that tell you? The answer would seem obvious that you're bothered by your nightmares and you want to get rid of them, or you know someone else who suffers from disturbing dreams. The fact you've taken the step of reading this book, then, shows you your attitude is already geared toward getting better.

Or is it? This is a key question to getting better. In the first two sections of the book, you've read about other people's nightmares and you've learned you're not alone with this problem. But somewhere else in the back of your mind in a corner that maybe hasn't really been touched by this new knowledge, there's a place where you have an attitude about what's going to happen next.

But is that attitude based on facts and reason, or is it based on the many long years of suffering that have led you to believe you'll never get rid of your nightmares? If your attitude tells you things will never change, and that you'll never be without bad dreams, then there's a good chance we won't be able to guide you down the right road.

Why is that? Because, by and large, people do not change unless they want to change or they're forced to change. No one's forcing you to read this book, so if there's going to be a change, it will happen because you're willing to consider the possibility that you can get rid of your nightmares.

Suppose you're standing in line outside a nightclub, waiting to see a comedian. It's bitter cold and raining, and the doorman says, "It won't be much longer, so just relax and enjoy yourself." You'd look at him kind of funny, right?

After all, freezing outside in the cold and rain probably isn't your idea of entertainment. Your attitude wouldn't be geared for having a good time. Suddenly, the door opens up and you move inside into a whole new world. It's warm, there's good food and drink, and plenty of other people who are looking forward to sharing the humor of this great comic. Your attitude's completely different now. You're ready for something good to happen.

We want to help you get rid of your nightmares, but we need your help too. We need you to take a step inside where it's warm and friendly, and where you'll believe something good is going to happen.

If you're having trouble taking that step, this next question may help you along.

WHO'S REALLY IN CHARGE?

You are!

In psychological jargon, there's a phrase known as "locus of control." It refers to a belief about how much control you have in a given situation.

Let's look again at people who suffer from tension headaches. One way for them to view their problem is that they are victims of stresses that lie outside their control. It's not their fault they get tension headaches. The fault lies with the stress—the boss, a spouse, perhaps children—that's causing the tension that in turn causes the headaches.

They might say, "I'm powerless to do anything about it. This just keeps happening to me." In this case the locus, or center, is now outside—it's external. The power is outside the person's control.

Getting stress out of your life is no easy matter, and we would not suggest otherwise. But we can recommend that the headache sufferer relate to the problem in a way that might make the stress less potent. For example, some people get tension headaches because they clench their teeth in response to frustration. Suppose they learned instead to relax their jaw muscles, thereby preventing the headaches. It's true they wouldn't have removed the stress, but they would have gained more power over the effects of that stress by learning to relax their jaws.

When you do that, you have an *internal* locus of control, that is, the power is controlled by you.

Many situations in your life can be analyzed in this way, sorting out the control and power in any given set of circumstances. Often, you find out you have more control in some cases, and less control in others than you would have previously thought. This is especially true with regard to your health.

Moving the locus of control onto your own shoulders helps you take more responsibility for things that happen to you— good and bad. In dealing with your bad dreams through guided self-management we want you to realize you have some control over your nightmares. This will improve your chances of success.

WHAT TO EXPECT?

Success!

When you first learned how to drive a car, was there ever any expectation you wouldn't get your license? Maybe there was a fear you'd never learn how to parallel-park, or you'd do something stupid to fail the test, but you probably believed sooner or later you'd be out there on the road with the rest of us crazy drivers.

What was it like to actually learn how to drive? Can you remember learning how to turn the steering wheel hand over hand? Or how about learning to drive the car in reverse? At first you didn't know how to do these things, then later you did. In between, you were gradually improving your skills, although some days were better than others. Maybe there were days you thought you'd never figure out how to parallel-park. Finally you got the hang of it and you took your driver's test.

Most of us expected we'd get it right and pass the test. We expected to succeed, and we did. Driving a car may seem like too simple an activity to compare to something as complex as a nightmare, but the principle holds. That is, we have expectations going into the treatment, and those expectations can help us a lot if we expect to succeed. Or, they can hinder us even more if we expect to fail.

Suppose, in working on your nightmares, things don't go well for you right from the start. If you believe you can succeed, then practice will take care of your problems. Or, suppose things go extraordinarily well in the beginning, but then you have problems later. Going back to the lessons ought to fix this if you genuinely believe the work you're doing can help you. Starting with the right expectations is going to help you succeed.

So why should you expect success?

Because the rehearsal method has proven to be an extremely effective way of dealing with chronic nightmares. If you stick to the program that's outlined, you can expect to eliminate or markedly reduce your nightmares.

It will work for you!

RECORDING DATA

If you're in business, you have to keep a record of your profits and losses to know how you're doing. It's a clear way of measuring your success.

Recording information about your nightmares will serve as a similar yardstick. It will give you the feedback to see what progress you're making. Feedback is an important principle in improving. It will allow you to review what you've done with each lesson and gain new insights so you can build on each of your successes. Sometimes the process of recording itself may prove especially useful as a part of your treatment. We'll say more on that later.

Now we'll ask you to grab a notebook to use over the next week. We'd like you to consider the following seven questions on the next page. Please answer them with a yes or no. You may want to write down the questions and answers on the first sheet in your notebook. Getting into the habit of writing things down will improve your chances for success.

ATTITUDE SURVEY

1. Do I understand the basic concept of guided self-management?
2. By the end of treatment do I want to be able to manage my problems with nightmares?
3. Do I have a positive attitude about trying to get rid of my nightmares?
4. Do I expect to successfully rid myself of my problems with nightmares?
5. Do I understand that in order to rid myself of my nightmares, I must accept more responsibility for the things that go on within me?
6. Do I understand the importance of a positive attitude, especially when things aren't changing as rapidly as I'd like?
7. Do I understand the importance of recording information in providing me with feedback about my progress and success?

Congratulations if you've been able to answer each question with a yes.

If you answered any of the questions with a no, we don't want that to deter you from proceeding to the first step. However, we would like you to think about reviewing some of the points in this chapter before continuing so you can remove any obstacles in your path to banishing your nightmares.

CHAPTER 13

The First Step:
Activating Your Imagination

SEEING WITH YOUR MIND'S EYE

Imagery and imagination are concepts that will provide the basis for the first step in getting rid of your nightmares. An image is something visual we can easily relate to: the image of a sunset, a mountain, or a tree. We can see these things in our mind's eye if we choose to focus on them.

Imagination suggests something more complex than mere images because we can imagine in different ways. We're not limited by the sense of sight. We can imagine the taste of good food, the sound of a beautiful symphony, the touch of a great massage, or more involved things like our feelings associated with any of these sensations.

We can go further with our imagination by combining all our senses and feelings into complex pictures in our mind. Imagine what it might feel like to walk barefoot across a log straddling a stream of water. A few things come quickly to mind: the touch of your bare soles against the tree bark, the sound of the water rippling underneath and your fear of falling.

Many people imagine with a predominant sense. Some are geared towards visualizing in great detail, while others have a greater sense of feeling things. Still others have a fine sense for hearing sounds in their imagination.

No one way of imagining is more correct than other ways. Each person may naturally lean more on one particular sense than another, but the important point to understand is that your imagination can be broadened with practice. We'll teach you how to do just that, because the more you activate your imagination, the better your chances for erasing your nightmares.

The reason for this is that your dreams and your imagination have a lot in common. In your dreams, good and bad, you see and feel things in ways that are similar to how you see and feel when you use your imagination. You'll learn to take advantage of this similarity later; but now let us focus on the first step of learning to use your imagination to its fullest.

GETTING STARTED WITH A PRACTICE FANTASY

We would like you to create a special situation to improve your performance in using your imagination.

You'll need to attend to three things.

First, find a quiet place so you won't be distracted by noise.

Second, make arrangements so you will not be interrupted.

And third, you must choose a position for relaxing, either sitting or lying, which feels the most comfortable.

Accomplishing these three things will facilitate your efforts to broaden your imagination.

Now we'd like you to imagine a practice fantasy, so please find your spot and get comfortable. You should also have your notebook to record some information afterwards. When you're ready we want you to slowly read the following *three* paragraphs:

I'm standing on a narrow road overlooking a wide expanse of beach. I see the surf, and I hear the sound of the waves. I smell the clean, fresh air as the sea breeze blows across my face. There are small islands off at an angle, but as I look out, I know the nearest land is really Japan, far, far away across the Pacific.

Then, I walk down a small embankment to the sand. I take off my shoes and socks. I feel the sand beneath my bare feet. Towards the water, I see sandpipers scurrying along the beach. I walk to the water's edge and look back. I see large trees looming up against the sky. A few of the trees have bare limbs with nests for bald eagles.

I turn back to the water and walk along the beach until I come across some large logs half-buried in the sand. The wind has blown fine sand over the logs, creating a variety of sculptures. Several catch my eye, so I decide to stop here and lie back against one of the logs. Studying the sculptures, I see many different shapes and forms, as if I were watching clouds. Eventually, I close my eyes and rest my head against the log. I listen to the waves, and think about all the things I've seen.

Now that you've completed the reading, we want you to remain in your comfortable position, close your eyes, and imagine what you've just read about. If you want to reread the three paragraphs again, that's okay. Do that now. Then, close your eyes and spend five to seven minutes reliving the images in your mind. Use all your senses in your imagination as you try to recall everything.

Remember, if you've arranged things to your benefit, you will have found a quiet place where you won't be interrupted, and you'll have found a comfortable position—sitting in a chair or lying on a couch.

The goal is to relax and enjoy yourself while using your imagination to its fullest. It's important that you take five to seven minutes for this practice session. Please don't continue reading until you're done.

EVALUATING YOUR SUCCESS WITH IMAGERY

You've completed the exercise, and we hope it was relaxing and enjoyable. For some, a few unpleasant images and anxieties may have intruded into your mind's eye. We'll have more to say about that, and if it occurs again we'll show you how to deal with it.

Now let's take a closer look at the way you use your imagination. Let's go through a series of questions about the feelings and images you thought of during this first practice. We suggest you write out your answers in your notebook, as this will enhance the process of building your imagination.

Here are the questions:

What was the color of the water as you looked out across the
    ocean?
Did you taste salt on your lips from the sea spray?
How loud were the waves as they lapped upon the shore?

What kind of clothes did you see yourself wearing?

How hot was the sand on your bare feet?

How many sandpipers did you see running on the beach?

How large were the bald eagles' nests?

What kinds of forms did you see in the sand sculptures?

What feelings did you experience as you relaxed against the
    log with your eyes closed, listening to the waves?

What else did you notice that wasn't asked in the above
questions? Please jot down anything you saw, heard, touched,
tasted, smelled, sensed, or felt in your imagination.

Obviously there are no correct answers to any of these
questions. Still, your responses reflect how you use your
imagination, and which particular sense you rely upon most.
As we've mentioned before, some people sense certain kinds
of things more keenly in their dreams and in their imagination.
For some, it might be the *feel* of the sand on your feet. For
others it might be the *sound* of the waves or the *smell* of the
breeze. For many, the *visual* sense of the trees and the beach
will be the strongest.

If you focus on one particular sense, it's useful to understand
it doesn't mean anything specific about *you*, nor does it suggest
anything specific about your treatment for nightmares. It does
mean this is the way you've learned to use your imagination.

If you find it easier to focus on your natural preference
for one sense more than others, then it's perfectly okay to
emphasize that sense for the rest of the steps. Whether you
focus on one mode or try expanding all your senses, it's the
attention itself that's important. As long as you maximize your
attention on the exercise, your imagination will improve.

This exercise can be repeated as often as you like, using the
same example we've written, as well as additional scenes you
create. Think about your favorite vacation spot or park where
you go to relax. Make up a whole scene and write it down. Or,
if you're very industrious, you can tape-record your scenes and
play them back to yourself to guide you through the images.

PRACTICE MAKES PERFECT

To complete step one, repeat this imagery of pleasant
scenes at least once a day for the next three days. What-

ever scene you choose, record your impressions in your notebook directly after the session. Please record your impressions with as much detail as possible.

Remember, recording itself can be a fundamental part of your treatment, both for the feedback it provides you with and in unconscious ways. So please work carefully at writing down everything you see and feel. If you need keys to help you think about what to write, then jot these words in your notebook: FEEL, SEE, HEAR, TOUCH, TASTE, SMELL, SENSE. Before each session, review these words to get yourself imagining in an expanded way.

We recommend picking certain times of the day to repeat the exercise: first thing upon waking up, before or after lunch, or in the evening before bedtime. Pick the time that will be most convenient and quiet with no interruptions.

At each session, expand your sensory images in a way that works best for you. Doing this over the next three days will help you to appreciate the incredible power of your imagination.

Again, as your guides, we want to encourage you as much as possible on this first step. In our experience, when people try out something new, they tend to think negatively about themselves, and about how they're doing. We want you to feel confident about spending the time and energy on this first step in expanding your imagination. And, we want to reemphasize that there's no right or wrong way of doing it. Any effort you put into the exercise qualifies as a success!

In the next chapter we'll review specific problems you may be having in performing the exercise. We'll recommend solutions to these problems to help you on your way. We want to make sure you're getting the most out of the lesson. And we encourage you to read the next chapter carefully if you're not satisfied with how well you're using your imagination.

Most of you have probably done well enough on this first practice to realize that with some effort you can sense a lot in your imagination. If you feel good about this, then you may want to skip Chapter 14, and go on to step two in Chapter 15 *after* repeating the exercise in imagination over the next three days.

If you have questions or problems, we suggest a careful reading of the next chapter.

CHAPTER 14

Perfecting Your Mind's Eye

DREAMS AND IMAGERY

Dreaming happens naturally. Most of us are reasonably good dreamers. That is, we imagine things creatively and with a wide range of senses—sounds, feelings, sensations, smells, and, of course, visual images. The dreaming mind's eye knows how to conjure up whatever it needs without difficulty. But this is an unconscious process. We want to affect our conscious mind's eye by directing your imagery.

Perfecting your ability to perform imagery involves many things: creating the right environment, dealing with distractions, and intensifying your images. If you've attempted a practice fantasy exercise over the last few days, you may have been tremendously successful, or you may have experienced some frustration. Regardless, we want to spend time now teaching you how to improve your imagery skills so you can become more successful, or so you can eliminate what's been holding you back.

We will review a few things already mentioned, then we're going to introduce some new ideas. When you read about what you already know, we'd like you to check on yourself. Ask if you've been applying what you know to get the best results. Remember, the process of imagery seems to form a direct link with your unconscious. Through this link, your nightmares will be conquered.

CREATING THE RIGHT ENVIRONMENT

Using your imagination is a lot like relaxing. It's not something you make happen, it's something you allow to occur. You facilitate relaxation by creating the right circumstances. This includes finding a quiet place, making enough time, arranging not to be disturbed, and, lastly, arranging your physical position in such a way you'll be totally comfortable for ten to twenty minutes.

Let's talk about each of these factors. The right place can vary considerably. Ideally, you'll have a quiet time at home where you can settle into an easy chair without any worries. "Ideally," however, rarely exists in most home environments, and therefore you have to be creative.

One working woman found the best place was in her car. After work, she knew she'd have her hands full with her children clamoring for attention. She'd drive home, turn off the motor and sit quietly under the carport for ten or fifteen minutes. Another man chose to incorporate his imagery exercises into his lunch break at work. Other people have set their alarm clocks a few minutes early. Several individuals have intended to do their imagery while in bed at night; however, they often fall asleep instead. This shortens their true practice time. Finding a quiet time will require a close look at your daily schedule.

Time also refers to the best time when you know you won't be disturbed so you can direct your full attention to the exercise. Ultimately, this means you have to *make* time. You'll have to give this a priority equal to many other daytime activities, like getting washed and dressed. You wouldn't dream of not doing these, so make your imagery session just as important.

You need to do this for a short time so commit yourself to finding the ten to twenty minutes necessary to practice. For those of you who feel guilty about doing something for yourself, rest assured the benefits you receive will be passed on to others through your increased well-being from controlling your nightmares.

You must also arrange not to be disturbed. Don't leave this to chance. Be bold—take the phone off the hook if you have to, or at least request your family take phone messages. Be so demanding as to ask members of your family to respect your quiet time for the twenty minutes. Consider locking the door to your room if that's what it will take. Do everything in your power to prevent external interruptions.

You must also watch for internal distractions. Ask yourself if there is anything you have to do in the next twenty minutes. Make an agreement with yourself that no matter what thought comes into your mind, you'll let it go until after you practice. Tell yourself that nothing that comes into your mind or awareness will have to be acted on. We make exceptions for house fires or rebellious bladders. Speaking of which, it's a good idea to empty your bladder, brush your teeth, turn off the stove, or whatever else you need to do to feel physically and mentally comfortable before you practice.

It's funny how these little things serve as wonderful excuses not to practice. That's why we're spending this time talking about them. We want to cover all bases so you can be prepared to avoid these simple pitfalls that will limit your success. You may have experienced some of these problems in your initial attempts.

Now let's continue with how to make yourself physically comfortable. Two things about position are important. One is having yourself fully supported. Some chairs, such as a La-Z-Boy, are designed to do this, but if you do not have one, create the same effect with chairs, sofas, beds, or pillows.

If you lie down on your back, it's best to have your knees slightly bent. This will promote relaxation of your legs and back. Put a large pillow under your knees and a small, soft pillow under your neck with your arms down at your sides. If you prefer lying flat, place a cushion under your leg from the heel to the back of your knee and a small soft pillow under your head.

If you prefer sitting up in a chair or sofa, rest your feet squarely on the floor. Feel your weight evenly distributed on your feet, thighs, and buttocks. Your back and head should be supported. Again, use pillows if needed.

Some people let their heads fall completely forward. For most of us less limber people this will produce uncomfortable pulling at the back of the neck after a few minutes. Whichever position you choose for your head—forward or back—pick *one*, and not something in between. If your head is leaning slightly forward or backward, you'll have a tendency to tighten your neck muscles.

Avoid positions where you feel a strong pressure at one part of your body. Crossing your legs will cause this sort of pressure on the supporting knee and thigh. Keep your body symmetrical.

Having the right and left side of your body in the same pose will promote balanced positions that won't create undue pressure on one body part.

A final word about indoors versus outdoors. Indoors is usually preferred because you can predict the temperature. If you want to try outside, generally avoid direct sunlight, as you'll get too warm. Keep a blanket close by, as an unexpected breeze may cause a chill.

DEALING WITH DISTRACTIONS

Now that we've dealt with housekeeping items, we can go back to the imagery itself. When doing your imagery you may have noticed your mind wandering to other thoughts. Problems you may have experienced during the day are common intruders begging for attention. You may also hear your children, a radio from another room, or an ambulance siren in the distance.

Absolute silence is not essential for success, but plan on dealing with inevitable distractions. Actually, the plan is simple. To minimize the effect of distractions, acknowledge they're interrupting the picture you're drawing in your mind's eye, then simply choose to return to your imagery exercise. Sometimes the distractions will lead your mind astray without your noticing. However, when you realize you're drifting, simply choose to return to the exercise.

Don't put yourself down for letting your mind wander. It's a natural tendency. We all do it. Some people practice special meditations for years and still their minds wander. It's okay that your mind wanders. You just have to agree to come back to your imagery.

It's like walking down a forest path where you intend to stay on the trail. Suddenly a beautiful bird flies up, and, as you watch it, you wander off the trail. When you notice you've wandered off, you can simply let go of looking at the bird and return to the path. This is a simple concept, but one many people have problems mastering.

Often a patient says: "I just can't concentrate." Our reply is, "That's great—you're not supposed to concentrate. Focus on the imagery and when you notice your mind wandering, let go of the thought or sound or whatever, and return to the imagery." Demanding you stay with the imagery 100 percent of the time will only frustrate you. Doing the imagery 20 percent of the time and having your mind wander 80 percent will still give you good results. You will improve your percentages to get better results over time.

A few people will have their minds "wander" into unpleasant territory. People with posttraumatic nightmares and PTSD, for example, are more prone to bad memories which may surface and compete with the pleasant images. These unpleasant thoughts, feelings, or images may induce anxiety and, in a few people, outright panic attacks. In a few instances, you may suffer anxiety or panic feelings without any particular images as the cause. Any of these occurrences can be particularly unnerving because for most of you an imagery exercise will have been a pleasant and positive experience.

If unpleasant images crop up and you become upset, the first thing we want you to recognize is that you have not lost control of the situation. As in dealing with other distractions, you still have a choice you can make. You can let go of the negative pictures in your mind's eye and you can choose to renew your interest in the positive pictures. Sounds too easy, we know, but you can achieve this ability with practice.

If you have a problem with unpleasant images, you may want to practice your ability to select the right images. For example, imagine your positive scene is a beautiful drive by the lake. Then, conjure up some negative scene, such as your boss hassling you at work, or whatever you think appropriate. Now picture first the positive scene, then the negative one, and then go back and forth a few times. Eventually, spend more time with the positive and less time with the negative, but consciously try to go back and forth to give yourself confidence in being able to control the imagery.

You don't have to push yourself to perfection to get good results from this exercise. Practicing back and forth between positive and negative will prepare you if you have an unexpectedly unpleasant image crop up in your mind's eye. You'll know how to turn away from the negative thoughts and feelings and return to your positive images.

One cause of these unpleasant images may be an unresolved conflict of some sort that surfaces for no apparent reason during the imagery exercises. Another explanation is that a particular trauma you've suffered in the past continues to express itself as a memory.

Whatever the reason, most who have the problem with unpleasant images will be able to deal with it successfully. If, however, you find a session unsettling, you can always stop your practice until later in the day or the next day. If you're still not satisfied with your efforts, this is an occasion where a mental health professional trained in relaxation and visualization exercises may be especially helpful in overcoming this hurdle.

SELECTING YOUR IMAGERY

We've previously suggested a beach scene. You may want to try different images. Use your own fantasies if you find them more appealing. If, for whatever reasons, you're having trouble selecting imagery, consider the following suggestions.

Try reliving a satisfying and memorable event. You might recall a song that was of special significance in an early romance. How about the quiet and serenity of a good fishing trip? Perhaps you remember some cold night by a fireplace with a loved one. By letting yourself recall a fond memory you will automatically begin the imagery process.

You can choose to build on this memory by focusing on the details of the experience. Let all the sounds, sights, and feelings come to you. Think about how good listening to that song made you feel. Remember those schools of fish darting under your boat. How about that fire crackling in the dark while you embraced your loved one?

For your initial practice session, spend your whole time recreating this memorable experience in detail. Then the next time, recall it as your imagery exercise. You can also use these types of memories as springboards to create other fantasies and images. Make it fun by recalling your past, or by creating a new fantasy.

If you're still having problems selecting a fantasy, consider creating something on a tape recorder. Use your own voice, or a friend's, and try describing a pleasant scene. If this works, record several variations. Also, speak slowly and pause regularly. Listening to this self-made tape can get you over the hump if you've been having trouble getting a good seat to the theater in your mind.

IS ONE SENSE STEALING THE SHOW?

Most of us have strong visual images in our dreams, yet we may have problems perfecting our visual imagery. It may be easier to imagine music or feelings. Mozart was a good example of this; he described "hearing" the music before writing it down.

If you find one sense predominates, you need to decide whether you want to focus on that sense or whether you want to try to branch out. Either way is acceptable.

John is a musician and composer who felt comfortable "listening" to the sounds in his images. He had trouble with visual imagery, which frustrated him, because his nightmares were so visually graphic. He thought he needed to practice his imagery in a way that would resemble his highly visual nightmares. Because John was so sure about this idea, we decided to work with him on it instead of correcting his mistaken belief.

John started by imagining music; then we instructed him to imagine what the keyboard looked like. Then we had him imagine the brand name inscribed on the keyboard. Then he progressed to imagining other members of the band, and on to other images of the audience and friends listening.

John progressed over the course of the week and was ready to tackle the nightmares. So, as John's case points out, you can start with the form of imagery you are most familiar or comfortable with, then add other sensory modes as you progress. In time, branching out will come easier. But you can also branch out to begin with and go from there.

ARE YOUR IMAGES TOO VAGUE?

Some people report images but see them as vague, diffuse, or nondescript. Although this is not really a problem for getting rid of nightmares, the exercise can be made more enjoyable by learning to create more vivid imagery.

Vividness can be enhanced by the same things that facilitate imagery in general—quiet, peacefulness, limited distractions, and relaxation. There is also a simple technique that can help. The key is to select simple images or geometric forms when you start practicing with your mind's eye.

For example, imagine a circle, a square, or a rectangle. Then pick one solid color for the object—let's say, a red circle. If you try to hold that simple image for a few moments, it may suddenly turn into a red ball. That red ball may quickly find itself bouncing up against a wall. In this way the imagery sort of comes alive, even though you started with something simple.

If the notion of geometry brings back unpleasant school memories, choose a simple structure. A common one is a staircase. Try imagining a straight wooden staircase with about ten steps. Now walk up the steps and listen to your footsteps. Can you hear the creaking of wood? Let those creaks echo. Here you started with a simple image—staircase, then you imagined a single sound—footsteps on wood. By slowly moving into the state that facilitates clear forms of imagery, you will often find they become more complex.

Intensifying the imagery can also be attempted. This is similar to dealing with vague imagery. Can we return to geometry for the moment? Don't worry, we're not handing out grades! Let's look at that circle again. Now make it a ball with a pale, washed-out pink color. Then darken the pink to a light red. Now make the red darker, and, finally, let the red get bright and fiery.

For the sense of hearing, start with the sound of a small creek. Let it progress through the sounds of a small stream, then to a river, the ocean, and, finally, Niagara Falls. For taste, try running the gamut from ice cream to a jalapeno pepper. For touch, imagine cool water running over your hands and move onto jumping into a cool mountain lake on a hot summer day.

Despite these efforts you still might feel that you're not able to visualize well in your mind's eye. Some of you will have a tendency to *verbalize* or *talk* about the images in your mind instead of actually *seeing* them. For example, you might describe a beautiful scene to yourself, but you can't really picture it. That's okay because you are still using your imagination and that will be enough to treat your nightmares. And, if you practice regularly, your imagery will improve over time. So let your imagination run free and have fun with the process.

ARE YOU FLOATING?

Don't worry.

Imagery causes changes in both mind and body. These changes produce sensations that you may not ordinarily be accustomed to experiencing. You may have noticed a warming sensation in your arms or legs, or you may have felt a tingling in your hands.

These feelings are caused by vascular relaxation, that is, blood vessels dilating to let more blood flow through. When blood vessels in your arms and hands relax, the increased flow produces this sense of warmth and tingling.

Another common experience is the sensation of mild heaviness. As you relax, the nerves connecting your muscles to your nervous system will sense the change. A relaxed muscle is sensed by the nerve endings as feeling heavier than a tense muscle.

This feeling of heaviness relates to the experience of floating. The nerve endings that pick up the sensation of heaviness are call proprioceptors. These proprioceptors act without our thinking about them. They give feedback to the brain, telling us where our position in space is. For example, are we seated, lying down, standing up, or, most importantly, about to fall on our faces. Along with this sensation of position, proprioceptors are fine-tuned to the effects of gravity and the sense of movement and acceleration. If you're in a car and step on the gas, you can feel yourself pulled back into the seat.

When you do imagery, the muscles relax and feel heavier. When you *stay relaxed* for a few minutes, the nerves will shut down and stop sending messages of heaviness. When they've stopped sending the signal, you feel the opposite of heaviness. Instead, a lightness, often experienced as a floating sensation, ensues.

Most people enjoy this feeling. If you experience floating as unpleasant, you can counter it by wiggling your toes or briefly making a fist. This activates the proprioceptors and stops the sensation of floating.

CHAPTER 15

The Second Step:
Recording Your Nightmares

In this chapter, you are going to learn the importance of recording your nightmares, and how to record them.

We hope you've had the time to work on your imagery of pleasant scenes. For the best results, we suggest you continue these exercises while you work on step two. Also, to maximize your success, we recommend you follow the stepwise plan we're outlining here. Progressing through the steps one at a time without jumping ahead is usually more effective in dealing with nightmares.

WHY YOU NEED TO RECORD YOUR NIGHTMARES

Dreams tend to be elusive. If you've ever read another book about dreams and dream interpretation, you will invariably find a section talking about *how* to remember your dreams. These "how-to" sections appear because, for many people, it's difficult to recall their dreams. Some people report they never dream at all, or at least can never remember a single dream they've had. This certainly would make it difficult to interpret your dreams.

If you suffer from chronic nightmares or you just happen to have one really bad dream some night, you know the problem of recall doesn't apply. Bad dreams often stick with us throughout the day and sometimes for weeks at a time. However, because of the unpleasantness of the nightmare, sooner or later the mind's ability to suppress will take hold and try to put the bad dream out of your consciousness.

This process of suppression is natural. We do it every day when we are faced with unpleasant situations which we don't want to deal with. The ability of the mind to suppress is so good, sometimes it sets to work right away in blocking the unpleasantness. It is for this reason we must be attentive to our bad dreams when they first occur. In this way, we are assured of remembering them accurately and with greater detail.

Nightmares recorded at night shortly after experiencing them tend to have the most information and details. Those dreams that are recorded in the morning have less detail. If you wait until later in the day, you will remember even less. The longer you wait to write them down, the greater chance you'll have of distorting or losing the dream.

Freud noted this process with the technical term "secondary revision" or "secondary elaboration." This process of revision refers to two major effects the waking mind will have on the recall of the dream.

The first reflects the nature of dreams themselves. They are often disjointed and bizarre, or at least appear that way to the waking mind. As our waking mind tries to make sense and logic out of this confusion, it will fill information into the dream as if connecting a jumbled story. As you might imagine, this process is fraught with inaccuracy. The dream tells its own story from your unconscious mind, and it tells the story in its own peculiar and particular style. If you try to "fill in the gaps," more than likely you'll alter the story significantly to where it no longer represents the original intent of the dream.

The second major effect of the waking mind involves the tendency toward censorship. This is suppression at its finest. We try to suppress certain parts of the dream from our first recollection. Why do we do this? Mostly for the obvious reason—we find the material unpleasant. It is common to report a particular anxiety dream to someone else and leave out details you might find embarrassing. Taken further, as we describe the dream back to ourselves, we may leave out details for the same reason. In a short time—as short as a few seconds—we no longer remember those unpleasant details and they are essentially gone from our consciousness.

This tendency to suppress can be demonstrated remarkably well if you happen to tape-record your nightmares directly after dreaming them. When you awaken the next morning, take a moment to recall the dream and ask yourself if you've left out anything important. Then play back the tape. Sometimes the difference is astonishing between what you thought was the dream and what you had recorded moments after experiencing the dream.

When you begin recording your dreams, regardless of the method you choose—tape-recording, typing them, or writing them down in pen or pencil—pay careful attention to this process of secondary revision. Even the most frightful nightmares and anxiety-producing dreams, which you would only too quickly forget, can be distorted by this process. Dreams, of whatever flavor, by their nature seem predisposed toward conscious revision and distortion.

Let's finish up this section on why you must record your nightmares with two more points. First, recording your nightmares provides a delightfully unexpected blessing. Simply put, recording your nightmares may get rid of them!

How does this work?

One theory focuses on the process of externalization. When you write down a nightmare you externalize it outside yourself. Instead of a memory festering within your mind, it now becomes something concrete you can focus on outside yourself. When something is outside ourselves, it is easier to objectify. In other words, it is easier to deal with it.

We have seen a number of patients who have spontaneously lost their nightmares after beginning the recording process without any further treatment.

Janet recorded her nightmares for a month before she was scheduled to begin treatment. However, when the time for her appointment arrived when she was to be taught imagery rehearsal, she was unable to come to the doctor's office because of a family conflict. Rescheduling would be difficult for this busy mother with three kids, so she elected on her own to continue writing down her nightmares. During the next month her nightmares diminished. She then continued to write them down whenever she had one, and this method worked well in relieving her bad dreams.

Arlene's case was a simple misinterpretation that worked out well. She mistakenly thought the research study only included the recording of nightmares. She presumed that no special treatment would be offered. How did she arrive at this conclusion? Very simply. Most of her nightmares went away when she started recording them. Therefore, it logically occurred to her that recording must be the treatment. She was partly correct.

Writing down the bad dreams seems to have a therapeutic effect, independent of the rest of the treatment. Several patients in our studies noticed a decline in their nightmares after recording them.

The last reason for recording is to make it easier on you in step three of the treatment. Having a written record of the nightmares that trouble you will make it simpler to carry out the remainder of the program. Recording will also provide you with a definite sense of your success in getting rid of your nightmares.

HOW TO RECORD

In using the three-step cure, you need only record your nightmares and anxiety dreams. If you have time and want to pursue further study of your dreams you may want to record your regular dreams as well.

To record your nightmares and dreams you must recall them. These are some things that will help:

At bedtime, suggest to yourself that you will remember your nightmare when you awaken in the morning.

Have a pen and paper at the bedside. Special books are available known as dream diaries. These may prove helpful.

Try to awaken spontaneously. Avoid alarm clocks if you can. Dreams are often lost if you are awakened suddenly in the morning.

After waking, lie quietly for a few minutes and visualize the nightmare as fully as possible. Only after it is clear in your mind, write it down.

Those who have a tape recorder may want to record the nightmare at night. Then transcribe it from the tape in the morning. A voice-activated recorder is ideal. It is standing by, ready to go. All you have to do is face the recorder, speak clearly, then go back to sleep.

A word of caution: When you use a tape recorder in a half-asleep state, you're likely to mumble so badly, you'll swear somebody must have stuck marbles in your mouth while you were speaking. If you use the voice-activated tape recorder, speak slowly and clearly.

Here are some guidelines that will help you keep your written records clear and understandable, including some dos and don'ts:

DO:

Write clearly, print, or type, double-space, and leave a margin on the left. The margin allows you room to write comments about your dreams.

Write down everything you remember about your dream, even details that may seem trivial, funny, or embarrassing.

Include everything you noticed *while dreaming*—feelings, thoughts, actions, scene changes, sensations.

Describe the dream in the order it occurred as best you can. If you have more than one dream, put the dreams in the order they occur.

Write down dream fragments. If you wake up and remember something about a cat, then jot down, "Something about a cat."

Write your dream in the FIRST-PERSON, PRESENT TENSE, for example, "I am walking along a path. I look up and see . . ."

DO NOT:

Write in the past tense "I *was* walking," or start by saying, "I was dreaming about . . ."

Write down your waking thoughts and feelings you had about the dream, but wait until you've finished recording the dream. In other words, keep the awake feelings or ideas about the dream separate from the feelings you had *in* the dream.

A SAMPLE NIGHTMARE

"A yellow hideous spider crawls onto my arm and bites me. I feel the sting through my green coat. I scream, it is a shrill piercing cry, and I am extremely scared. I can't get the spider off me, it is biting me again."

Notice the above nightmare is written in the present tense. This makes it easier to describe things and it seems to promote fuller and more accurate recall of the dream events. With regard to detail, notice the *green* coat might initially seem insignificant. The dreamer, however, later recalled that her mother had given her a similar green coat when she was fourteen years old. This proved significant in the dream's interpretation.

USING ALL OF YOUR SENSES

Looking at the sample nightmare, notice she put several sensory modes into her recollection. What she *saw*—"the yellow hideous spider"; what she *felt*—"feel the sting"; her *feelings*—"scared"; and what she *heard*—"a shrill piercing cry"; even when it was her own voice. Including the different senses will lead to a descriptive recording of the nightmare. When you progress through the treatment program, you will see that recording all your senses will help you in step three by giving you different options to help you get rid of your nightmares.

Lastly, leave space between each nightmare you write down. This will allow room to jot down your thoughts or associative memories about the dream. You might also wish to make a drawing of the nightmare. Some people prefer to write the dream on one side of the page and leave the back blank for note-taking or drawings. Either way is fine.

Now that you have the basics of recording, we suggest you grab another pen and a pad of paper. Put them beside the bed or in a place where you can reach them. Then record your nightmares during the next week. Remember, during this week practice your imagery exercises as well.

With a few nightmares recorded and your imagery of pleasant scenes drawing standing-room-only crowds to the theater in your mind, you'll be ready for the final step in getting rid of your nightmares.

CHAPTER 16

The Third Step:
Conquering Your Nightmares

You have completed the initial steps of the three-step cure by practicing imagery of pleasant scenes and by recording your bad dreams. You're now ready to conquer your nightmares. We've got a nice surprise for you with step three—it's the easiest step of all and it requires little extra time.

If you have not had any nightmares during the past week, it's still important to continue with step three. Some people may have eliminated their nightmares by recording them. If for any reason your bad dreams have diminished, please forge ahead. We think you'll find step three very interesting.

If you're recently without nightmares, you'll need to select one you've recorded or else select one you remember from some other time. If you've had one recently, use that.

Now, let's say goodbye to those nightmares!

CHANGING THE NIGHTMARE

We want you to establish a clear picture of the nightmare you're going to work with. Obviously, when you awake in the night from a bad dream, the picture is all too clear. If that happens, you can work immediately on step three. Right now, since you're reading the book, we'll offer two suggestions for picturing the nightmare.

First, consider using the imagery you've been practicing on pleasant scenes. Image the nightmare to produce a clear picture. For some, this will be distressing. Let us assure you that you only have to do this once, and only do it for as short a time as needed to see the dream clearly—perhaps a minute or so.

If you find this too distressing, then *don't* image the nightmare. Instead, think about the bad dream by reviewing what you've recorded. Read your notes a couple of times through to give yourself a clear understanding or picture of what takes place in the dream.

So take a few moments to be clear on the nightmare you're going to work with. Then read on.

Okay. So you have a clear impression of the nightmare.

Now *CHANGE* the nightmare in *ANY WAY* that *FEELS RIGHT* for you. For now, we'll leave this open-ended. We really do want you to *change* the nightmare in any way you choose.

In the next chapter we will provide plenty of examples to show how other people changed their nightmares. We think you'll have better results if you're not influenced by their ideas. One of the keys to this method appears to be that *you* decide *how* to change your nightmare.

Take your time. Work on changing the nightmare until you feel right about it. Once you decide on your changes, write down the changed version in detail. Think of it as a "new dream" and write it in the first person, present tense.

IMAGING YOUR NEW DREAM

With your new dream in hand, you are ready to create a new image in your mind—an image that's going to replace the old nightmare image. This is the essential step to getting rid of either your current or any future nightmares.

Now prepare yourself for an imagery exercise. Find your quiet place. Insure that you will not be interrupted; take care of any distractions.

Relax in your comfortable position. When you close your eyes, we want you to image only the new dream. Forget about the nightmare. Image just the new dream. Go over it at a normal pace, neither rushing it nor pondering it too slowly.

Read on after you've imaged the new dream at least once.

Now that you've imaged the new dream, check on how it made you feel.

WAS IT RIGHT FOR YOU?

If it wasn't, take time to change it further. When you've changed it to your satisfaction, write it down. Then, image it again, rehearsing it in your mind's eye *two more times* today. As always, pay attention to detail and enhancing the images. Spend at least five minutes rehearsing the new dream. If it's short, you might rehearse it several times.

If you want to spend more time—ten or twenty minutes—that's okay, too. Remember, you're only working with the new dream. Do not use imagery on the old nightmare.

Please schedule practice sessions for each of the next three days. In each session, work only with the new dream—the one you now feel right about.

We are finished for today. We suggest you put this away until tomorrow.

A Day Later

If you had no nightmares last night, congratulations. You're on your way to conquering your bad dreams. Ten percent of our research subjects and patients have eliminated their bad dreams with just one day of practice. If you had none, we still suggest you repeat the imagery of the new dream you created yesterday.

If you had the same nightmare as before, you also need to repeat your imagery of the new dream. Make sure you feel okay with your new version. If not, go over it, change it again and write down the new version. Then rehearse the *new dream* three times.

If you had a new nightmare, then get a clear picture of it by imaging it or reviewing your recording. Then change it and write down the changed version. Then image the *changed* version—the new dream—three times.

Some of you may have multiple nightmares in one night. If so, don't put pressure on yourself by trying to change all of them. That's too much work and it's unnecessary. You only need to work on one of your bad dreams.

Repeat these directions for the next two days.

Two Days Later

Some of you will have already cured your nightmares. Others will need to work on this program for several weeks. A few may require months.

Don't be discouraged if you're one of those people who needs more time. If you're a chronic nightmare sufferer, chances are you've had bad dreams for at least five years, if not twenty years. Hang in there; relief is just around the corner. This simple method will banish your nightmares, so please keep up your practice.

For those of you who have no nightmares, we suggest you practice your imagery of the new dream twice this week, then once a week for the next three weeks.

If you have a nightmare at any time during this period, then go back to three successive days of working on the new dream. If it's a new nightmare, you'll have to change it again. If it's an old one that you've previously changed, make sure you're satisfied with your changed version.

Let us emphasize that you *don't* have to work with every nightmare. Suppose you have five or ten or more nightmares every week. You can achieve excellent results by working on two bad dreams per week. What's important in this phase of the three-step cure is that you build confidence in using the technique effectively—learning to change your nightmare into a new dream and learning to image the new dream.

So, for every night you suffer a nightmare, you want one practice session to image a new dream. You can do this as soon as you wake up from the bad dream or later the next day. Either way, practice at least three successive days after any night you've had bad dreams. When you go a few days without nightmares, you can schedule fewer sessions.

SUMMARY OF TREATMENT STEPS

Imagery of Pleasant Scenes. This step teaches imagery rehearsal. You can practice imagery of pleasant scenes at any time regardless of what's happening with your nightmares. Some people find it relaxing, especially if you do it for ten or twenty minutes. Others describe imagery as useful in such activities as problem-solving, golf or treating insomnia. Regarding the nightmares, if you have trouble in step three imaging your new dreams, please consider scheduling some separate sessions to practice imagery of pleasant scenes.

Recording. Recording helps in two ways. For some, it eliminates bad dreams. For others, it provides a clear picture to use in step three when you create a new dream. You may record a nightmare at any time after you've had it. The sooner you record, the more details you will remember.

Changing/Imaging of the New Dream. Change the nightmare in any way you wish, then image only the new dream. You can do this at any time. If you are awakened in the night, you will already have a clear picture of the bad dream. You can immediately decide how to change it. Then, write down your new dream and image it. This is an ideal time to practice for three reasons.

First, many people complain of insomnia following a bad dream. If so, use this time to your advantage by changing the nightmare, then imaging the new dream. This produces confidence because it provides an immediate plan of action for dealing with bad dreams that awaken you.

Second, some people discover that imaging the new dream promotes relaxation that will help you return to sleep.

Third, many nightmare sufferers report the upsetting experience of returning to sleep after a bad dream only to find themselves right back in the same nightmare. We know several individuals who have prevented this "instant nightmare replay" by using imagery of the new dream before returning to sleep.

If it proves more convenient you can change and image the new dream the next morning. This is an ideal time, too. You can also practice later in the day. Remember, though, the longer you wait to work on the dream after you've experienced the nightmare, the more likely your busy daytime schedule will interfere with your sessions.

Step three seems so easy many people have difficulty believing it will work. We have a one-word response to this:

BELIEVE!

It really works this simply. If you have any doubts, we hope to put them to sleep in the next chapter when we tell you about the fascinating stories of other nightmare sufferers. You'll hear how they changed their nightmares and how they achieved great success.

In the meantime, keep up your practice sessions.

CHAPTER 17

Seven Stories of Success

GETTING BETTER

We'd like to show you the ways other people have turned their nightmares into dreams, because your experience will share similar features. Once again, let us stress that it may be more profitable for you to spend time working on your own nightmares first before reading this section.

Why do we suggest this?

We believe the treatment revolves around how *you* choose to change *your* nightmare. Your conscious and unconscious thoughts select the necessary changes to help resolve your problem with the nightmares.

This is similar to interpreting your dreams—the interpretation ultimately must resonate with *you* to be considered accurate. Therefore, your attempts at changing bad dreams will likely carry a great deal of insight from within yourself, regardless of whether your decisions are conscious or unconscious. We'll take up this point repeatedly as we discuss these next cases.

The stories also show how different one person's experience can be from another's, even when following a stepwise treatment plan. This leads us to the belief that there is *no single right way* of changing your nightmares. There are many paths leading to success, and the level of success may be variable for different people as well.

One thing stands clear: the key for continued success and improvement for most people is continued practice.

EASY DOES IT: MAUREEN'S HARROWING ESCAPE

"I am trying to escape from a man who is carrying a handgun. It is dark and there are trees to hide behind. He has trouble finding me. I am terrified and running for my life. He is drunk and yelling at me, hoping I will give him a clue to my whereabouts. The gun shoots off into the darkness, but the bullet doesn't hit me. I run down the long lane where there are fewer trees. He is now in a fit of anger. He catches up to me, grabs me . . . I wake up."

Maureen is a fifty-year-old writer whose nightmares began following a terrible incident in her life where she was falsely accused of a crime, handcuffed, and taken to jail. The nightmares awakened her at least twice a week, but she could never return to sleep, and consequently suffered regularly from fatigue. Many of her bad dreams had similar themes. Often she was chased or beaten by figures of authority such as policemen.

When Maureen was asked to create her new dream in treatment she had a lot of questions. "Can I make it shorter? Do I make it longer? Can I change any part of the dream? Should I change just the ending? Should I change the whole dream entirely?"

We responded in vague fashion for the reasons we've stated: An individual's changed dream comes best from his or her own mind. Asking for too much direction from someone else, whether a friend or professional, is probably a mistake.

We will add, though, that the answer is "yes" to all Maureen's questions. If you want to make your dream shorter, do so. If you want to make it longer, go right ahead. If you want to change just the ending, that's fine. And so on. Whatever feels right is probably the best change you could make.

Here's her changed dream: "I am with a good male friend. He is neither drunk nor carrying any weapons. His children are with us and we go for a night walk. The kids hide behind trees and try to scare us as we stroll down a long lane. One child climbs an apple tree. The limb he stands on snaps and he falls to the ground unhurt. We walk back home."

For Maureen it was important to change almost the entire

set of images, although it's interesting she also put in a little scare scene involving the kids hiding behind trees coupled with a nervous moment where the tree limb snaps. Whatever her motivations behind her changes, within one week, Maureen's nightmares were completely eliminated. She only practiced rehearsal a total of three times in the first week; then she quit practicing, because the nightmares were gone.

That's how easy this can be for some people, although we suggest you continue your imagery for awhile longer.

CHANGING THE ENDING: ROLAND'S HORSE PLAY

"My wife and I are driving a rental car in San Francisco just south of Golden Gate park. It's windy and rainy. We drive on slowly and arrive at Fisherman's Wharf; however, it seems odd the sun is out and everything is dry. We park the car and go for a walk. We come upon a team of horses in the street and one of them suddenly kicks out at me. I shift my body to avoid his hoof. This movement awakens me and my wife who I've bumped up against in bed."

Roland often dreams of animals lashing out at him. Usually it's snakes or other vicious animals that threaten him with direct attacks. In these episodes Roland would describe a fairly mellow dream scenario; then out of the blue an animal would attack. Roland would respond the same way—desperately trying to avoid a bite or a claw or, in this case, a horse's hoof.

Roland's behavior may represent a type of disorder we will discuss in Chapter 21—the REM behavior disorder—where the dreamer acts out portions of the dream while actually dreaming. In some cases, rehearsal may be effective in the treatment of this problem. In other cases, medication is required.

To change the dream, Roland took the same situation and changed one detail. "We park the car and walk down the street. On our side of the street we spot a team of horses. We cross over to the other side of the street to avoid the horses. We continue down the Wharf until we find our favorite restaurant where we enjoy a delicious seafood dinner."

Notice how closely Roland sticks to his original dream and simply changes the ending. This is the obvious thing to do with your dreams, but it doesn't mean it's the only way. Changing the beginning of the dream also works for some people.

Roland wasn't the only one to praise the success of rehearsal. In a few weeks his nightmares were virtually gone, resulting in this comment from his wife: "It's marvelous. We haven't slept this well together in years." Considering how she used to get slapped and bumped throughout the night, we can understand why she was so pleased.

CHANGING EVERYTHING: ISABELLA'S JOY-LESS RIDE

"I am driving a car through a heavy rainstorm on a dark highway. I'm driving too fast, but I'm telling myself to slow down. I can't. My foot's on the gas pedal, but it's numb and I can't move it to the brake. I spot a lot of traffic going in my direction, but they're going much slower. It's crowded— I steer onto the shoulder of the highway to speed past them. I'm panic-stricken as I fly by.

"There's a traffic signal, turning yellow, then red. I roar through the intersection, narrowly missing a semi, only I lose control of the steering wheel. The car spins, then flips and smashes against something. The car begins to crush in around me. There's blood everywhere.

"My vision is blurred from the blood streaking down my face, but I spot a priest coming towards the car. He's throwing holy water on the car. I scream at him to help me out, but he doesn't see me or hear me. He continues praying. The car is being buried somehow. It's getting darker. I start banging my hands against the windshield.

"The priest throws a black prayer book onto the windshield and leaves. I wake up in a sweat."

Isabella is a thirty-year-old social worker. Her nightmares began after her parents divorced when she was five. The situation deteriorated further as neither parent could handle the responsibilities of parenthood. In fact, before Isabella reached her teens she was without either parent, raised instead by her maternal grandparents. She's had nightmares at least twice per week and with greater frequency when she finds herself in stressful situations. Starting a new job almost always causes her nightmares to increase. Marriage has proven stressful as well, with no letup in her bad dreams.

Isabella described in her dream diary a variety of nightmares showing little similarity in terms of content, dream figures, scenarios, or the specific stories themselves. If this is so for your bad dreams, you may need to change several different nightmares to achieve the best results. Those with the recurring bad dreams can work over and over again with their similar dreams.

Isabella commented that her dreams often had vague images which she had difficulty remembering, even though they awakened her in fear. She selected the "car out of control" dream because she had a clearer picture of its content. She often had this type of dream when she experienced an "out-of-control" feeling in her everyday life. Here again we see an individual who changes nearly everything in the dream.

"I am driving my car in no traffic. I'm passing through an old neighborhood with lots of trees and manicured lawns. I am cruising slowly so I can look at all the beautiful homes. It's early afternoon, the sun is out, and I can see everything clearly. I have no trouble controlling the car. I'm just out on a pleasant joy ride, listening to music, and having a great time."

Despite suffering so many different bad dreams, Isabella achieved complete success in a couple of weeks. What's more fascinating is that at the beginning of her treatment, a significant family crisis developed which required marriage counseling for her and her husband. In the past, this kind of situation triggered her nightmares. Instead, she practiced her treatment and got rid of the bad dreams.

RECENTLY DEVELOPED NIGHTMARES: AUDREY'S TRIP TO THE CEMETERY

"I am walking to the cemetery to visit Patsy—a friend of mine who died recently. People are working at various gravesites and in one place they're digging up coffins and setting them in rows, like parking places for coffins. Although Patsy is dead, she gets out of her coffin and we visit for awhile. The conversation lasts a long time though I can't remember what was said.

"Now it's time to go. Patsy's mom is in another coffin nearby. She gets up and tells me to look at Patsy's thumb. Patsy picks up her hand and shows me her thumb—it looks like a white coral reef. A second later Patsy's voice changes. It turns into the devil's voice and says, 'Never ask to see my thumb again.' I wake up very scared."

Audrey's nightmares began recently—within a year of seeking treatment. The inciting incident was the death of her close friend Patsy in a car accident. Audrey had many dreams about her friend, some scary, others less so. Often there was a macabre element, such as visiting Patsy in a mortuary or cemetery. Audrey's anxiety stemmed from the persistence of the dreams and the continued presence of her dead friend in her unconscious. So, in this instance, a traumatic episode appears to have caused the bad dreams.

Here's how Audrey altered her dream. "I go to visit Patsy at her house, not at the cemetery. It's some time in the past when she is alive. I visit her in her room and we talk about old times. During the conversation her voice doesn't change. We have a nice visit and then I leave."

Audrey's nightmares disappeared after only two practice sessions. She was surprised how easy it was, but certainly delighted. Plus, she found an added bonus. The imagery exercises taught her how to relax. She often visualizes a favorite fantasy at work in the middle of a stressful day.

GETTING THE MOST FROM YOUR IMAGES:
RITA'S WALK IN THE PARK

"I am walking in a park in Belgium. It is sundown and there is a strange golden glow in the sky. I am heading toward a monument when suddenly the park lights come on. The monument is about twenty feet tall and is made of concrete with a rough surface. I notice a reflecting pool off to the side surrounded by a waist-high metal railing. I bend over the fence and look at my reflection. I notice deep beneath the surface of the pond three sculptures of Indian figures. They are also made of concrete. As I look closer I realize they look like a cross between mummies and sculptures. They are lying on their backs, all three in a row. I peer deeper into the water trying to get a better look.

"An arm from one of the sculptures rockets out of the water and tries to grab me and pull me into the pond. I wake up."

Rita is a forty-seven-year-old artist. In her whole life she cannot remember going two nights in a row without nightmares. On average, she has more than *twenty* bad dreams every month. From her childhood, she remembers a great deal of physical and psychological abuse heaped upon her by her schizophrenic mother. Her nightmares often portray her under attack by some unknown figure trying to kill her.

Here's how she changed her dream. "I am walking in a park in France with my two dogs. It's a beautiful summer day. I'm wearing a light summer dress and sandals. The sun is directly above and puffy white clouds are floating through the blue sky. The air smells of wonderful French cookery. I walk along the grass past some trees up to a beautiful monument of a woman riding a horse.

"Off to one side there is a small pond with beautiful white swans frolicking about in the water. I plop down on the grass with my dogs and take out some French bread from my shopping bag. I break the bread into small crumbs and toss them to the swans. I watch as they eat. I lie back on the grass and stare up into the sky thinking about how beautiful it is. Somehow I realize I am dreaming and I wake up smiling."

Rita certainly gets an "A" for her efforts in imagining the scene as richly as possible. We know she's an artist, but the process of enhancing your imagery by using all your senses can be attained by anyone with practice. Enhancing the images may also improve your results.

Rita also gets an "A" because she practices her imagery every day. The results for her were equal to her effort. The nightmares significantly decreased within one month's time and after three months of steady practice she has been experiencing only a few bad dreams each month.

CHANGE IT AGAIN . . . AND AGAIN: FELIX'S HOSPITAL VISIT

"I am in a hospital as an observer, not a patient. It's busy—lots of commotion and noise. I see a young woman who is suffering a great deal from a terminal illness. I realize I know how to cure her, but no one will listen to me. I am not permitted to cure her. I think up various subterfuges so I can get to the girl to help her, but somehow my actions cause more commotion.

People are running everywhere, shouting and pushing, and I can't get to the girl."

Felix suffers from nightmares every other night. His dreams show a recurrent pattern of extreme frustration and usually he awakens feeling depressed and anxious. Typically, he is trying to resolve some problem with his work, but he can never get it solved to his satisfaction.

In Felix's first attempt at changing his dream he concentrated on his power of cure for the young girl with the terminal illness. "I am in the hospital and I realize I have the power to cure a young girl with a terminal illness. I exercise this power and she gets better. No one else knows I have done this."

After practicing this new version for less than a day, Felix noticed he was dissatisfied with it. So he changed it again. In the next version, the young woman was never sick and she doesn't need to be cured. This too proved unsatisfying, so Felix changed it again. In the third attempt, he imagined a hospital where many people were cured. This too proved unsatisfactory. In the fourth attempt, he imagined many patients and other people in the hospital learning to cure themselves. This proved more satisfactory, but Felix still wanted to deal with one more issue—the hectic quality to most hospitals. In his last attempt he also included a vision of a hospital as a pleasant place to be.

Felix's multiple attempts at changes bring up an important consideration in using rehearsal. It's important to create a vision for yourself which yields a new dream you feel is the right one. For some people this is as simple as changing one single element in the nightmare, but for others such as Felix it required wholesale changes throughout the dream. There is nothing wrong with either approach. You must proceed according to your instincts.

We offer one suggestion concerning multiple changes. It probably can be taken too far. You might get so caught up in making changes you never give yourself the opportunity to practice the imagery of the new dream.

Remember, the link between the conscious and the unconscious appears to be forged through this process of imagery. Changing the nightmare on paper is only one step of that process. If you make a lot of changes and find your concentration diminished when you attempt to focus on the new dream, then you may not get the best results.

Felix has no complaints as his frequent changes proved successful. He experienced only two or three more nightmares after beginning treatment. In working with these remaining bad dreams, he had to go through multiple changes again to find satisfactory new images. When he finally settled on a vision for his imagery, his nightmares disappeared entirely.

INTERPRET IT OR CHANGE IT?
CAROL'S GOLDEN EYES

"I am suddenly aware gold is hidden on the inside of my contact lenses. I remove part of the lenses from my eyes to look at them and then realize they've turned into glass. They break in my hands and I realize I still have broken glass in my eyes and it's covered with gold on the inside. I also realize these lenses can give me special vision, which worries me, because somehow I know I need the gold to see.

"The scene switches abruptly to a department store where I'm in front of a big bin loaded with sunglasses. Many of the glasses are weirdly shaped and many are cheap, but in another second I spot the one pair of gold sunglasses. I realize instantly there are special gold lenses hidden inside these sunglasses. I must have these glasses because they will give me the gold I need to see.

"I lunge for the bin, but at the same time many shoppers crowd around the same spot. Everyone grabs at the sunglasses. My gold glasses fall deeper into the bin. Things are getting hot and sweaty and more chaotic. I feel desperate about getting the glasses, but it's no use. I wake up."

Carol is a thirty-five-year-old graphic artist. We've selected her story last because it highlights how some individuals come for help for their nightmares after they've been working on their problems in a therapeutic setting. Because of this we don't feel rehearsal can take as much credit for the person's success when they were in a position to get rid of their bad dreams anyway.

Many of Carol's dreams had a recurring theme. One in particular involved her murdering an unidentified man, then having to cover up the crime in assorted ways. In the dreams she would become cruel and heartless in her attempts at getting rid of the body and in ordering others involved to keep their silence. She would often wake up feeling guilty and ashamed of herself.

Carol was an introspective person and she had enjoyed interpreting her dreams in therapy. She also felt she had learned some valuable insights by analyzing her dreams. She found her golden eyes dream particularly revealing on some issues she had recently worked on in therapy, so she spent some time interpreting the dream, garnering some valuable insights. Afterwards, she raised the intriguing question: "Now that I've analyzed my dream, can I still change it?"

Absolutely.

Ideally we would all have the time, energy, and inclination to work with our bad dreams in both ways—interpreting them and changing them. This double-barreled approach would undoubtedly give you tremendous insight into your conflicts and provide you with a great boost of confidence by overcoming your nightmares. We encouraged Carol just as we encourage you to consider interpreting *and* changing your nightmares.

Here's how Carol changed her nightmare. "I possess special golden contact lenses which I can use to gain incredible wisdom. I can literally see other people's thoughts and feelings. At night I take out the gold lenses and place them in a fancy jewelry box, then store them safely away.

"In the morning I go to a department store with my boyfriend, Ted. In a display case, I see a beautiful pair of gold glasses which I know can help me keep my special vision. I go on about my shopping while Ted secretly sneaks back and purchases the glasses for me. Later, on the way home he gives the gold glasses to me in a beautifully wrapped package. I am delighted. I put the glasses on and realize I will have extra-special vision for as long as I want."

Notice that Carol's changed dream included virtually all the same elements as the nightmare. There was a strong desire in the original dream to succeed—to get those special golden glasses. In Carol's new version she altered the events so she could succeed, not to mention bringing in an interesting romantic twist with her boyfriend.

Carol's nightmares went away in the first week of treatment. She's had virtually none since. She was pleased rehearsal worked so well for her. She was feeling better about herself and experiencing less anxieties.

The combining of techniques is an intriguing idea. At present, we have only a few cases to report. One person felt he needed to interpret the nightmares first, then integrate the material before feeling all right about letting go of the dreams. This took him several days. Another person was comfortable interpreting the dream, then changing it in the same session.

SUMMARY

With these seven cases we've demonstrated a number of ways in which nightmare sufferers approach the step of changing their dreams. You probably noticed many people chose to stick to the same elements in the dream, altering only a few details to twist the story around to something more comfortable. A few dreamers changed the story radically as if everything in the dream were disturbing.

There is no right or wrong way of altering the dream, that is, in the formal sense of right and wrong. If you're not successful, however, in abolishing your nightmares, it's possible you're not selecting the best images to penetrate your unconscious. It's also possible this technique alone will not be sufficient for your particular problem with nightmares. But assuming for the moment that this is not the case, what else can we suggest if you're still having problems?

There are several points we'll review, but it's important first to determine if you've given your practice a chance to work. Most people using this technique required, on average, two weeks to two months of practice before they noted a significant reduction in their nightmares. So please give yourself ample time to see improvement.

In the next chapter, we'll review cases where individual problems created obstacles to immediate success. We'll show you how these people were able to overcome these hurdles and achieve success with rehearsal.

CHAPTER 18

Problems Along the Way

We hope you're sleeping better and feeling better about yourself now that you've said good-bye to your nightmares.

However, in medicine virtually nothing is 100 percent guaranteed. Yet imagery rehearsal works for a sizable number of people, especially when they make the commitment to practice the technique. It would be convenient if everyone could practice for two weeks or less and have their nightmares go away. For some, that does happen.

But practice makes perfect, and, over time, most who stay at it will have fewer and fewer disturbing dreams and nightmares. For many of you, the only real obstacle you'll face is finding the time, energy, and situations to continue your practice.

Some, though, will encounter other types of obstacles or distractions that limit how fast you can achieve success. We want to review assorted problems so you can see if you're doing things that might be hindering your progress.

HOW YOUR BELIEFS AFFECT YOUR RESULTS

Edna's best friend had nightmares and got rid of them using rehearsal, but Edna thought it was a fluke. Three months after her friend's success, Edna's own nightmares increased. She'd had disturbing dreams for ten years, one of which was a recurring dream about her son's arm caught in a power saw. In real life, her son had three different surgeries for a badly broken arm. Now he was able to play baseball again, but recently he'd been involved in an automobile accident which triggered another round of nightmares in his mother. At her friend's urging, Edna decided to try the treatment.

Edna had trouble rewriting the nightmare of her son's arm stuck in the power saw. She decided to change the whole thing. Now he had a minor cut on his elbow, then suddenly she switched scenes to him playing baseball, making long throws from centerfield with his powerful arm.

Edna's skepticism continued. She insisted rehearsal was so much nonsense, but she also practiced for the next few months. At three months she was asked how she was doing. Her reply was, "Doing with what?—the nightmares? Don't make me think about them. They've gone—good riddance. I'm not sure why they went away."

So here we have someone who continued doing something she said she didn't believe in, and yet things got better.

For Henry, however, his negative beliefs formed an impossible barrier to success. Most of his nightmares were vague— "Something chasing me." Henry wasn't from Missouri, but he was a "Show me" type of guy. He couldn't accept that imagining something in his mind could affect the nightmares. Henry came to treatment at the urging of his wife. He did try, but he only spent a week practicing. The last we heard, Henry was still having nightmares.

So beliefs are extremely important and serve as a major obstacle to overcoming your bad dreams. Once again, you must ask yourself: "Do I really want to get rid of my bad dreams?" We suspect that Henry and a few other individuals we've worked with are getting some kind of benefit from their nightmares. By constantly complaining about their bad dreams, they have a ready-made source of attention-getting.

Without the nightmares Henry might have to invent something else to be upset about. Perhaps this sounds like we're being harsh on him. After all, it's certainly possible the technique just won't work for him. True enough. And it's possible Henry's nightmares are caused by deeper emotional problems and that this simple behavioral method won't work on his dreams.

Every person who attempts imagery rehearsal will have to make a decision about letting go of their old beliefs about nightmares and taking a look at some new ideas. Letting go of your bad dreams may not be an easy thing, but it can be done if you believe it's all right to let go.

DO YOU FEEL YOU'VE CHANGED THE NIGHTMARE IN THE RIGHT WAY?

"I am walking across the river with my dog. The water is running low, but a big breeze is holding me back. The water now starts getting higher and running faster. My dog is going down with the water. I try to catch her. I can't, and she's gone. The water is deep but now becomes still. I wake up feeling very sad."

Dottie is a twenty-year-old Native American. She has had nightmares for twelve years. They began after an injury to her ribs while climbing trees. She ended up in bed for a few days and had nightmares about how she was going to get sick and never recover. The nightmares occurred every night for several months, then they decreased to a couple of times a week, but they never disappeared.

Dottie changed two significant dream elements in her nightmare. She got rid of the dog and replaced it with a cat, and she altered the scenario completely by getting rid of the river. "I am walking with my boyfriend. I am holding my cat, Miffy, in my hands, but she jumps out to chase after a field mouse. I start running after her but my boyfriend holds me back. I call out to Miffy and she comes back when I call her name. We walk back home and go inside."

Notice how Dottie changed much of the nightmare. The river seemed to frighten her, therefore she simply took it out of her dream. This is a perfectly legitimate approach; however, it raises a question. Is it better to work with the nightmare by confronting the elements in the dream? Or is it okay simply to discard those elements that you are afraid of?

This is a tricky question to answer. Another patient, who dreamed of being chased by a man with a knife, changed her nightmare in a most unusual way. She created a new image where the man stabbed her to death! She explained she felt more comfortable with this image because she no longer had to live with the fearful image of being attacked. Amazingly or not, her nightmares vanished quite rapidly.

Dottie, on the other hand, took longer to get rid of her nightmares. The process was a gradual one with noticeable improvement every few months. So, there may be something to working through the elements in your dreams instead of discarding them. For now, though, we can't state categorically that you have to do it one way or the other.

WHAT IF YOUR NIGHTMARES RETURN AFTER INITIAL SUCCESS?

Seline had no problem banishing her nightmares, but three months later she had a car accident. She chipped her teeth, and suffered a back strain and neck whiplash. The nightmares returned in spades. She felt miserable, couldn't sleep, and had no energy to work on the dreams. We suggested she do nothing for a while, take something for pain, allow herself to heal, and start her treatment later.

She renewed her imagery techniques six weeks after the accident. This time it seemed harder and it took longer, but the nightmares were eliminated again. Although most people we've worked with have not had a return of their nightmares, some people will have bad dreams re-triggered by new stresses.

This is not always the case, as we've had several patients describe new stresses occurring just as they had begun treatment, or a few weeks into treatment. These patients still achieved success in reducing or eliminating their nightmares. This boosted their confidence because, in the past, new stresses had always worsened their bad dreams. Eliminating the nightmares during tough times inspired them with a sense of mastery and self-control.

If you achieve initial success, then a new incident occurs in your life, it's appropriate to evaluate the incident to see how you feel about it. Divorces, separations, and loss of a loved one need time for anger, grief, and healing. Bad dreams may be a natural stage to go through in that healing process.

Other stresses, such as job changes, or moving to a new city, will usually be easier to put behind you once you've adapted. If your nightmares return after a change in your situation, consider a time limit of a few weeks to a few months to see if the bad dreams reflect important information about your new environment. After that, consider using rehearsal again if it seems appropriate.

DOES WORKING ON YOUR NIGHTMARES
CAUSE TOO MUCH ANXIETY?

Alice had very predictable nightmares. She worked as an executive secretary; her job was writing business reports. Her bosses gave her the material in rough form with little time to meet the deadline. The nightmares would always occur one or two days before the deadline, as she never felt she had enough time to do a good job.

Alice also suffered from anxiety. She didn't have full-blown panic attacks, but she'd suffer cold sweaty hands, a rapid heart beat, and that uncomfortable feeling of a lump in her throat. When she would work on her nightmares, all these feelings would return. By the time she recorded her changed version of the dream, she couldn't face the imagery exercises.

Alice was advised to write down the nightmare, change it, and then put it away!

We had her do something else for a while—for several hours, if need be. When she returned to her practice, we had her first imagine a favorite holiday place. She would stay with this imagery for several minutes or longer to relax. Then she switched to the changed version of her nightmare which she'd already prepared. This process took a few sessions before she could relax, but it solved the problem and within a few weeks her nightmares were gone.

ARE YOU REPLACING YOUR NIGHTMARES
WITH DAYTIME ANXIETY?

Clifford is a forty-year-old calligrapher who's had nightmares for thirty years. He could not recall going without nightmares for more than one to two weeks at a stretch. He awakens from nightmares occasionally, but he always feels depressed and anxious over his dreams. His wife noticed his mood changes and could predict when he'd had a nightmare. He had only vague memories of some of the images, but the feeling of horror was clear and pronounced.

"I am in a suburban neighborhood. Inside each house something bizarre is going on. I feel horror. There are monsters in the house."

Clifford practiced rehearsal and his nightmares went away quickly—too quickly for Clifford. He began to worry. Maybe he needed the nightmares. Maybe something worse would happen because he had gotten rid of his bad dreams. So Clifford put his nightmarish activities of self-doubt and negativity into his daytime events as if this would somehow "balance out" his psyche. He stopped practicing, and gradually the nightmares returned.

When we saw him again he explained his predicament. He was encouraged to resume his treatment and was reassured there was no evidence that getting rid of nightmares would cause any harm. He accepted this, but it still took him two months of being miserable in the morning with his nightmare hangovers to get back to the treatment. At six months he felt he could take control again. This time he wasn't worried about needing his nightmares to keep himself "in balance."

SHOULD YOU CONSIDER PROFESSIONAL HELP ALONG WITH IMAGERY REHEARSAL?

Most people handle their own treatments without professional help. But a few people cannot. They would get more out of the imagery technique in working with their bad dreams by seeking out a mental health professional to guide them.

Sonja was a French Canadian who, as a child, moved to Vancouver with her family. Her father had been active in the movement to free Quebec from Canada. Sonja remembers the meetings, the political rallies, but also the abuse. Her father took his frustrations out on her and her brother, physically and sexually. Her nightmares started when she was ten years old.

After moving to Vancouver, her father divorced and remarried. Sonja told her stepmother about the abuse. Right after that, both her father and stepmother warned the neighbors that Sonja had been accusing the neighbors of sexual abuse—an obvious coverup to protect them so no one would believe Sonja's story.

Sonja, a bright and attractive girl, tried to extricate herself from her family, but couldn't get away. The abuse continued into her midteens. Finally, she married at eighteen and had two kids in the next few years. She raised them while starting her musical career. She was a talented pianist and worked weekends in piano bars. Her life was busy, and, although her nightmares continued, she was able to cope.

Then, while her children were entering adolescence, her husband died in a boating accident. A few years later, her son left home and, though the daughter stayed, Sonja decompensated. She became depressed and the nightmares worsened. She had some counseling to help with the depression, and later entered an intensive group therapy program. She had periods where she felt better, but the nightmares were now horrendous.

"A vicious dog is biting a cat's head. No one will help and I am paralyzed too."

"I am living underground. My son and daughter can leave, but I can't. I am in extreme panic as I realize the walls can cave in, burying me alive."

"I wake up in the morning and am paralyzed. I can feel my bed move. This entity comes inside me and looks out of my eyes. It is horrible; I struggle to move. It leaves as I free myself from the paralysis."

The nightmares and sleep paralysis plagued her and she was put on a tranquilizer. This failed to work and she heard of the rehearsal method and wanted to try it. She recorded her nightmares, but found it too difficult to go through them visually. We arranged to do a simple imagery exercise of something pleasant.

In trying this simple exercise she had a horrible daymare-type experience. She envisioned a small man coming out of her body—it was her father. This frightened her and she could not continue. We could go on with the worsening images that developed in Sonja's attempt to free herself from her nightmares, but we're sure you get the picture. Sonja's past was just too unforgiving. She needed to work through many difficult issues of which the nightmares were just one.

Unfortunately, some people cannot get the relief they so desperately seek by using only behavioral methods. Instead, they must consider the old adage, "The longest way round is the shortest way home." In this case, the long way is extensive and intensive psychotherapy to deal with the bad experiences you may have encountered for so many years. If your mental health problems are so consuming, it would be wise to consider the nightmare treatment while working with a therapist as well.

CHAPTER 19

Complexities, Catalysts, and Conclusions

COMPLEXITIES OF TREATMENT

To share with you the complexity of another human being's life we are often forced to condense the information into a few paragraphs or a few pages. Yet, we know each person's experience with his or her nightmares produces its own unique story. We also know that much of the background for each person may have included months, if not years, of both painful as well as rewarding life experiences. It is not only satisfying for us to see the tremendous gains that people make in their treatment of their nightmares, but it is a fascinating experience as well to see how much they have gone through in their quest for improved mental health.

Still, the question arises: With all this complexity, how can we really know what caused the treatment to be so successful? Was it the simple behavioral technique? Was it that each person who came to treatment was finally ready to give up the nightmares and had adopted the right attitude? And, if so, how did they reach that right attitude?

Consider the situation of Anita. She was one of the most difficult cases we worked with in our research study—difficult because she had no less than three nightmares every night. When she began recording her bad dreams she had to stop because she filled up a book with over 100 nightmares in less than a month! She had suffered this way for years with a wide range of disturbing dreams of violence, frustration, anger, depression, and anxiety.

Her life actually got worse before she even had a chance to use rehearsal. She was hospitalized for depression and suicidal thoughts. During her three-week stay in the hospital, she underwent intensive psychotherapy. We told her to postpone any further work on the nightmares until things had stabilized and she'd had a chance to talk things over with her therapist.

A few weeks after discharge from the hospital, she wanted to pursue working with the bad dreams again. And this time, she decided she wanted to do it all in her head without further recording. She visualized the dreams, then changed them and revisualized them every morning after she woke up. She also changed her attitude about the dreams. She admitted earlier to being one of those people who just couldn't give them up. There had to be something to them and she was afraid to let go.

Within a mere two months, Anita had almost completely eliminated her bad dreams. And her whole attitude has changed; now she actively looks for solutions to problems that show up in her dreams and she does some of this while she's dreaming!

So what caused her turnaround? The technique? Her attitude? Her psychotherapy? Perhaps all three.

We suspect in many cases there are numerous factors involved in the success of the individual. In fact, it is probably the complexity of each person that is the more typical pattern for the average person. Nowadays, because of the nature of oversimplified self-help books, we often get the feeling of quick cures and simple successes.

We're not downplaying the excellent results we've achieved with imagery rehearsal, nor are we suggesting it isn't a powerful technique. It's just that there's always more going on than we can ever convey in the format of this short book.

To give you one more taste of this complexity, we'd like to share another case.

Sara's "Quick Cure"

Sara is a thirty-two-year-old student and housewife—a mother of a five-year-old girl. She works as a fire patrol ranger in an isolated wilderness area during the summer months.

Both her parents are alcoholics and they fought a great deal when Sara was growing up. Her nightmares began when she was less than five years old. She's had them ever since. Her nightmares wake her up with feelings of panic. When she worked with us, she was having bad dreams four or more times a week.

Sara had a difficult time adjusting and maturing for a number of reasons. Her early family life had many unsettling features, prime among them the tendency for the kids to mimic the fighting nature of their parents. No one ever learned how to get along and enjoy themselves as a family.

This was exacerbated by their frequent moves around Vancouver and Vancouver Island in British Columbia. Her father was a logger, spending time away from home at logging camps. His work was seasonal and money was either in abundance or lacking. Her mother worked part-time as a waitress, often leaving the kids home alone to fend and fight for themselves.

The result of these stresses led to a tumultuous adolescence. At age eighteen, suffering from depression, Sara made a serious suicide attempt. Wisely, she sought psychotherapy after that and her life began to settle down. She worked as a waitress on a large ferry. And she went to college part-time where she met her future husband. Their courtship was stormy but two years later they married.

Sara took courses in forest service management for a year, then got pregnant and had their first child. She described this as a happy time in her life with only minor conflicts in their marriage. But the nightmares continued three to four times a week, usually with the same theme. The dream would start out okay. Then a problem would arise and she'd have to find a solution. When she'd figured out a solution, more problems would crop up in the dream. Eventually, the problems would come faster and she'd panic.

From her psychotherapy she had a good idea of what this meant. It was a repetition of her earlier years as a child when her family life was filled with frustrations and anxiety. It reminded her of the lack of support she'd constantly suffered through, leaving her with an uncertainty about what each day would bring.

This insight exposed another problem which Sara recognized in herself—she had trouble relaxing. Even when things were good, she would expect something bad to happen. Most of the time she could control these feelings, but certain events triggered a bad reaction. When her husband came home late from work, she would feel jealous and hurt. Anger, frustration, and hopelessness would come flooding back, reminding her of her family life as a child.

Sometimes, her husband, knowing her past, would help her out of those feelings, but other times he would be irritable and would respond by yelling and the evening would deteriorate. Sara could expect a severe nightmare on those nights. The next day she would feel guilty, depressed, and the suicidal thoughts would return.

A year after the baby was born they bought a house. Real estate prices were inflating and they thought it best to buy before prices shot up again. Sara got a job with the forest service during the summer to help with the new costs of a home. She liked the job even though she was in isolated areas away from her daughter and husband for several days at a time. But she knew they needed her to work to keep up the house payments. It also allowed her to continue her studies in the fall and winter, taking a few courses each year.

The marriage continued to be good with intermittent squabbles—usually over finances and child care. Things seemed to be on a steady course. In light of Sara's upbringing and difficult adolescence, she certainly had made progress in her life. Yet despite all these stabilizing factors, Sara suffered mentally from a number of symptoms.

She felt a range of emotions and feelings throughout the day: fatigue, nervousness, hopelessness, annoyance, anger, and a sense of being a failure or unworthy. She was troubled about these negative thoughts, especially because she couldn't push them from her mind. She knew rationally that her feelings didn't fit with her improved life situation. But, like her nightmares, she couldn't control these irrational thoughts. She felt she'd worked hard at making her life much better. Having these symptoms and the persistent nightmares seemed unfair to her.

Sara heard about treating nightmares from a coworker and, although she didn't have much faith in the idea, she thought it couldn't hurt to try.

Her first recorded nightmare did not seem traumatic. It related to work and awakened her with anxiety. "The sky is bright blue. There are bushes and trees and something about a forest service truck. I am anxious about the time. How long before they discover I am gone? How far away will the truck be? I know I am not with the truck, but it's important the bosses find the truck missing. How long will that be?"

The next night Sara had a recurrent dream, one she'd had frequently in the past. "A disembodied hand appears, holding a gun. It is dark . . . all I can see is the hand and the gun. I am not afraid. The gun fires and an object hits me in the chest. The force knocks me backwards, my chest hurts. I can see nothing. I am aware of nothing but the pain in my chest."

This nightmare might cause fear and anxiety in most people. Sara responded differently because she had experienced the dream before. She complained of awakening with a terrible pain and tightness in her chest.

Three nights later, Sara had a more disturbing nightmare. "I see still pictures of children lying on the ground. Some are huddled next to women, probably their mothers. Lots of dust and flies. Children bloated and laid out in rows. I am not there, I only see these pictures. Pictures are passing in front of my eyes. Pictures of children. I am not in these pictures. My child is not in these pictures. I am just looking at them. Pictures of holocaust skeletal children. Ethiopia, shriveled bodies, flies, bloated bodies. India, children laid out in rows, massacred children—killed for god and politics. Stab wounds. I know these children! These children whose lives can't be. I know them—but I don't. The pictures keep flashing by."

You can appreciate the turmoil Sara would suffer from these nightmares. And you probably suspect as we did that children's tragedies could certainly reflect the emotional state of her own childhood.

Sara had thirty-nine nightmares during the four weeks she recorded her dreams. She continued to feel trapped and irritable, and suffered from perpetual low energy. Because Sara had joined our group she had learned that others had achieved success in conquering their nightmares. This motivated her to work hard using the three-step cure.

She enthusiastically embraced the imagery exercises and

practiced enhancing the images. She chose one of her recent nightmares to work on. "I am working on a house project with my husband and my younger sister. The two of them are in an old truck which has a rope tied between the back of the truck and a wooden fence. But something is wrong. The fence is bending. The boards are straining to snap. I am screaming at them to stop. But the noise of the truck's engine is loud. I wave my arms for them to stop, but they don't see. I am yelling wildly, but all they do is gun the engine louder. I realize suddenly I'm on the fence. I scream one last time, but the engine revs louder. Then I woke up."

Sara changed the nightmare very simply: "We start the truck and pull down the fence. It feels so good to get rid of that old fence. It opens the yard and gives me a sense of freedom."

Sara rehearsed her new images only twice during the next week. Yet, over the next six-month period after her very first attempt at practicing, Sara had only two nightmares. At her follow-up visits, she said she repeated the treatment two more times for the two additional nightmares. She also had one type of experience, which we will describe more fully in a moment, where she aborted a nightmare while she was dreaming. She literally woke herself up before it got to the bad part.

Sara had only practiced a few times and by the end of six months she was virtually free of the bad dreams that had plagued her several times a week for years. She noticed her daytime anxieties responded as well. "When I get anxious I use rehearsal to change the way I am thinking. It has made me feel so much more functional."

The treatment was a resounding success for Sara. But can we pinpoint why this was so? Was it strictly the effects of the imagery? Certainly, rehearsal caused some of her success, but it's possible it was also the right treatment at the right time.

Sara had survived a tumultuous childhood and was left feeling insecure and unworthy. She had worked hard in psychotherapy and continued striving, working, and going to school. She worked faithfully to make a good marriage and raise a child. The tremendous amount of energy Sara put into understanding herself and her problems was probably the real foundation for success. It provided the key she needed to get over the last big hurdle.

What does this mean? Did Sara have to do all this work to succeed with rehearsal? Our clinical impression is that if there is a great deal of either physical or psychological trauma, it may need to be worked through and understood to enhance the chances of success.

You will have your own complexities to deal with as you work on your own nightmares. For some of you, there will be other stresses clearly related to your nightmares and you may need to deal with the stresses as much as you work on your nightmares.

Some of you may suffer from the oversensitivity that appears in certain chronic nightmare sufferers. In this case, you may have to work on establishing more definite boundaries in your relationships with other people.

All of this raises the obvious question of what's really happening in our brains as we do the exercises. We believe the process of dreaming and the use of imagery exercises are functions that are closely linked in the brain. And therefore, by processing the imagery information, brain functions are somehow altered to change the nature of the nightmare, perhaps turning it into a less threatening dream.

Imagery itself, then, appears to be therapeutic. How it shifts the brain from a relatively unhealthy state towards a healthy one is unknown. Using the behavioral model, we could speculate that this process simulates the initial learning that occurred at a previous time which led to the mental aberrations that resulted in nightmares. By practicing the imagery rehearsal, then, you are changing the effects of the initial negative learning into something more positive, and simultaneously erasing the nightmares.

Lastly, we raise these issues of complexity to reassure you in the event that you find your own treatment going slowly. Remember, nearly a third of the people we worked with required several months before they considered themselves successful in ridding themselves of their bad dreams. It may take less time for you, or it may take longer. If you persist in your practice and consider all the aspects involved with your nightmares, we think you'll achieve success.

Perhaps an old Sufi saying applies here. "If happiness is in your destiny, you need not be impatient."

NEW EXPERIENCES CATALYZED
BY THE TREATMENT

Many of you will encounter new experiences as you continue to use your imagery techniques in the treatment of your nightmares, or for other things, like relaxation. Three common events are lucid dreaming, out-of-body experiences, and a greater interest in your dreamworld. Some of these processes are a bit eerie, but they are also common, so we want to make sure you're comfortable with them in case you experience one or the other.

Lucid Dreaming

Lucid dreaming means being aware you are dreaming while you are dreaming. In other words, a part of your "waking" mind recognizes you are dreaming without necessarily waking up. This has been described in a variety of recent books about dreaming. Some experts still scoff at the notion, while others are convinced it's a real phenomenon meriting further research. We have encountered many people who have lucid dreaming experiences. And, imagery techniques seem to make a person more prone to lucid dreaming.

Martha noticed she could recognize she was dreaming while having a nightmare. At the moment of recognition, she would wake herself out of the bad dream. She remained slightly anxious from the nightmare, but less so than before because she had not let the nightmare progress.

Repeated awakenings at the beginning of each new nightmare interrupted her sleep, so Martha applied the principles of rehearsal immediately after each awakening. She would review the bad dream, change it, rehearse the change, then drift back to sleep, all within a few minutes. This prevented the original nightmare from returning.

However, when she failed to do this, she would return to sleep only to find herself back in the nightmare. This motivated her to continue practicing her imagery during the daytime and also at night if she awakened herself at the beginning of the nightmare.

One night, an interesting development occurred. As the nightmare scenario began, she became aware she was dreaming, but instead of awakening, she modified the nightmare as it was occurring! It had been a simple dream. "I was walking down a street. In the middle of the road was a child. It was going to be hit by a car if I didn't do something. I suddenly realized I was dreaming and decided to go pick up the kid and put it safely on the curb. I didn't awaken then, but the next morning I remembered the whole thing."

Lucid dreaming showed up in a modified way in a number of other patients. Instead of waking themselves up out of fear, they simply recognized they were dreaming and *chose* to awaken themselves. In this situation, you perceive the nightmare and its threat, but you simultaneously perceive you're dreaming. Then, you choose to awaken yourself—not because you're afraid of the threatening figures in the dream—but because you don't wish the dreaming experience to continue.

Lucid dreaming is thought to be a common phenomenon, although the scientific research in the field is limited. Many of you will experience some level of lucid dreaming because you are paying such close attention to your dreams. This is a naturally occurring process, that is, people who spend more time and energy investigating their dreams have a greater tendency to dream lucidly.

Martha's initial awareness of her nightmare while she was dreaming is the most basic aspect of lucid dreaming. The next step for her was waking herself out of the nightmare. She was controlling her state of consciousness, causing herself to go from the dream state to the waking state. Many of you will be involved in these first stages of lucid dreaming where you will gain the ability to be aware of the nightmare or dream and wake yourself out of it if you choose.

Later Martha learned to stay in the dream and change the course and content of the nightmare while dreaming. This is the second level of lucid dreaming. Some of you may find you can go to this second stage and actually begin to change the nightmare yourself while you're having it.

A third level of lucid dreaming is suggested by Stephen LaBerge in his book, *Lucid Dreaming*. He reports in detail on the process of awakening *in* the dream rather than *from* the dream. In his discussion of nightmares, he focuses on the conflict model. He suggests that a nightmare represents a conflict that could be dealt with while dreaming. He attempts to link the waking and dreaming thoughts during the course of the dream in an attempt to deal with the conflict.

This sounds somewhat complex and difficult and it probably is. Still, it's something any person might experience without necessarily expecting to. While you are dreaming you might initially alter the nightmare, and then while you are still dreaming you might look over your new version.

For example, the conflict might have been portrayed as an unknown man attacking you with a knife. You then change the dream (while dreaming) to a known man who now offers you a gift. Using this technique as a treatment for nightmares has been suggested by LaBerge and may be helpful to some people who naturally find themselves lucid dreaming; however, there is little substantive that has appeared in the medical or psychological literature to support lucid dreaming as a valid treatment.

This is clearly a difficult and complex process. Many people are unable even with prolonged practice to enter into a lucid dream state. From our experience, lucid dreaming may be enchanced by imagery techniques, as there appears to be an overlap between the two.

First, things that make you more aware of your dreams will help you facilitate lucid dreaming. By recording your dreams, you will become more aware of them, not only because you write them down, but because you will also spend time reflecting on them.

Second, imagining yourself in the dream state will help you to lucid-dream. Intensifying and enhancing images with rehearsal creates this feeling as you feel yourself go deeper into your imagination. The deeper you go into your imagination, the more you may notice the similarities to the dreamworld. In fact, try to ask yourself, "Am I dreaming?" or, as you drift off to sleep, ask the same question. This will program your mind to dream lucidly.

Third, repetitive exercises seemed to work to induce lucid dreaming. In rehearsal, you repeat exercises throughout the day or week. Use this same repetition to feed yourself ideas about lucid dreaming. Suggest to yourself you will have a lucid dream. This is best done in a relaxed state, just before bedtime.

Fourth, rehearsal also autosuggests that you have control over your nightmares, which is a superficial form of lucid dreaming.

Arriving at the lucid dream state is only half the battle. Maintaining a lucid dreaming state appears to be more difficult. There is a tendency to move out of the lucid dreamworld quickly. Practicing imagery techniques may assist in maintaining the state.

Intensifying your images with rehearsal may enhance lucid dreaming. You start by imagining a vague color, then proceed to more intense and definite colors. You can also start with two-dimensional shapes and progress to a three-dimensional shape. Then move on to various objects, then to faces, and then on to scenes.

As you imagine a scene and it becomes more vivid, try to "slide yourself into the scene, becoming part of it." If you do this at night you may slip into a hypnotic dreamlike state in which you are also conscious and aware of the dream. This same awareness will then develop when you enter your normal REM dream state.

Another technique for maintaining lucidity was described by Don Juan in Carlos Castaneda's *Journey to Ixtlan*. While dreaming, he suggests you try to look at your own body, specifically your hands, and use this as a cue to remind yourself you are dreaming. Programming yourself to think about your hands in your dreams will get you searching for your hands as you dream, and that will trigger you to realize you are dreaming. In some cases, hands are not easily seen and therefore you can focus on another part of your body.

A final suggestion to maintain lucid dreaming is to imagine moving outside your own body or imagine you are floating out of your real body. If you create this feeling, you then "watch" yourself. Imagining this out-of-body sensation while you're awake allows you to be aware of it in a dream.

Some people become afraid with this experience. This occurs when they feel they are out of their body and have a sense they cannot get back. This is easy to resolve. As soon as you find you're worried about it, you'll probably come right out of it. The person wills himself back to his body spontaneously. Another suggestion we've given people is to move their big toe or their finger—one small part of their body—and as soon as that occurs they regain the sense of being back in their body.

Some advice is necessary at this point for those of you who want to try expanding your lucidity in dreams. We suggest you do further reading on the subject to acquaint yourself with the methods and follow any guidelines that LaBerge may suggest in his book.

To summarize lucid dreaming, it is a fairly common experience that can be induced with various techniques practiced over time. One big question remains: Is there a significance to changing your dreams while you're having them? We don't know the answer, nor has anyone done any research on this question. For chronic nightmare sufferers it may hold out promise as another method for dealing with disturbing dreams.

Out-of-Body Experiences

If you've ever felt the sensation of being outside your body, you probably know it can be an eerie experience. Many people have such episodes. And many of these out-of-body experiences occur while in the dream state. As you become more interested in your own dreamworlds, this may happen to you, and we want you to know a little about what to expect.

This phenomenon is nicely described by a university student who was living in one of the author's homes during the time we were writing this book. "I remember sleeping in my bed. I knew I was sleeping, but I could feel myself getting lighter as if I was waking up. But I didn't wake up even though I kept hearing noises outside my bedroom window.

"I felt myself wanting to wake up to investigate. So I 'got up' and walked out of my bedroom. The noise got louder as I got closer to the back door. But when I reached the door and looked out the window the noise stopped. I looked outside. There was a grayish light everywhere. When I saw nothing was there, I went back to my bedroom through the dark house.

"As I reached my bedroom door the noise started up again, so I headed for the back door again. I got closer and the noise got louder, then stopped again as I reached the back door and looked out the window. Finally, after repeating this three or four times, I was getting angry and decided to take action.

"After looking out the window I would go halfway to my room, then run back to the window and try to catch whatever was making the noise. I ran back and saw a girl standing about four feet away from window. She was fiddling with a plant. I stared at her. We were both a bit startled. Then she kept looking at me and her look shifted slowly to an evil smile.

"I looked out the window at her and it was crystal-clear. After a few seconds of her staring at me with that devilish smile I felt threatened for myself and the family I lived with. It's hard to explain, but I had this overwhelming feeling. I had to do something about it. So I tried to get at her. My crystal-clear picture started to blur as I worked frantically to unlock the door. The harder I worked to unlock the door, the more difficult it became. After beating on the door for about a minute, it all suddenly stopped, and I was standing there in my bedroom again.

"I turned to go to bed and saw myself still sleeping. That somehow calmed me down. Then I walked toward myself and the closer I got, the more unclear my image of myself became. It was like I slowly fell deeper and deeper back to sleep. Just the opposite of what had happened at the beginning.

"Then I woke up. I felt scared. It was as if it had really happened. Then I kept telling myself it was just a dream, and concentrated on other things. It took time before I was able to go back to sleep again."

This describes a very physically oriented out-of-body experience containing many of the phenomena that are commonly described. One of these is the vividness of the experience. Some people describe it as "being more real than real." Another aspect is his return to the bedroom. As he got closer to his body, things became more blurry. This also is a commonly described effect.

There are several questions raised by this experience. In coming back into the bedroom did he experience his "dreaming" body which lay there on the bed? Or, was he actually having a sense of his own "real world" body lying there in bed? Some people have described seeing themselves, then upon wakening they find they are in a different position from the one they witnessed from their dream.

Some have described being able to do what they call astral traveling. A group of these people claimed to be able to induce this at will. They were asked to visit a particular spot. After they went to this predetermined place through astral traveling, they returned and were asked to describe what they saw. The experiences as reported by the different people during the astral traveling were different.

What might this mean?

Could we assume their experience does not relate to viewing the actual structures as one would while they were awake? Or perhaps astral traveling or out-of-body experience is purely a mental phenomenon which does not relate directly to waking experiences or things in the real universe? Another interpretation is that while we are in the astral plane during an out-of-body experience, our mental experiences somehow color our interpretation of the real universe.

Whatever, this phenomenological experience deserves further research. It would appear the dreaming experience may be a valuable aid in our further study of these experiences.

New Attitudes Toward Dreaming

One of the experiences we hope you definitely encounter is a new attitude toward your dreams. We know for many of you with chronic nightmares or frequent disturbing dreams, the dreamworld is not one you've looked forward to visiting.

But we hope using the imagery techniques of rehearsal has reduced your bad experiences with dreams to a minimum or completely eliminated them.

So how might this change your dreamworld?

One of our patients, Maria, a thirty-year-old pediatric nurse, had a very interesting experience following the banishment of her nightmares. Her dreamworld suddenly came alive with a new array of colorful and exciting images. She now is an avid dream recorder and has developed excellent recall of her dreams. A whole new world has opened up to her and she cherishes it a great deal.

What happened? Could it be that all along she was a vivid dreamer, but the terror of her nightmares forced her to see things more vaguely to protect herself? Or, could the relief of having the nightmares vanish make her less defensive in her sleep so she is able to approach her dreams with less caution?

One dream Maria shared with us is incredibly rich and

inspiring. "I am in a long rectangular room. At the end of the room I see a beautiful rug on the wall. The rug is formed with striking colors of gold, red, and blue woven into an intricate geometric design. As I turn away from the rug, the image remains in my mind."

In real life, the image remained in Maria's mind as well. She was literally inspired by the vision of the rug and all its colors and intricacies of design. The thought of it produced other thoughts and images relating to art. Maria had always been interested in art and decided to have some children in the hospital draw pictures. She also had her own nieces and nephews draw pictures. She became intrigued by the differences in the artwork of those who were healthy and those who were sick.

Now that her nightmares had stopped, Maria was eager to discover new visions awaiting her in her sleep. This new flow of positive images sparked an even greater interest in art. And a short time later, Maria decided to advance her career by pursing course work in art therapy.

We hope you find yourself with such uplifting dreams as well. Perhaps your new dreams will inspire you toward achieving that time-honored adage:

Follow your dreams.

CONCLUSIONS

In writing this book, we have chosen an eclectic approach. That is, we have selected a variety of theories and methods to put together information that we believe can help all nightmare sufferers.

In the first part of the book, we discussed many different theories on the causes and meanings of nightmares, including Freudian, neurochemical, and biological, as well as a few cultural perspectives.

In the interpretation section, we looked at dreams and nightmares from a more psychoanalytic approach, which presumes dreams and nightmares represent meaningful expressions from our minds, conscious or unconscious.

And in this section we've moved into the behavioral realm where we've focused on nightmares as a distinct problem that can be treated by changing behavior and thinking patterns.

We've purposely chosen this eclectic approach because we think it provides you with the greatest amount of information to deal with your nightmares. If we had only selected a psychoanalytic approach, then we would not have been able to offer you much in the way of treatment, because analysts focus on interpreting nightmares as a way of abolishing them. This is not a very practical approach for most people, and it can be very expensive.

On the other hand, if we had provided only the behavioral view in our book, then we could not have offered much in the way of dream interpretation techniques. There is no particular dream interpretation method promoted by behavioralists.

These two approaches—behavioral and psychoanalytic—would seem to be at odds with each other. Furthermore, in discussing other theories, especially those in the first part of the book, these too seem to be in conflict with each other.

With so many different theories, we might ask whether this tells us something about the range and depth of modern man's understanding about dreams and nightmares.

It is our view that the current understanding of how dreams and nightmares function is very limited. The fact that you can simply alter your nightmare while awake, then reimagine it and have it go away is astonishing to us. It suggests something about the power of the technique, but more importantly it suggests that there is much we really don't understand about dreaming.

Or, looking at the psychoanalytic approach, it is equally awe-inspiring that people can work through their dreams and learn incredible insights into their characters and personalities, and that these new insights can serve as a guide to lead them toward a new horizon in their life.

Again, some people would view all of this as being in conflict. How can something that is so easy to erase from your unconscious also have so much value?

In science, we often find theories that appear to indicate conflicting views, only to find out later—often years and decades later—that we just didn't understand enough about the processes to see that in fact no conflict existed.

We wonder if that's where we really are now with our current understanding. Dreams have only been researched seriously over the past century, and nightmares less than half of that time. It seems much more likely that our knowledge and understanding of the dream universe is very limited, and that we just can't arrive at one all-encompassing theory to explain everything about dreams and nightmares.

We are left with a view that dreaming is a multidimensional process and that each of its dimensions has validity.

This is what makes the field so intriguing and fascinating. There is so much to learn about the workings of the mind and about our understanding of human nature. We hope that exploring your nightmares has led you to new and interesting dreams.

Let us leave you with a story about another dreamer.

A poor fellow named Vaclav lived in a small village many miles from Prague. He was so poor his home was a one-room hovel with a dirt floor. He heated it with an old stove that barely stood erect on three cracked metal legs. Despite his poverty Vaclav did not complain, for he was a man of faith and hope who counted his many blessings—good health, enough food to keep from starving, and a home that kept him warm.

One night Vaclav dreamed that a great treasure awaited him, buried beneath a bridge in Prague. Dreaming it one time did not spur him to investigate, but when the dream recurred three times, he set out for Prague on foot. After a tiring journey, he arrived several days later.

The bridge, however, was guarded day and night by the king's men. So every morning Vaclav walked back and forth across the bridge. He did this for three days in a row, for there was nothing else he could do.

Finally, the captain of the guards questioned him. "Poor man, why do you walk back and forth across this bridge?"

Vaclav replied timidly, "I must confess I am here because of a dream I kept having. I dreamt a special treasure lay buried beneath this bridge."

The captain of the guards burst out laughing. "And so to please the dream, you wore out your shoes to come here! Poor fellow! Why, if I were to follow my dreams, I would have ventured to some silly village far from Prague, and there I would look for the hovel of a poor man named Vaclav who has a three-legged stove standing above a dirt floor. And beneath that I would have dug up my own buried treasure."

The captain of the guards laughed again. "I had this very dream three times, but you don't see me leaving my post to dig for treasure that doesn't exist. Now be gone with you, poor fellow, and do not let your dreams get the best of you next time."

Vaclav bowed to the guard, traveled home, then dug up the dirt beneath his stove. There he found a treasure of gold and silver which made him wealthy for the rest of his life.

We hope that by turning your nightmares into dreams you will have the same opportunity to find the treasures that await you in your dreams.

PART IV

Wrapping Up the Night

CHAPTER 20

The Nightmare Family of Troublemakers

Now we'll cover those other nightmarelike experiences we've mentioned throughout the book. Many of these problems are often confused with nightmares. Most are very disturbing and a few can lead to serious physical injury. Nearly all of these problems must be treated differently from REM nightmares.

To give you an easy way to lump these conditions together, we've grouped the various nightmarelike experiences according to where they occur in the sleep cycle. As you may recall from Chapter 2, the sleep cycle is divided into two worlds: REM and NREM. We dream mostly in REM and sleep in NREM. NREM is further divided into four numbered stages which correspond to how deeply you're sleeping.

For the REM stage, we'll talk about one problem known as the REM behavior disorder. For NREM, we'll discuss several problems which arise in the deepest phase of sleep—Stage 3/4. We'll begin with several conditions seen in our lightest phase of sleep—Stage 1 of NREM.

LIGHT SLEEP

"It happened during the summer when I visited my grandfather in old Mexico. I was sixteen years old and he let me sleep in this large bedroom with a huge bed. It was raining that night and at first I thought I'd been awakened by lightning.

"I saw her as she approached my bed—a haggard old woman. I could hear her footsteps on the wooden floor. She came up to the edge of my bed. I was filled with horror as she pointed her finger at me.

"I wanted to destroy this vision, but I was unable to move. I was paralyzed and felt my heart racing. But then she disappeared. I got up and walked around the house, then I went back to sleep. A short while later, she returned again pointing her finger at me. But as my panic increased, she disappeared again."

Hypnagogic Hallucinations

Alfredo's experience isn't really a dream—it's a *hypnagogic hallucination* (abbreviated HH). The hypnagogic state is the lightest phase of sleep—Stage 1—where we are falling asleep or waking up. Because we're more awake than asleep, the visions are termed hallucinations instead of dreams.

Many people describe the presence of the vision after awakening. Jerome had such an episode. "I saw a large, reddish monster. It was threatening me. I couldn't make out much detail, but then I awoke and the weirdest thing was the monster was still there. I'm sure I was awake. I know my eyes were open. The room was dark and the image of this reddish thing was floating motionless in front of me." People observed during these episodes have their eyes shut, or else open with a blank expression.

Shaking yourself out of the hypnagogic state is sometimes difficult. Often, you feel paralyzed because you are simultaneously suffering from a second condition—*sleep paralysis* (abbreviated SP).

Sleep Paralysis

Sleep paralysis is an exceedingly common experience. Fifty percent of the population may have experienced it at least once. It occurs separately or with hypnagogic hallucinations. It also occurs in Stage 1. You may experience sleep paralysis without hallucinations and still be frightened because you really can't move. This is *real* paralysis, not imagined.

How can you be paralyzed in your sleep?

Looking at REM sleep physiology provides an answer. The REM dream stage exhibits two cardinal features which distinguish it from NREM stages. One is known by the name itself—*r*apid *e*ye *m*ovement. The other is the absence of muscle tone, that is, through your nervous system, an inhibitory network is activated which prevents your muscles from moving while you dream.

Some dream researchers believe this *REM-onset sleep* theory explains how SP and HH occur. REM sleep invades this light phase when we are falling asleep. Normally, REM is a separate stage, distinct from any of the four NREM stages; and REM usually does not occur until after the sleeper cycles through all the NREM stages. Somehow the normal REM muscle paralysis slips into Stage 1. Since we are not quite asleep, we sense this inability to move, become frightened, then jerk ourselves awake.

This is only one theory, and we wonder if these phenomena are really something quite different. Dreams and nightmares have a tremendous amount of variability in their content, yet the SP and HH experiences are often described in surprisingly similar terms—some sinister character threatening the individual. When the episodes recur in the same person, they are often identical, and among different cultures and peoples in other lands the episodes are also described in this same manner.

So the process may be related to REM in that it makes the person susceptible to the attack. But the episode itself might be a separate process—either intrapsychic, that is, coming from within ourselves, or extrapsychic, that is, coming from some force outside ourselves.

One study of a few thousand college students in Newfoundland showed nearly half had experienced sleep paralysis at least once. A Japanese study showed an incidence of 40 percent among more than 600 students. In a small study of blacks, 25 percent were affected by sleep paralysis once a month. In our research of chronic nightmare sufferers we found more than 20 percent experienced episodes of SP and/or HH.

Sleep paralysis usually lasts no longer than ten minutes, but often stops in less time. The victim becomes aware of the paralysis and attempts to break out of it. Moving any part of the body seems to release you, as will being touched or spoken to by a bed partner. Often the paralysis stops on its own. If you return to sleep after an episode, the paralysis may come back. And for whatever reasons, nappers are prone to the attacks.

Numerous people report preventing the episodes by *not* lying flat on their backs. For some, it has been as simple as lying on their side or abdomen. For others, sleeping upright in bed with lots of pillows or leaning face down over a chair or stool has prevented SP.

The Old Hag

A special type of attack is known as the *Old Hag*—a cultural term used in parts of Canada and the U.S. The Old Hag is an ugly old witch who attacks people in their sleep. It is believed to be an instance of supernatural assault.

Other cultures throughout the world have similar legends of monsters or mythical figures that attack people while sleeping. When Alfredo experienced his attack in old Mexico, it was shortly after the death of his grandmother. Before he'd ever heard of SP and HH, he wondered if the old woman who visited him was the spirit of La Llorona. La Llorona is a well-known legend in Hispanic culture. In this legend, a woman who was spurned by the conqueror Cortez returns to kidnap children and drown them. She is sometimes referred to as the ditch-witch.

Although we cannot refute nor prove the theories of supernatural assault and other mythical legends, the Old Hag and similar experiences closely match the experiences of sleep paralysis and hypnagogic hallucinations. There are numerous folklore traditions to combat the Old Hag, ranging from prayer rituals to placing a container of your own urine under your bed. David Hufford's intriguing book, *The Terror That Comes in the Night* provides an in-depth analysis of the Old Hag experience.

Regarding medical treatments, most people do not seek medical attention for either the Old Hag experience or for SP and HH. In fact, most victims believe they've had some sort of nightmare. Victims will describe the experience as if recounting a bad dream. Yet there remains an interesting difference in that people will remember their SP and HH experiences more clearly than they do many of their dreams and nightmares.

When Jerome described his reddish monster, we had asked him, "Do you have nightmares?" He replied that he rarely recalls his dreams and almost never has nightmares; but then he said, "There was this time . . . I must have been about seventeen years old, there was this reddish monster . . ." So

Jerome remembered his HH experience even though it occurred only one time, and that was twenty-five years ago.

Many researchers note that HH and SP are commonly confused with REM nightmares, so much so that we don't have a clear picture of who suffers from these conditions and how often they occur. We suspect hypnagogic episodes of SP and HH and the Old Hag experience are very prevalent.

Narcolepsy

Additional confusion surrounds sleep paralysis and hypnagogic hallucinations because they also occur in narcolepsy. Narcolepsy is an intriguing ailment characterized by four specific problems: hypnagogic hallucinations, sleep paralysis, sleep attacks, and cataplexy.

Sleep attacks are episodes of overwhelming drowsiness which result in the narcoleptic falling asleep in as little as a few seconds, even if the person is driving a car, making love, or engaging in a heated argument. *Cataplexy* is a waking equivalent to the absence of muscle tone we experience in our dreams. Often triggered by emotional responses, such as laughter or anger, a standing narcoleptic may suddenly fall down as his or her knees buckle. Both HH and SP are prominent features of narcolepsy.

Much of our research on SP and HH has come from studies on narcoleptics. Unfortunately, this has led some people to assume that if you have either an HH or SP episode, you must be evaluated for narcolepsy. This just isn't so. Researchers have studied SP extensively throughout the world. Their findings show SP occurring in large numbers of healthy people who suffer no sleep disturbances. So if you've had an episode of sleep paralysis, don't think you automatically need to be evaluated for narcolepsy.

To distinguish properly between the two problems, some experts use the term *independent sleep paralysis*. Although independent sleep paralysis attacks rarely last longer than ten minutes and result in no obvious harm, they are so disturbing to some chronic sufferers that therapy may be needed. Many of these chronic sufferers notice an increase in episodes during periods of stress. Some people have been successfully treated with meditation or hypnosis.

Others require medicines. Through the study of narcolepsy, researchers discovered that antidepressant drugs were highly effective in combating sleep paralysis. The specific drugs are from a chemical family known as the tricyclics. Some of the names of these tricyclic antidepressants are imipramine, clomipramine, and desipramine. Newer drugs of the same or similar classes are currently being tested and used in narcoleptic patients. Perhaps one of these newer drugs will prove more effective for those who suffer from independent sleep paralysis.

DEEP SLEEP

Now we'll look at several disturbances that occur in our deepest sleep, including *night terrors, sleepwalking, and sleep-talking*.

Night Terrors, Sleep-Talking, Sleepwalking

Night or sleep terrors are perhaps the most dramatic of all nightmarelike experiences. From the deepest slumber, the sleeper abruptly sits up in bed with an expression of absolute horror etched on the face. A second later, he yells out with a terrifying scream of utter panic. The amazing thing about sleep terrors is that victims usually don't remember any of this. Nor can they figure out what had them screaming bloody murder.

Children with sleep terrors often fall right back to sleep. An adult may do so as well; however, a bedmate is sure to be awakened by the commotion. The bed partner then attempts to rouse the victim, believing it's a nightmare, but this can worsen the attack. The sufferer is experiencing complete disorientation and may feel the bedmate is a threat.

The older term for night terrors was *pavor nocturnus*. The current psychiatric term for the chronic condition is the *sleep terror disorder*. In the typical account, the person shows an intense fear or anxiety reaction—dilated pupils, sweating, skin hair standing on end, hyperventilation, and a rapid pulse. And all of this comes out of the blue. Sleep lab recordings of night terror victims show virtually nothing abnormal, even seconds prior to the attack.

Night terrors occur in Stage 3/4—the deepest level of sleep. This accounts for victims' striking disorientation. One moment they are lying calmly in their most restful sleep, then a moment later they're abruptly brought to consciousness by some terrorizing force. It may take several minutes for them to realize they were asleep. Because the person goes from sleep to waking, night terrors are classified as *disorders of arousal*. In other words, the unusual awakening itself is what's abnormal.

Because most of our deepest sleep—Stage 3/4—occurs in the first half of the night, we expect to observe night terrors within the first few hours of bedtime. In fact, nearly two-thirds of all night terrors erupt in the first NREM cycle.

What causes night terrors?

One theory is night terrors are not really dreams at all. Rather, the nervous system, acting on its own, suddenly goes haywire, causing the heart and breathing rates to double or triple. When the person unconsciously experiences this rapid, unexpected change in vital signs, especially during sleep, it brings on a state of anxiety.

This theory explains why the person doesn't remember much about the events because there probably isn't much to remember. According to this theory, night terrors are *not* brought on by unconscious psychological conflicts. Other experts dispute this autonomic nervous system theory. Instead, they have looked to see if dream content can be uncovered in night terror victims.

In their studies, night terror victims have recalled definite images and memories immediately after an episode. Usually, these are threatening images, such as feeling trapped or crushed, or the feeling that someone will hurt them. Choking and falling sensations, as well as fears of dying, were also detailed. While this resembles REM nightmare themes, the images are rarely depicted as dreams. Rather, they are expressed like thoughts, without the fantastic or bizarre imagery we see in our dreams and nightmares.

This raises the interesting question: Do we dream or think in other stages of sleep? Several studies show that mental activity in the form of dreams or thoughts could be recalled in virtually every stage of sleep. Dreaming predominated in the REM phase, while thoughts or thoughtlike memories predominated in the NREM phases.

Does the victim experience some dreadful thought or memory seconds before a night terror?

Looking at individuals suffering from both night terrors and nightmares helps answer the question. If a person describes similar threatening themes in both episodes, this would suggest the threat is the cause of the nightmare *and* the night terror. Sleep lab studies have confirmed this by monitoring individuals who've suffered a nightmare and a night terror on the same night. After the attacks, they commented on the similar nature of the threats they recalled. At our present level of research we still don't know the specific triggers for night terrors.

Night terrors are common in children. In adults, they are much less frequent, so much less that there are few statistics to determine how often adults suffer these dreadful episodes. When an adult develops night terrors, they often begin in the age range of twenty to thirty. Rarely do they develop after the age of forty. Those who develop them as adults, however, often have them chronically.

Night terrors in adults often signal an emotional disturbance, and therefore psychotherapy is recommended to address the underlying conflicts which may be causing the attacks. However, night terrors usually cause the victim no harm or injury unless the attack is accompanied by additional activity.

What kind of activity? If victims of night terrors also develop *sleep-talking (somniloquy)* and *sleepwalking (somnabulism)* episodes, then they are at much higher risk for physical injury. However, this finding is confusing, because the overwhelming majority of sleep-talking and sleepwalking episodes are very benign, resulting in no problems whatsoever.

To clear up this confusion, we'll expand a bit on walking and talking in your sleep. Like night terrors, both sleepwalking and talking usually occur in the deepest stage of sleep. Sleep-talking is very common. In studies of college students, 50 percent reported that someone observed them talking in their sleep. Most research shows that the great majority of somniloquy occurs in normal people without any other sleep or mental disturbances.

Sleep-talkers usually speak in short phrases or merely a word or two. It is much less common to carry on for long, nor does much in the way of true conversation take place between the talker and an awake bed partner. Furthermore, the notion of secret telling in your sleep is considered a myth.

Sleepwalking is also usually benign when it involves simple actions such as dressing, eating, or going to the bathroom. There is no memory of the activity. If the walker wakes up away from bed, he or she will be disoriented and unable to remember how they got there. All this is done as if awake, yet the sleeper's face wears a blank expression as if in a daze. The sleepwalker may continue for thirty minutes, though most episodes last less than fifteen. The activity can stop spontaneously or the person completes the activity by returning to bed without awakening from sleep. There is no recollection of dream content associated with benign sleepwalking.

Sleep-talking and sleepwalking, however, can be worrisome if associated with night terrors. Much of the research on sleep-talking has focused on people who also suffer night terrors. Many episodes of sleep terrors are preceded by sleep-talking. The speech relates to the threatening images which the victim recalls from the actual terror attack. In one study, a man uttered several phrases at the outset of the attack describing someone stepping on him. When fully awake he recalled the image of someone trying to step on him.

In another case, a man screamed out: "Help! Hey! Help! Hey, get! It's near my throat! Things choking me! Something is stuck in my throat!" After awakening, he recalled something was trying to choke him. In fact, he used the phrase, "something is choking in my throat" to describe what he remembered.

Further agitation with night terrors can develop through sleepwalking. In these cases, the risks for injury are substantial. Cases have been reported of broken bones and severe cuts and bruises from people walking out of windows in multistoried buildings.

In adults, unlike children, frequent sleepwalking episodes may be associated with other mental health problems unless another cause is uncovered such as a medication side effect. In the elderly, sleepwalking appears in those suffering from dementia or other changes occurring in the brain, as with stroke patients.

Just how dangerous is sleepwalking? Coordination is poor, which accounts for the high incidence of injury. A person can easily fall down steps or trip over objects. One research study suggested that 70 percent of sleepwalking incidents may end in an injury.

Consider Tom's story. He had a history of night terrors and sleep-talking beginning at the age of seven. He remembered nothing about them and they became less frequent as he got older. When Tom's parents separated, the problem recurred at least once a month. Then he moved with his mother to another city, but they fought regularly and after six months Tom moved into an adolescent group home at the age of seventeen. His sleep-talking increased and the other teenagers in the home told him he was regularly crying out in his sleep. He discussed it with the counselor who felt it was a worsening of his night terrors and they made plans for Tom to see a specialist in sleep medicine.

The week before the appointment, however, Tom awoke one morning on the ground outside the home with a fractured arm and several small cuts on his arms and legs—he had jumped out the window of the two-story home! He remembered fragments to a bad dream, but there was nothing specific he could relate to his counselor. The counselor moved Tom to a first floor room and reorganized his bedroom to make it safe. They even put bars on the windows. Everyone thought this would solve the problem. But Tom had another incident a few days later—he walked out of his room and put his head through a glass aquarium. The cut on his scalp required 21 stitches.

Before treating sleepwalking with medications, it's important to be certain that a drug side effect is not the culprit. Medication side effects are usually seen in patients with more serious mental illness, such as schizophrenia and manic-depressive disorder, where they have been prescribed antipsychotic and mood-altering drugs.

For the average person, however, alcohol must be considered. Combinations of alcohol and sleeping pills, antidepressants or antihistamines have been observed to cause sleepwalking episodes. Combining alcohol with these other medications is always discouraged because these combinations can be deadly. Now we know one more reason not to combine them—sleepwalking.

While there have been recent studies showing that many patients with night terrors and/or sleepwalking don't suffer from serious mental illnesses, it would still be wise to consider a professional evaluation for any prolonged period of *new* night terror/sleepwalking episodes.

A large percentage of adult sleepwalking is preceded by major life stressors, such as a death of a spouse or loss of job. Often the patient has increased symptoms such as anxiety, depression, or irritability during the waking hours. All this should alert you to the need for a physician's consultation. Some may require further evaluations by a neurologist—a brain specialist.

Ultimately, three issues must be addressed to properly treat patients with night terrors and/or sleepwalking. The first is to make the environment safe in which they sleep. Sleeping on the first floor, barring windows, gating stairways, and removing dangerous objects from the room are essential steps to take, especially in the beginning of treatment if the problem is out of control.

Second, since many cases do reflect mental disturbance, psychotherapy and stress management methods such as relaxation exercises must be encouraged to target the stressful elements in the person's life. Hypnosis has been successfully used but so far it has only been proven effective in patients who seemed relatively free of psychiatric symptoms.

Lastly, medication is often needed. The three most commonly prescribed drugs in the past include diazepam and chlordiazepoxide (tranquilizers which most people know as *Valium* and *Librium*), and imipramine (an antidepressant). The drugs act on the sleep cycle in unknown ways, but are effective in reducing episodes. Doses vary according to the person's tolerance to the medication. Therefore, trials of the medicine are needed before one set dose can be fixed.

Clonazepam, a drug in the same family of benzodiazepines as *Valium,* has also been shown to be very effective in a recent study. Clonazepam is the drug of choice for the other adult sleep movement problem—the REM Behavior Disorder, which we'll discuss next. Clonazepam may also prove of equal value in treating sleepwalking.

REM SLEEP

Rem Behavior Disorder
Now let's return to the REM stage to discuss the recently discovered disturbance known as the REM Behavior Disorder.

Here's a dream from Ginny, a twenty-eight-year-old grad student who suffers from the REM behavior disorder. "Someone is watching me. I open my eyes but I can't see because it's too dark. I feel myself panicking. I jump out of bed and run. I can hear a man laughing, but I still can't see him although I feel his presence. As I run, the evil man pushes me and I fall. As I fall I can still hear the laughter. I start crying, then screaming. The next thing I know I'm lying on my bedroom floor completely awake."

This is a typical night's event for Ginny. She suffers from bad dreams so frequently she sleeps with her mattress on the floor. To make her environment safer, she puts bolsters and other pillows around the edges of the mattress so she doesn't hurt herself when she lands on the floor.

The REM Behavior Disorder (RBD) sounds a lot like sleepwalking with one huge difference. Now the dreamer is actually dreaming throughout the activities. It's as if you were carrying out the events unfolding in your dreams. If you experienced routine dreams this might not be such a problem, but patients suffering from RBD invariably have nightmares.

We know a patient who dreamed he was about to be drowned by a large flood tide. To save himself, he dove headfirst under the wall of water. When he awoke, he realized he had smashed his head against his bedroom wall. In the emergency room, X rays showed he had broken his neck.

RBD is thought to be relatively rare; however, because of the recentness of its discovery, there are no statistics available to show how many people suffer from it. We suspect it will prove more common than initially thought, because in our research on nightmares we've already turned up three people who describe behavior that closely matches RBD.

In some ways RBD is similar to a sleep terror because the person is capable of thrashing about in his or her sleep. And, it is similar to sleepwalking because of the increased physical activity. However, the significant difference is that the activity carried on by the dreamer in RBD reflects the events he or she is experiencing in the dream. So RBD occurs during REM sleep, unlike night terrors and sleepwalking, which occur in Stage 4 of NREM.

You may recall that we discussed the normal paralysis during REM sleep. EMG studies (tests of muscle movement) of dreamers with RBD, however, have shown the *absence* of paralysis. For normal dreamers this paralysis shows up on the EMG as no muscle tone. People with RBD not only show the presence of muscle tone, but some have hyperactive tone which probably contributes to the excess movements. These patients thrash about in their beds fifteen or twenty times during a thirty-minute REM dream period, while normal dreamers remain virtually motionless.

Much of this activity is consistently associated with dream actions involving chases or attacks or other aggressive incidents. Case reports from several researchers, as well as from our own patients, have described the following actions: thrashing and flailing of arms, shaking and jerking, punching and kicking, jumping, walking, running, talking, yelling, screaming, pointing with fingers, moving furniture, waving of hands, falling out of bed, staggering about the room, crashing into objects, striking at walls, searching, and reaching and grabbing.

While the dreamer is at risk for self-inflicted injury, it is often spouses who insist on the medical checkup because of the physical harm done to them. As the disorder has so far appeared more in men, there are several wives who have taken the brunt of the violent behavior. Several have been nearly strangled to death. Other women report being kicked and punched enough to move to another bed.

Still, it is the dreamer who is primarily at risk. We know of an individual who dreamed he was running from an attacker. He jumped through a closed window and suffered facial lacerations. Another individual dreamed he was trapped in a room from which there was no escape. He banged his head against the wall trying to break free and gave himself a concussion.

One large study examined 100 patients who sought help at a sleep lab center after suffering sleep-related injuries. While the largest group included fifty-four people who suffered from night terror/sleepwalking episodes, another thirty-six people were diagnosed with the REM Behavior Disorder. In one case, a man reported tying himself to his bed every night for the previous six years. Unfortunately, he was still able to break loose at times because of his violent thrashing.

Most cases of RBD in the scientific literature involve elderly male patients who suffered some type of brain damage, possibly blockages in the small vessels that supply blood to the dreaming centers in the brain. These could be very small strokes which can only be detected by special scanning equipment such as the newer *magnetic resonance imaging* machines known as MRIs.

According to this theory, the small blockages in the blood vessels result in damage to the area of the brain that sends the signal to paralyze the muscles while dreaming. In other cases of RBD, brain damage was also discovered which may have affected the brain's dream centers.

While most of the cases have been reported in elderly men, RBD occurs in younger, otherwise healthy men and women. It is therefore possible that some physiological problem with sleep may turn up as another cause of RBD. Overwhelming stress seems to have been a factor in some cases. Withdrawal from drugs such as alcohol, amphetamines, and tricyclic antidepressants may also contribute to the problem. For those who suffer from a combination of RBD and mental illness, psychological influences may turn out to play a greater role.

Many of these patients need extensive examinations, including sleep lab recordings, neurologic and psychiatric evaluations, and sometimes brain scans such as CT and MRI. Once the diagnosis has been established the good news is that there is a drug which has proven remarkably effective in controlling the problem.

Clonazepam—a tranquilizer and anticonvulsant—of the benzodiazepine family has been used for several years to treat RBD. Some patients are on record as having taken the drug for six years without serious side effects or reduction of effectiveness in controlling RBD.

A small dose of clonazepam is given at bedtime. Good results are achieved in the first week, often on the first night. While clonazepam is clearly the drug of choice, patients must still be directed to take maximal safety precautions, including the removal of dangerous objects from the room, placing the mattress on the floor, surrounding the mattress with pillows and cushions, sleeping on the first floor, and barring or covering windows.

SLEEP DISTURBANCES UNCLASSIFIED
BY SLEEP STAGES

Sleep Panic Attacks

Panic attacks are overwhelming episodes of anxiety lasting a few seconds to a few minutes. They more commonly occur during the waking state. If you've ever experienced one, you may have ended up in an emergency room convinced you had a heart attack. The symptoms can be so similar to cardiac chest pain that you may have been admitted to the hospital for overnight observation. Only after repeated episodes will it become easier for both the doctor and patient to distinguish between these overwhelming anxiety attacks and true cardiac chest pain.

In many ways panic attacks are like nightmares and sleep terrors because they provoke similar symptoms. The victim experiences shortness of breath, a smothering sensation, dizziness, faintness, palpitations, a rapid heartbeat, trembling, shaking, sweating, choking, nausea, abdominal pain, flushes, chills, chest pain, a fear of going crazy, and a fear of dying, to name some but not all of the symptoms.

What must be horribly distressing to panic-attack victims is that at least a third of them not only suffer during the day, but they will also suffer attacks in their sleep. In fact, some people suffer more attacks in their sleep than during wakefulness. Some patients have their first episodes occurring in sleep, which would be a frightening and unnerving experience.

Panic attacks affect at least 1 percent or more of the general population, but among families the rate can be as high as 20 percent to 30 percent. This shows the strong genetic predisposition to the problem.

At present, there is no research to show the relationship between sleep stages and panic attacks. They appear *not* to occur out of REM, nor out of Stage 4, which would eliminate nightmares and night terrors as the cause. Also, victims recall no dreams prior to the attacks and they are completely oriented when they awaken.

Treatment for sleep panic attacks is the same as for waking episodes. Medication and psychotherapy, particularly behavioral techniques, are often required. Many patients respond to psychotherapy as the sole means of treatment and prevention. Others, however, require medication for as long as six months to a year to prevent early relapses.

Many drugs have proven effective in treating panic attacks. However, each drug may work more or less effectively for a given patient. Side effects must also be considered. Therefore, it may take several trials on different medicines before finding the best one.

Drugs that have proven effective include the tricyclic antidepressants, phenelzine, alprazolam and clonazepam. Some other drugs include verapamil and newer antidepressants, such as clomipramine and fluoxetine.

Nocturnal Seizures

Seizures are a common disorder and nearly 80 percent of all those suffering from epilepsy suffer convulsions while they sleep; however, some people suffer their seizures *only* during sleep, making it more difficult to pin down the diagnosis.

Following a seizure from sleep, the patient may awaken disoriented and then proceed to move about the environment in an aggressive manner. Sometimes incoherent speech with mumbling and screaming are a part of the picture. This would make the diagnosis difficult because of the similarity to night terror/sleepwalking episodes.

Unfortunately, the EEG, which is the best laboratory tool for studying seizures, doesn't always record seizure impulses on the brain tracing. In fact, in regular epilepsy, where there has been no trauma to the head or no underlying problem such as a brain tumor, the EEG may only help to make the diagnosis in 10 percent of cases. Patients with only nocturnal seizures may continue with their problem for a while until they have a witnessed seizure during the day.

Dream recall in seizures is absent; however, there are a few cases where the sufferer reported a nightmare *prior* to the seizure. This may be similar to the aura effect in awake seizure patients. Just prior to the seizure they notice tingling sensations in one arm, or they see flashing lights. In the same way, a nightmare could precede a nocturnal seizure.

Concerning treatment, the problem with nocturnal seizures is making the diagnosis. In some cases, because the patient has no daytime seizures, the doctor must make a decision to use *empiric* treatment, that is, the physician suspects nocturnal seizures and proceeds to treat with anticonvulsant medicines to see if the problem resolves.

There are a number of medications which are used in the treatment of seizures, including *Dilantin*, phenobarbital, carbamazepine, valproic acid, and *Mysoline*. Depending upon the type of seizure activity, a neurologist would be the specialist trained in selecting the specific medication.

Daymares and Flashbacks

Daymares are essentially daydreams that turn sour. Daydreaming is a ubiquitous phenomenon—everybody does it. Most of us have reasonable control over our daydreams, but people who suffer chronically from nightmares seem to be more susceptible to daymares. For them, frightening thoughts and images invade their waking fantasies.

Hartmann noted that if he asked people who had good dream recall, but did not suffer from nightmares, whether or not they suffered from daymares, they invariably responded "No," or "I don't know what you mean." So it may be that daymares occur mostly in people who suffer chronic nightmares. Daymares share some of the qualities of flashbacks—an experience often seen in people with traumatic nightmares and PTSD.

Flashbacks occur as vivid and disturbing memories of traumatic events. In effect, the person relives—at least for the moment—the painful episode in an intensified and condensed fashion, dredging up the horrible emotions he or she experienced when the event happened.

Concerning treatment, daymares are treated by working on the chronic nightmares; however, there is little information available to know the effects of treatment. Flashbacks are treated by working on the traumatic nightmares and other aspects of PTSD and may improve with treatment.

Traumatic Nightmares

While writing this very chapter, we were involved in a most dramatic case in our emergency department. George is a Vietnam veteran who has suffered from the posttraumatic stress disorder for years. He served in Vietnam in 1965 and developed PTSD about 10 years later—for very understandable reasons.

Entering Vietnam as a teenager, he found himself in a unit that ultimately had several members prosecuted for war crimes. George admitted his involvement in this and it regularly flared up in his nightmares. When we saw him, he described the following dream: "We are hanging them up . . . the bodies . . . in the trees, like always. We start hacking away at them. I'm using my machete to cut off their limbs . . . I can't take it anymore. I feel sick. I want it to stop. I look at the machete. I realize there is only one way. I point it at myself and begin chopping at my belly."

George woke up shortly thereafter with a metal coat hanger stuck three inches into his abdomen. He was rushed by ambulance to our trauma center where an evaluation revealed he was stable. He had missed puncturing any large blood vessels. He was then admitted to a psychiatric facility where he has undergone intensive therapy for PTSD.

Posttraumatic nightmares are vivid re-creations of painful events from the past. Though occurring in sleep, they often feel like a relived memory instead of a dream. They occur in people who have suffered from war-related horrors, motor vehicle accidents, rape, or other forms of assault in childhood or adulthood. They also occur in survivors of natural disasters such as earthquakes and any other types of trauma.

Consider the recurrent nightmare of Ellen, a forty-year-old secretary. "I am alerted by a sound at the door. A man is trying to get into my home. I am afraid to confront this situation but force myself to go downstairs and look. It's nighttime but the lights are on in my house. As I approach the door, I see he's already part way in—his hand and arm are reaching through the doorway. I push against the door trying to keep him out. It's strength against strength, but I feel myself weakening. I need help! Someone please help me! I yell for help over and over and then I wake up."

Ellen's nightmares occur in sporadic episodes. Sometimes she has them once a week for months, then they'll disappear for no apparent reason. Her nightmares are almost always the same, identical to the one described above—and for a good reason. A similar encounter occurred twenty years ago when a man broke into her house. In real life she used common sense to lock herself in the bathroom, then she opened the window and screamed for help. A conscientious neighbor heroically subdued the burglar at gunpoint until the police arrived.

A simple psychological interpretation of Ellen's recurring dream suggests she has experienced a trauma which she's never been able to forget. Notice in the dream how she chooses more of a confrontation than what occurred in real life. This notion of unresolved conflicts and feelings goes to the core of most theories about traumatic nightmares.

Hartmann has extensively researched traumatic nightmares. He notes that the victim's dreams may be different than ordinary dream images. Sometimes they will take on a memorylike quality, as if the person were reliving the episode and not just dreaming about it. It's as if they were "replaying" the event. And sometimes they will alter one significant detail from the real-life event which changes the dream into something more nightmarish.

Hartmann also notes the difficulty in classifying these dreams by sleep stages. They may appear in various stages with some overlap. While most occur in REM, other nightmares have been documented in Stage 2 or Stage 4 of NREM sleep. In these stages, the dreams take on the qualities of night terrors. Furthermore, the memories can be replayed during the waking state as flashbacks. These are more common in sufferers whose traumatic nightmares are part of the posttraumatic stress disorder.

An important consideration for treatment is to distinguish between people who have only the traumatic nightmares versus those with all the symptoms of PTSD. Most things in medicine are never clear-cut and people often have combinations of symptoms. Some will have a few symptoms of PTSD but frequent nightmares. Others will have a few nightmares but most of the other symptoms of PTSD. And, there will be patients with any combination in between.

If you suffer from posttraumatic nightmares without other symptoms, then you can use the treatment section where we've outlined the technique of imagery rehearsal. Many of our patients in both our research studies and our clinics have responded well to this form of treatment.

If your posttraumatic nightmares are just one aspect of PTSD, then more comprehensive treatments involving psychotherapy and medications are usually required. Treatment is best received under the guidance of a therapist and, in many cases, a special unit designed for this disorder. Several veterans' hospitals around the U.S. have developed programs to treat PTSD in Vietnam veterans. These hospitals are conducting research to improve treatment.

Special centers have also been established to treat PTSD caused by other traumatic events besides war-related incidents. These programs teach patients how to become socially engaged again because so many of them have become disengaged from family, friends, and society. They teach patients to deal with their anger and to communicate their feelings more effectively.

Some use a technique known as *implosion*, which involves reliving the experience in detail. Though painful, this helps to verbalize the horror and, it is hoped, lay it to rest. *Biofeedback* is commonly used. With biofeedback, you learn to decrease your physiological arousal in response to the memories. You learn to feel more comfortable in general and if the memory recurs, you'll have a less intense response.

A group therapy format is helpful, as many people with PTSD feel isolated. Going through treatment with other people provides support. Also, working through the painful memories with other people who've shared similar experiences can build a sense of camaraderie which in turn can reconnect you with other people. Establishing relationships with people in the group promotes renewed relationships with your own family and friends.

Special treatments are also designed to deal with other symptoms of PTSD, such as insomnia, anxiety, agitation, and, when drugs and alcohol are involved, drug and alcohol counseling and treatment. Most programs have treatments for all these problems and will tailor the program to fit the individual needs.

Of course, the nightmares can be treated as a specific symptom, using imagery rehearsal, at the same time the other problems are addressed. Another method called *desensitization* has also been used on posttraumatic nightmares. The patient is taught to relax, then go over the nightmare, and then relax away the tension that surfaces while reviewing it. Over time, you learn to relax to the point that the images no longer bother you.

We do not know which of the two treatment methods—desensitization and imagery rehearsal—works best for posttraumatic nightmares. We do know that both have been used successfully.

CHAPTER 21

The Children's Hour

WHY DO KIDS HAVE NIGHTMARES?

Bad dreams and nightmares are so common in children, they probably represent a normal phase of development. Nearly 90 percent of those between the ages of one and five cry or call out in their sleep at least once a week. And about 60 percent of these young children awaken from a disturbing dream once a week or more.

Although the REM phase garners a major portion of sleep during the first year of life, there is no way to determine if actual dreaming occurs. The infant must first pass the preverbal phase and begin speaking. Children will describe their earliest dreams between the ages of one and a half and two and a half years. Invariably, nightmares occur.

In these early years, children often experience falling dreams which may reflect fears of abandonment. How does this come about? Psychologically, the child faces a number of issues which revolve around seeing himself or herself as a separate object, for example, separate from mother or other nurturing adults. We see this in the child's fascination with his or her own body as well as the bodies of other adults and children.

We do not seem to be born with this ability to separate ourselves from others. On the contrary, we are born with an instinct that we are all united in some fashion—the world is at one, more or less. Specifically, we are attached to our mothers. Over time, we learn we are separate from our mothers and other beings and that other humans are separate from us. Once children learn this distinction, they are prone to anxiety of a special kind—*separation anxiety*. Nightmares of falling may reflect this anxiety in children's dreams.

Another explanation for falling dreams is that toddlers regularly fall as they learn to walk. Dreams of falling may reflect their concerns about their safety as they learn how to maneuver in their surroundings.

When the child reaches the preschool and early school years, roughly ages four to six, the incidence of nightmares peaks. Dreams of being chased or attacked are common. These dreams represent the increasing complexity of the child's interactions with the rest of the world. Now the child has developed significant sexual and aggressive impulses, many of which have already been repressed or at least routinely frustrated.

Nightmares of assaults could represent children's fears of injury, both physical and psychological, because they have reached the age where they know others can hurt them. But the dreams could also be projected wishes—the psychological process of placing your own impulses and emotions onto another person because you are unable to deal with those feelings. In an assault dream, the attack could represent the child's aggressive impulse toward a parent or sibling turned back on the child. These attack or chase dreams reflect the child's attempt to deal with other people—adults and children. And dreaming, in general, may be a means of problem solving for children.

During these peak years of nightmares, early signs of the rivalry between the child and his mother and father emerge. These are the so-called oedipal struggles or, in more common language, dealing with early "love triangles."

In the next phase of development—roughly ages seven to eleven—the child has submerged or repressed many of these aggressive and sexual impulses. This may be the reason nightmares appear less frequently during this phase.

Bad dreams reemerge during puberty, forming the second highest peak of nightmares, roughly between the ages of ten and thirteen. Pre- and early adolescence is a time of increased sexual tensions, new learning, peer pressure, parental conflicts, and other struggles of growing up. Nightmares may be attempts to cope with these problems. Sexual themes are especially common and may produce nocturnal emissions or wet dreams.

Earlier problems reappear as well, such as the preadolescent struggles with separation and body image. But the focus is now on identity. "Who am I? What am I? What does it mean to be a boy or a girl?" The rivalry in love triangles and other relationships also resurfaces as boys and girls struggle through early love affairs and increasingly complex and intense friendships.

Thinking about this, we may be reminded of our own experiences as children and adolescents. For most of us, there was a mixture of good and bad times. What was your experience like? How did you contend with all these problems of normal development?

And what about the "unexpected" misfortunes—deaths, divorces, marital separations, physical and mental abuse from parents who either attack their kids, sexually or otherwise, or who withhold love and affection from their children. If you experienced any of these traumas, how did you handle them? Also, let's not forget all those other experiences of "growing up"—our encounters with friends and enemies, teachers, doctors, other kids' parents, illness, hospitals, and so on.

With the complexities of development and the trials we must endure, it's not surprising that our children, just like ourselves, have had bad dreams at different stages in life.

WHEN SHOULD YOU BE CONCERNED ABOUT YOUR CHILD'S NIGHTMARES?

With the obstacles we must overcome to reach adulthood, it is always an intriguing aspect of human development to see how much we grow. In terms of nightmares, the majority of children grow out of them. But some won't, and the question arises: What does it mean if your child, at whatever age, develops chronic nightmares persisting for more than a few months?

Nightmares are not always a sign of disturbed mental health, but in most instances bad dreams should be taken with more than a grain of salt. Much depends on the situations in the child's life. There may be good reason for disturbing dreams. Children suffering through earlier-than-expected loss and separation seen with divorces and parental deaths may develop bad dreams as an appropriate and perhaps healthy response.

What if the occasional nightmare becomes frequent nightmares? And when do frequent nightmares require more attention?

There is no set answer to these questions, but we can use the notion of "children at-risk" to look at the problem. This term "at-risk" describes children susceptible to drug abuse, depression, suicide, mental illness, and other serious problems. We look at what's going on in the child's life and ask one central question: How are things changing? For example, when a student who consistently makes B-average grades, suddenly brings home a report card with scattered Cs and one D, we know something must be causing the change.

If we look at all aspects of the child's life, we get a general sense that things are improving or deteriorating. Has the school called you more frequently about some trouble your child has gotten involved in? Has your child missed more school because of illness? What's going on in the circle of friends? Have new friends entered the picture and, if so, what influence are they having?

You'll also need to look closely at what's happening at home. Has there been an increase in fighting between brothers and sisters, between child and parent, or between parents? Is homework completed on time, or are there more delays? What about your child's play behavior? Does the child maintain a strong zest for playing sports or other games after school? Is he or she active in extracurricular activities and programs outside of school?

Much of this seems obvious at first glance, yet in the course of family life, problems will evolve slowly without anyone noticing. This is not unusual because living together in a family makes us so close to each other we sometimes have trouble seeing the trees for the forest. And, with our own struggles as adults, there will be times when we'll be more caught up in our own lives and not aware of our children's.

We then develop *reactive* postures, that is, we *react* to what has already happened instead of preventing it. There's nothing wrong or abnormal with this way of life. In fact, sometimes it's a lot healthier, because it gives us all a chance to learn by making mistakes.

Still, there will be times in your child's development when you will want to determine his or her at-risk status. Whether the question is drugs, teenage pregnancy, violence, or chronic nightmares, you must take a break from your normal routine to assess the seriousness of the problem.

For some parents, a professional counselor can help you ask the right questions of yourself and your child. Moreover, many young people with chronic nightmares may be in need of short-term counseling to help them uncover their feelings about these problems. A few children and their families may require longer psychotherapy.

Is there something specific in the content and frequency of the nightmares that will clue you in to a potential problem?

Consider Maria and Jenny, eight-year-olds who are neighbors. They play together in an empty lot behind Maria's house. One day, an older boy with borderline retardation molested Jenny by touching her buttocks. A few days later, it happened again and Maria told her mother. The mother contacted the boy's family and reported him to the authorities. The girls gave statements and the boy was dealt with appropriately.

Although Maria was never touched, she was scared by the events. She stopped sleeping in her bedroom and was found on the living room couch three mornings in a row. Maria said she couldn't remember how she got there, which prompted her mother to bring her in for evaluation.

Maria was nervous about telling her mom about the boy because, like many children, she somehow believed she herself had caused the problem. In therapy, she confided she'd had a nightmare about him coming into her bedroom. After that, she'd been afraid to sleep there.

When Maria was asked if she wanted to deal with the nightmare, she was eager. She was offered a piece of paper and pencil and asked to draw what the nightmare was about. She hesitated, unable to respond.

Then, we held up the blank piece of paper and we said, "This is your nightmare, right?"

She smiled and said, "Yes, that's my nightmare."

"What do you want to do with it?"

She pointed towards a trash can, so we crumpled up the paper and threw it away.

She smiled.

Then we asked, "Where's the nightmare?"

She said, "It's gone."

She then drew a picture of a pleasant dream—a colorful picture of her room with her bed, her bookshelves, her dresser, and her dog coming in the door.

Maria was seen for a few more sessions to ensure she was coping properly as well as to allow her to express any other feelings. She was reassured this occurrence was not her fault, and that she'd done an excellent job in describing the events to the authorities. She was given advice on how to avoid such situations and what to do to protect herself. This reassured her and she had no further nightmares.

In this case a real-life event precipitated the nightmares like a posttraumatic stress reaction. And it proved worthwhile to work on the problem through therapy.

The frequency of nightmares may in itself mean a child needs help because increased nightmares could easily disturb a child's sleep and affect how he or she functions during the day.

Unless the content of the dream is specifically related to a previous traumatic event, content is not a specific reason for judging the need for treatment. The one exception is a nightmare whose content is so disturbing to the child and/or the parent that it needs to be addressed, such as dreaming about a death of a parent, sibling, or the child itself.

Lastly, if the child has any problems which seem to be reflected through the nightmares, professional guidance in working through both the problems and the bad dreams may be helpful.

HOW TO APPROACH INDIVIDUAL OR OCCASIONAL NIGHTMARES

Although nightmares are a normal occurrence in children, it may be wrong to assume that the nightmare is meaningless. Children certainly have a number of trials to go through and they have a lot of feelings to learn about. If your child mentions a nightmare, it may be a golden opportunity to explore how the child is feeling, how the child is perceiving the world, and what difficulties the child may be confronting.

Discussing the nightmare can lead to a nice heart-to-heart chat. The dream provides the child a way to express himself or herself in a less threatening manner. This is especially true when the child has negative feelings about a parent. It can also be true for other feelings the child is embarrassed to reveal.

A typical dialogue between a father and daughter may go like this: "Dad, I had a nightmare about a dog chasing me last night, and I woke up scared."

"That's interesting, what happened?"

"Well, Dad, see, I was walking down the road to school and just minding my own business along the sidewalk, and this big dog came barking at me and at first I didn't think it was a problem because there was a fence, but then it jumped over the fence and came running after me."

"Then what happened?"

"I started to run, and it kept getting closer and just about the time it was ready to jump me, I woke up."

"And how did you feel?"

"Really scared. It was one of those big boxer-type dogs, Dad."

"And you said you were on your way to school in the dream?"

"Yeah, it was just like our street, and seemed like any other day before the dog came running after me. So it was really scary."

"You said you were going to school in the dream. Is there anything at school that might be kind of scary for you?"

"Well, they are having this play. And it's supposed to be put on at Christmas. I'm trying out for one of the parts and I guess when I get up there, it's kind of scary to do that."

So the dog may represent a fear at school or something else. Most importantly, the nightmare provides the opportunity for the father to talk with his daughter about some problems that might be bothering her. In talking over a nightmare, you can give guidance and support to your child. Remember, though, the child's view of the world is very different from your adult perspective. Things that seem trivial to you may be larger than life to the child.

HOW TO APPROACH CHRONIC NIGHTMARES?

If your child develops chronic nightmares, you will want to consider a few things. First, think back over the past months of the child's life to see if there's anything causing stress. This could be something outside of home, such as school, sports, and other activities, or it might reflect some tension in the home or family life which the child senses.

Your child could be growing through a developmental phase that makes it more difficult for him or her to cope with situations that had previously been routine. Consider exploring what other people who work with the child have to say. Give a teacher a call, talk to a coach, or speak with someone about your child's behavior at religious school. If you're married, it's crucial to discuss what's happening with your spouse. If you're single, consider talking with other members of the household or other close friends or relatives who have contact with the child.

If you uncover specific problems, then you'd be wise to take some form of action at home or at school or wherever the case may be. If nothing is uncovered, but the nightmares persist, you might want to teach your child how to cope with the bad dreams. There are innumerable methods that have successfully worked with children.

You can have your child draw a picture of the nightmare, and then change it and draw a picture of the changed version. Or, ask your child to tell a story about the nightmare and have him or her come up with a solution to the story as a new fantasy. Then go over the solution with the child in detail to reinforce the solving of the problem in the dream.

It's helpful to start in a systematic way. This will help you feel competent in what you're doing. The child will sense your confidence and feel more comfortable.

Consider these steps:

1. Relax yourself so you're in a receptive state to hear the nightmare.
2. Ask the child to describe in detail exactly what the nightmare was about.
3. In a neutral tone, ask your child to expand on some of the details of the nightmare.
4. When you notice certain feelings expressed relative to the nightmare, mirror those feelings back to the child.

For example, after a particularly scary part you could say, "That must have made you feel pretty scared." This substantiates children's feelings and allows them to feel all right about what they're feeling. You're letting them know it's okay to have those feelings in those circumstances.

Once you've established what the nightmare is about and validated your child's unpleasant feelings, you can move on to the last step of problem solving. You could say, "I wonder if there might be a way of dealing with that situation in the nightmare." Most children are creative and will entertain all sorts of ideas on how to deal with what bothers them in the dream.

If they seem stuck, encourage them. If they stay stuck, offer easy alternatives which are only part of the solution. Usually, when children receive hints, they will build on them. When they suggest an idea, even if it seems strange or bizarre, offer them credit and praise. Once your child has a solution, or at least an idea of how to deal with the dream, have him or her recreate the dream and tell it to you as a new story.

For children who like to draw, let them draw the new story. As you're doing this, it's a good idea to say, "Well, it's nice that you have a solution. Now, put the nightmare behind you and get rid of it." After that, you could say, "Now, let's look at your new story." You will want to phrase this in a way appropriate to the age of your child.

This whole process can be fun for children. If you make it a game, they will enjoy it while gaining a sense of control over problems that arise. When children learn this measure of control in dealing with nightmares, it gives them a feeling of mastery for other situations in their lives.

Working with your child can be a pleasurable experience and can bring you closer. Ending the session with a hug and reassurance, or if you're doing this at night, a tuck into bed and a kiss, finishes the session on a positive note.

If the nightmares persist after doing this a few times and your child is upset about the bad dreams, consider professional guidance. If you are not sure where to get help, your family doctor or pediatrician will steer you in the right direction.

Therapists tend to be less directive in working with kids because children come up with their own ideas, images, and solutions. Our job is to facilitate this process, offering encouragement. Rather than searching for deep meanings in nightmares, we work in images, stories, and pictures to let the child provide the meaning as it evolves.

Some parents find this approach frustrating because they want to know the meaning of their child's nightmare. Patricia Garfield's book, *Your Child's Dreams*, provides specific interpretations for certain nightmares in children. Although this is a helpful way to look at your child's bad dreams, the author herself lists these as "usual meanings." We suggest using her book as a guide to interpreting and not for literal interpretations. By focusing on the personal aspects of your child's nightmare, you'll gain more meaning from the dream.

DEEP SLEEP PROBLEMS

Night Terrors, Sleep-Talking, Sleepwalking

From our deepest phase of sleep—Stage 3/4—there are a number of problems which affect children. These include night terrors, sleepwalking, sleep-talking and confusional arousals. All these activities engage the sleeper in a way that suggests partial awakening or arousal. Many experts therefore call these problems "disorders of arousal."

From deepest sleep, the child enters a state where actions and behavior suggest he or she is actually awake. Yet, attempts to communicate or otherwise engage the sleeper will result in a greater disturbance, prolonging the episodes. Moreover, the child rarely remembers anything about the episodes.

Night terrors are the most well-known of these deep sleep episodes. They occur more in older children. Although they last a few minutes, in that short span of time the intense reaction of fear to some "hidden attack" manifests in dramatic form. A bloodcurdling scream, accompanied by a horrific stare, racing heart, and profuse sweating are the trademarks of the typical attack.

As many as 5 percent of children suffer frequent night terrors at some point during childhood. More than 60 percent of young people suffer at least one episode. Boys experience the attacks more than girls and a variety of stress factors may increase the episodes. Fever, physical illness, fatigue, poor sleep habits, head or other physical injuries may all precipitate episodes.

The good news, however, is that night terrors in children, unlike adults, usually do *not* reflect serious psychological disturbance. Therefore, treatment with medications is rarely indicated for a child, even one with frequent episodes. Instead, it is usually the parents who must be reassured for if they are unfamiliar with these unnerving attacks, they assume a terrible illness has befallen their child. As we've mentioned, the child has little or no recollection of the episodes.

Once parents understand the problem, it is a simple matter of having a strategy to deal with an attack. The most important consideration is to avoid interfering with your children unless they might injure themselves. Perhaps you're now asking, "Interfere with what?"

During the attack, the child sits up in bed and seems to live out the terror strictly in his or her mind. It is difficult for a loving parent or a compassionate friend to sit idly by and watch this horror continue. But numerous studies reveal that if you try to shake children awake, there's a chance they'll scream louder or fight back. Remember, at this point the child is disoriented and it's possible any interference will be perceived as a threat.

Some episodes are not so stationary. For whatever reasons, the sleeper combines movement with the attack. Because sufferers remember so little about their night terrors, we don't know why they suddenly hop out of bed and bump into furniture, as well as performing many other potentially injurious activities.

This brings us to two more disorders of arousal—*sleepwalking* and *sleep-talking*. When the victim of a night terror attack thrashes about, it is a form of sleepwalking. And if there is more movement and more vocalizations—sleep-talking—accompanying the night terror, there is a greater risk of injury.

Many children sleepwalk and sleep-talk without any problems. As many as 15 percent of kids have walked in their sleep at least once. The disorder runs in families, but can hardly be called a disorder because it usually creates no disturbance at all. Most of the time, sleepwalking will resolve over time.

However, in combination with night terrors, sleepwalking and talking may be more agitated, frenzied, and ultimately aggressive, leading to a much greater disturbance of the household and to serious injuries. Medications to control these attacks can be used until the child grows out of them.

The three most commonly prescribed drugs include diazepam (a tranquilizer which most people know as *Valium*), a similar drug, *Librium*, and imipramine (an antidepressant). Dosages range according to the child's age, weight, and above all, their tolerance to the medicine. Therefore, trials of a drug may be needed initially to establish one set dose. Clonazepam, a drug in the same family as *Valium*, has also been very effective in a recent study.

Lastly, in deep sleep, there are the *confusional arousal* states. These occur in younger children, usually infants and toddlers, or those under five years of age. The attacks seem like "mini-night terrors." The episodes are not so intense and do not include the "look of terror" seen with night terrors. Instead, the child appears confused or upset. They may cry out or moan or look "possessed."

Like night terrors, children cannot be consoled by their parents and the episode may worsen if the parents interfere. The attack often ends with the child returning to sleep without any memory of the events.

One last word on the indications for psychotherapy in these deep sleep problems. While it is true most children suffering from these problems—night terrors, sleepwalking, sleep-talking and confusional arousals—rarely suffer significant injury, the question remains whether there might be some underlying psychological problem. Sleepwalking can be a sign that the child is experiencing increased stress in his or her life. And some studies show children with night terrors may repress their feelings, especially anger. So, in these instances, psychotherapy might prove beneficial.

HEAD-BANGING

Head-banging goes by the medical term *jactatio capitis nocturna*, which means to jerk the head at night. The infant makes repetitive and rhythmic movements of the head as if nodding continuously and may continue for as long as an hour or more with a frequency of up to 120 times in a minute. Most episodes last fifteen minutes or less and the frequency is usually less than one "beat" per second.

Most of these episodes occur with sleep onset, be it nighttime sleep or daytime naps, but they can occur during other times, such as when the child is resting or drowsy. The infant can forcibly bang his or her head against the pillow or the side of the crib. Injuries are surprisingly rare. In fact, children seem to gain pleasure from the activity. Head-banging usually starts at seven months and lasts for several months and sometimes a couple of years. This is distressing to parents because the child typically head-bangs every night.

Usually no treatment is required because injuries are infrequent. However, in mentally retarded children, injuries are more likely to occur and often require protective measures such as helmets or crib padding.

No one knows why or how head-banging occurs. Head-banging in normal children may be a different process than in retarded infants, especially so because the activity stops in the sleep of the retarded child, yet it continues in the sleep of normals.

Neither group has demonstrated specific causes to expand our knowledge of the process. Retarded children suffering from various brain and nervous system lesions which have caused their retardation do not show the same damaged site in the brain to account for the problem. And, in normal children, no underlying psychological or physical problems have been related to head-banging. Current theories suggest head-banging and other rhythmic body movements represent normal nervous system development seen during periods of transition, for example, between sitting and crawling, or crawling and walking.

The two other frequent body movements are "head-rolling"—the shaking of the head from side to side; and "body-rocking"—the movement of the whole body to and fro while on the hands and knees. All these activities have been recorded in children in sleep labs and are observed throughout all stages of sleep. While this certainly suggests a generalized nervous system process, we still don't know what that process might be.

Perhaps 5 percent of normal children are head-bangers or head-rollers, whereas about 20 percent are body-rockers. Interesting associations have shown that head-bangers have a much lower incidence of thumb-sucking, and body-rockers seem to reach certain developmental milestones faster.

Unfortunately, if these rhythmic body movements persist into later childhood or young adulthood, they can produce significant psychosocial effects on the individual. The person may avoid activities and interactions because of the embarrassing nature of the problem. If episodes continue past the age of three, further evaluation by psychiatrists and neurologists may be warranted. Behavioral therapy approaches, involving simple techniques of "rewards," may yield good results.

We have treated one case of body-rocking that persisted into adulthood. The patient described what sounded like a meditative state when she did the activity. In view of this, she was taught to do a mantra-type meditation, which produced a similar feeling. She was able to substitute this activity for the body-rocking prior to falling asleep.

In some cases, sedation with tranquilizers, such as the benzodiazepines, or with tricyclic antidepressants, may be helpful.

This completes the final section of the book. In the appendix which follows, we've compiled a list of medications that have been associated with nightmares. Please consult this if you think drugs are causing your bad dreams or those of some one you know.

Lastly, you'll discover a lengthy bibliography in the appendix. It contains articles and books to guide you toward additional information about nightmares and other sleep disturbances.

We invite you to join us in the exploration of the dream universe. We feel it will lead all of us to a fuller understanding of ourselves and the world around us.

Bibliography

Books

Arkin, A. 1981. *Sleep-Talking: Psychology and Psychopathology*. Hillsdale, N.J.: Lawrence Erlbaum Associates.

Arkin, A., Antrobus, J., and Ellman, S. eds. 1978. *The Mind In Sleep: Psychology and Psychopathology*. Hillsdale, N.J.: Lawrence Erlbaum Associates.

Breger, L., Hunter, I., and Lane, R. 1971. *The Effect of Stress on Dreams*. New York: International Universities Press.

Corriere, R., and Hart, J. 1977. *The Dream Makers: Discovering Your Break Through Dreams*. New York: Funk & Wagnalls.

Corriere, R., Karle, W., Wolderberg, L., and Hart, J. 1980. *Dreaming and Waking: The Functional Approach to Dreams*. Culver City, CA: Peace Press.

Delaney, G. 1988. *Living Your Dreams*. San Francisco: Harper & Row.

Downing, J., and Marmorstein, R. eds. 1971. *Dreams and Nightmares: A Book of Gestalt Therapy Sessions*. New York: Harper & Row.

Drazan, J. 1979. *The Nightmare: A Checklist of the World Literature to 1976*. Palo Alto, CA: R & E Research Associates.

Faraday, A. 1973. *Dream Power*. New York: Berkley.

Faraday, A. 1974. *The Dream Game*. New York: Harper & Row.

Foulkes, D. 1966. *The Psychology of Sleep*. New York: Charles Scribner's Sons.

Freud, S. 1965. *The Interpretation of Dreams*. Strachey, J., translator and editor. New York: Avon Books.

Freud, S. 1952. *On Dreams*. Strachey, J., translator. New York: W.W. Norton.

Freud, S. 1952. *The Major Works of Sigmund Freud*. Great Books of the Western World. Hutchins, R. ed.-in-chief.

Chicago: Encyclopedia Britannica.

Fromm, E. 1951. *The Forgotten Language*. New York: Grove Press.

Garfield, P. 1984. *Your Child's Dreams*. New York: Ballantine Books.

Gastaut, H., Lugaresi E., Ceroni, and Coccagna, G. eds. 1967/1968. *The Abnormalities of Sleep in Man*. Proceedings of the XVth European Meeting of Electroencephalography. Bologna: Aulo Gaggi Editore.

Guilleminault, C., Dement, W., and Passouant, P. eds. 1976. *Advances in Sleep Research, Vol. 3: Narcolepsy*. New York: Spectrum Publications.

Hadfield, J. 1973. *Dreams and Nightmares*. Baltimore: Penguin.

Hall, C. 1954. *A Primer of Freudian Psychology*. New York: World Publishing Co.

Hall, C. 1966. *The Meaning of Dreams*. New York: McGraw-Hill.

Hartmann, E. 1984. *The Nightmare: The Psychology and Biology of Terrifying Dreams*. New York: Basic Books.

Hauri, P. 1981. *The Sleep Disorders*. Current Concepts Scope Publication. Kalamazoo, Michigan: Upjohn.

Hoffman, E. 1981. *The Way of Splendor: Jewish Mysticism and Modern Psychology*. Boston: Shambhala.

Hufford, D. 1982. *The Terror That Comes in the Night*. Philadelphia: University of Pennsylvania Press.

Jones, E. 1971. *On the Nightmare*. New York: Liveright.

Jung, C. 1964. *Man and His Symbols*. Garden City, N.Y.: Doubleday.

Jung, C. 1974. *Dreams*. Princeton: Princeton University Press.

Kellerman, H. ed. 1987. *The Nightmare: Pyschological and Biological Foundations*. New York: Columbia University Press.

Kiessling, N. 1977. *The Incubus in English Literature: Provenance and Progeny*. Washington State University Press.

Klagsbrun, F. 1980. *Voices of Wisdom: Jewish Ideals and Ethics for Everyday Living*. Middle Village, N.Y.: Jonathan David Publishers.

Kraul, E., and Beatty, J. 1989. *The Weeping Woman: Encounters with La Llorona*. Santa Fe, N.M.: The Word Process.

Kryger, M., Roth, T., and Dement, W. 1989. *Principles and Practice of Sleep Medicine*. Philadelphia: W.B. Saunders.

LaBerge, S. 1985. *Lucid Dreaming: The Power of Being Awake and Aware in Your Dreams*. New York: Ballantine.

Langs, R. 1988. *Decoding Your Dreams*. New York: Ballantine.

Lincoln, J. 1935. *The Dream in Primitive Cultures*. London: The Cresset Press.

Loehrich, R. 1978. *Exercitium Cogitandi*. Vol. 1–6. Oxford: The Centre for Medieval & Renaissance Studies.

Loehrich, R. 1956. *Modus Operandi*. McHenry, Ill.: The Compass Press, Inc.

Loehrich, R. 1953. *Oneirics and Psychosomatics*. McHenry, Ill.: The Compass Press, Inc.

Loehrich, R. 1964. *Systematic Oneirics*. McHenry, Ill.: The Compass Press, Inc.

Loehrich, R. 1953. *The Secret of Ulysses*. McHenry, Ill.: The Compass Press, Inc.

Meier, C. 1967. *Ancient Incubation and Modern Psychotherapy*. Monica Curtis, translator. Evanston, Ill.: Northwestern University Press.

Mack, J. 1974. *Nightmares and Human Conflict*. Boston: Houghton Mifflin.

Neidhardt, E. J., Weinstein, M., and Conry, R. 1985. *No Gimmick Guide to Managing Stress*. Vancouver: Self-Counsel Press, Inc.

Perls, F. 1974. *Gestalt Therapy Verbatim*. New York: Bantam.

Ratcliff, A. 1923. *A History of Dreams: A Brief Account of the Evolution of Dream Theories*. Boston: Small, Maynard & Co.

Roscher, W., and Hillman, J. 1979. *Pan and the Nightmare: Two Essays*. Irving, Texas: Spring Publications.

Schneider, D., and Sharp, L. 1969. *The Dream Life of Primitive People. Anthropological Studies*. Goodenough, W. ed. Washington, D.C.: American Anthropological Association.

Shain, R. 1984. *All for the Boss*. Jerusalem: Feldheim Publishers.

Shulman, S. 1979. *Nightmare: The World of Terrifying Dreams*. New York: Macmillan.

Stekel, W. 1967. *The Interpretation of Dreams: New Developments and Techniques*. Translated by Eden and Ceder Paul. New York: Washington Square Press.

Von Grunebaum, G., and Caillois, R. eds. 1966. *The Dream and Human Societies*. Berkeley: University of California Press.

Weiss, L. 1986. *Dream Analysis in Psychotherapy*. Psychology Practitioner Guidebooks. Goldstein, A., Krasner, L., and Garfield, S. eds. New York: Pergamon Press.

Williams, T. ed. 1987. *Post Traumatic Stress Disorders: A Handbook for Clinicians*. Cincinnati: Disabled American Veterans.

Wiseman, A. 1986. *Nightmare Help: A Guide for Adults and Children* (Dream Exploration Series). Berkeley, CA: Ansayre Press.

Zolar. 1963. *Zolar's Encyclopedia & Dictionary of Dreams*. New York: Prentice Hall.

Reference Books

American Psychiatric Association 1987. *Diagnostic and Statistical Manual of Mental Disorders (DSM-III-R)*. 3rd edition—Revised. Washington, D.C.: American Psychiatric

Association American Society of Hospital Pharmacists. *International Pharmaceutical Abstracts*. 1985–1989. Bethesda, Maryland: American Society of Hospital Pharmacists.

Dukes, M. ed. 1975, 1980, 1984. *Meyler's Side Effects of Drugs*. 8th, 9th, 10th editions. Amsterdam: Elsevier.

Dukes, M. ed. 1978–1989. *Side Effects of Drugs Annuals*. Amsterdam: Elsevier.

Physicians' Desk Reference, 44th Edition, 1990. Oradell, N.J.: Medical Economics Company.

The Oxford English Dictionary. Second Edition 1989. Prepared by J.A. Simpson and E. S. C. Weiner. Oxford: Clarendon Press.

Stedman's Medical Dictionary. 23rd edition. 1976. Baltimore: The Williams & Wilkins Company.

Articles

Allen, R. M. 1983. Attenuation of drug-induced anxiety dreams and pavor nocturnus by benzodiazepines. *Journal of Clinical Psychiatry* 44(3):106–7.

Andrisani, M. 1969. Nocturnal angina pectoris (letter). *Journal of the American Medical Association* 208(1):152.

Arkin, A. M., Toth, M. F., Baker, J., and Hastey, J. M. 1970. The degree of concordance between the content of sleep talking and mentation recalled in wakefulness. *The Journal of Nervous and Mental Disease* 151(6):375–93.

Arkin, A. M., Toth, M. F, Baker, J., and Hastey, J. M. 1970. The frequency of sleep talking in the laboratory among chronic sleep talkers and good dream recallers. *The Journal of Nervous and Mental Disease* 151(6):369–74.

Arkin, A. M., Antrobus, J. S., Toth, M. F., Baker, J., and Jackler, F. 1972. A comparison of the content of mentation reports elicited after nonrapid eye movement (NREM), associated sleep utterance and NREM "silent" sleep. *The Journal of Nervous and Mental Disease* 155(4):427–435.

Aserinsky, E., and Kleitman, N. 1953. Regularly occuring periods of eye motility and concomitant phenomena during sleep. *Science* 118: 273–279.

Belicki, D., and Belicki, K. 1982. Nightmares in a university population. *Sleep Research* 11:116.

Belicki, K. 1985. The assessment and prevalence of nightmare distress. *Sleep Research* 14:145.

Bell, C. C., Shakoor, B., Thompson, B., Dew. D., Hughley, E., Mays, R., and Shorter-Gooden, K. 1984. Prevalence of isolated sleep paralysis in black subjects. *Journal of the National Medical Association* 76(5):501–508.

Bell, C. C., Dixie-Bell, D. D., and Thompson, B. 1986. Further studies on the prevalence of isolated sleep paralysis in black subjects. *Journal of the National Medical Association* 78(7):649–659.

Berlin, R. M., and Qayyum, U. 1986. Sleepwalking: diagnosis and treatment through the life cycle. *Psychosomatics* 27(11):755–60.

Betts, T. A., and Alford, C. 1983. Beta-blocking drugs and sleep: A controlled study. *Drugs* 25 (Supplement 2):268–272.

Bishay, N. 1985. Therapeutic manipulation of nightmares and the management of neuroses. *British Journal of Psychiatry* 147:67–70.

Bixler, E. O., Kales, A., Soldatos, C. R., Kales, J. D., and Healey, S. 1979. Prevalence of sleep disorders in the Los

Angeles metropolitan area. *Medical Journal of Psychiatry* 79(11):1257–1262.

Boxer, S. 1989. Inside our sleeping minds. *Modern Maturity*, October–November: 48–54.

Breger, L. 1967. Function of dreams. *Journal of Abnormal Psychology Monograph*, 72(5):1–28.

Broughton, R. J. 1968. Sleep disorders: Disorders of arousal? *Science* 159:1070–8.

Cartwright, R. D. 1979. The nature and function of repetitive dreams: a survey and speculation. *Psychiatry* 4:131–7.

Cautela, J. R. 1968. Behavior therapy and the need for behavioral assessment. *Psychotherapy: Theory, Research, and Practice* 5(3):175–9.

Cellucci, A. J., and Lawrence, P. S. 1978. Individual differences in self-reported sleep variable correlations among nightmare sufferers. *Journal of Clinical Psychology* 34(3):721–25.

Cellucci, A. J., and Lawrence, P. S. 1978. The efficacy of systematic desensitization in reducing nightmares. *Journal of Behavior Therapy and Experimental Psychiatry* 9:109–14.

Cernovsky, Z. Z. 1985. MMPI and nightmares in male alcoholics. *Perceptual and Motor Skills* 61:841–42.

Cernovsky, Z. Z. 1986. MMPI and nightmare reports in women addicted to alcohol and other drugs. *Perceptual and Motor Skills* 62:717–18.

Choi, S. 1973. Dreams as a prognostic factor in alcoholism. *American Journal of Psychiatry* 130(6):699–702.

Chollar, S. 1989. Dreamchasers. *Psychology Today* April:60–61.

Culebras, A., and Moore, J. T. 1989. Magnetic resonance findings in REM sleep behavior disorder. *Neurology* 39:1519–1523.

Dahlman, K. 1989. Approaching the dream image within the therapeutic group context. Department of Art Education. University of New Mexico.

De Koninck, J., Christ, G., Rinfret, N. 1990. Language learning efficiency, dreams and REM sleep. *Psychiatric Journal of the University of Ottawa* 15(2):91–92.

Dement, W., and Kleitman, N. 1957. Cyclic variations in EEG during sleep and their relation to eye movements, body motility, and dreaming. *Electroencephalography and Clinical Neurophysiology* 9: 673–690.

Dolnick, E. 1990. What dreams are (really) made of. *The Atlantic Monthly* July:41.

Doyle, M. C. 1984. Enhancing dream pleasure with Senoi strategy. *Journal of Clinical Psychology* 40:467–474.

Dreistadt, R. 1972. A unifying theory of dreams, a new theory of nightmares, and the relationship of nightmares to psychopathology, literature, and collective social panic behavior. *Psychology* 9(4):19–30.

Dunn, K., and Barrett, D. 1988. Characteristics of nightmare subjects and their nightmares. *Psychiatric Journal of the University of Ottawa* 13(2):91–93.

Dworetzky, T. ed. 1989. The Omni book of dreams: A guide for the bewitched, bothered, and bewildered. Supplement to *Omni* magazine. November:8 pages.

Eccles, A., Wilde, A., and Marshall, W. L. 1988. In vivo desensitization in the treatment of recurrent nightmares. *Journal of Behavior Therapy and Experimental Psychiatry* 19(4):285–288.

Erman, M. K. 1987. Dream anxiety attacks (nightmares). *Psychiatric Clinics of North America* 10(4):667–674.

Erman, M. K. 1987. Insomnia. *Psychiatric Clinics of North America* 10(4):525–539.

Faraday, A., and Wren-Lewis, J. 1984. The selling of the Senoi. *Lucidity Letter* 3(1):79–81.

Feldman, M. J., and Hersen, M. 1967. Attitudes toward death in nightmare subjects. *Journal of Abnormal Psychology* 72(5):421–25.

Fisher, B. E., and Wilson, A. E. 1987. Selected sleep disturbances in school children reported by parents: Prevalence, interrelationships, behavioral correlates and parental attributions. *Perceptual and Motor Skills* 64: 1147–1157.

Fisher, C., Kahn, E., Edwards, A., and Davis, D. M. 1973. A psychophysiological study of nightmares and night terrors. I. Physiological aspects of the stage 4 night terror. *The Journal of Nervous and Mental Disease* 157(2):75–98.

Fisher, C., Kahn, E., Edwards, A., Davis, D. M., and Fine, J. 1974. A psychophysiological study of nightmares and night terrors. III. Mental content and recall of stage 4 night terrors. *The Journal of Nervous and Mental Disease* 158(3):174–189.

Flemenbaum, A. 1976. Pavor nocturnus: A complication of single daily tricyclic or neuroleptic dosage. *American Journal of Psychiatry* 133(5):570–572

Fleming, J. 1986. The successful use of imagery to treat nightmares associated with posttraumatic stress disorder. *Sleep Research* 15:80.

Fleminger, R. 1978. Visual hallucinations and illusions with propranolol. *British Medical Journal* May:1182.

Fodor, N. 1951. Nightmares of cannibalism. *American Journal of Psychotherapy* 5:226–35.

Foulkes, D. W. 1962. Dream reports from different stages of sleep. *Journal of Abnormal and Social Psychology* 65(1):14–25.

Freeman, D. 1967. Shaman and incubus. *The Psychoanalytic Study of Society* 4:315–325.

Fukuda, K., Miyasita, A., Inugami, M., and Ishihara, K. 1987. High prevalence of isolated sleep paralysis: *Kanashibari* phenomenon in Japan. *Sleep* 10(3):279–286.

Geer, J. H., and Silverman, I. 1967. Treatment of a recurrent nightmare by behavior-modification procedures: a case study. *Journal of Abnormal Psychology* 72(2):188–90.

Gorton, G. E. 1988. Life-long nightmares: An eclectic treatment approach. *American Journal of Psychotherapy* XLII (4):610–618.

Greenberg, R. 1967. Dream interruption insomnia. *The Journal of Nervous and Mental Disease* 144:18–21.

Gregor, T. 1981. The dream symbolism and dream theories of the Mehinaku. *American Ethnologist* 8(4):709–720.

Hall, C. S. 1955. The significance of the dream of being attacked. *Journal of Personality* 24:168–180.

Halliday, G. 1987. Direct psychological therapies for nightmares: A review. *Clinical Psychology Review* 7:501–523.

Harris, I. D. 1951. Characterological significance of the typical anxiety dreams. *Psychiatry* 14:279–294.

Harris, I. D. 1960. Typical anxiety dreams and object relations. *International Journal of Psychoanalysis* 41:604–611.

Hauri, P., and Van de Castle, R. L. 1973. Psychophysiological parallels in dreams. *Psychosomatic Medicine* 35(4):297–308.

Harary, K., and Weintraub, P. 1989. Life is but a dream. *Omni* 12(2):November p. 43.

Haynes, S. N., and Mooney, D. K. 1975. Nightmares: Etiological, theoretical, and behavioral treatment considerations. *The Psychological Record* 25:225–236.

Herr, B. 1981. The expressive character of Fijian dream and nightmare experiences. *Ethos* 9(4):331–351.

Hersen, M. 1972. Nightmare behavior: A review. *Psychological Bulletin* 78(1):37–48.

Hersen, M. 1971. Personality characteristics of nightmare sufferers. *The Journal of Nervous and Mental Disease* 153(1):27–31.

Hishikawa, Y., Sugita, Y., Teshima, Y., Iijima, S., Tanaka, K., and Tachibana, M. 1981. Sleep disorders in alcoholic patients with delirium tremens and transient withdrawal hallucinations—Reevaluation of the REM rebound and intrusion theory. *Psychophysiological Aspects of Sleep* Proceedings of the Third International Congress of Sleep Research, pp. 109–122.

Hobson, J. A., and McCarley, R. W. 1977. The brain as a dream state generator: an activation-synthesis hypothesis of the dream process. *American Journal of Psychiatry* 134(12):1335–1347.

Howard, C., and D'Orbán, P. T. 1987. Violence in sleep: Medico-legal issues and two case reports. *Psychological Medicine* 17:915–25.

Hurwitz, T., Mahowald, M., Schenck, C., Schluter, J., and Bundlie, S. 1991. A retrospective outcome study and review of hypnosis as treatment of adults with sleepwalking and sleep teror. *The Journal of Nervous and Mental Disease* 179(4):228–233.

Kales, A., Beall, G. N., Berger, R. J., Heuser, G., Jacobson, A., Kales, J. D., Parmelee, Jr., A. H., and Walter, R. D. 1968. Sleep and dreams. Recent research and clinical aspects. *Annals of Internal Medicine* 68(5):1078–1104.

Kales, J. D., and Kales, A. 1975. Nocturnal psychophysiological correlates of somatic conditions and sleep disorders. *International Journal of Psychiatry in Medicine* 6(1/2):43–61.

Kales, J. D., Kales, A., Soldatos, C. R., Caldwell, A. B., Charney, D. S., and Martin, E. D. 1980. Night terrors:

Clinical characteristics and personality patterns. *Archives of General Psychiatry* 37(12):1413–17.

Kales, A., Soldatos, C. R., Caldwell, A. B., Charney, D. S., Kales, J. D., Markel, D., and Cadieux, R. 1980. Nightmares: Clinical characteristics and personality patterns. *American Journal of Psychiatry* 137(10):1197–1201.

Kellner, R., 1987. A Symptom Questionnaire. *Journal of Clinical Psychiatry* 48(7):268–274

Kellner, R., Abbott, P., Winslow, W. W., and Pathak, D. 1989. Anxiety, depression, and somatization in DSM-III hypochondriasis. *Psychosomatics* 30(1):57–64.

Kellner, R., Krakow B., and Neidhardt, J. The treatment of nightmares. (submitted for publication)

Kellner, R., Singh, G., and Irogoyen-Rascon, F., 1991. Rehearsal in the treatment of recurring nightmares in post-traumatic stress disorders and panic disorder: case histories. *Annals of Clinical Psychiatry* 3(1):67-71

Kellner, R., Neidhardt, J., Krakow, B., and Pathak, D. 1992. Changes in chronic nightmares after one session of desensitization or rehearsal of instructions. *American Journal of Psychiatry* 149:659-663.

Kostis, J. B., and Rosen, R. C. 1987. Central nervous system effects of beta-adrenergic blocking drugs: the role of ancillary properties. *Circulation* 75(1):204–212.

Lennartsson, O. J., Lindquist, O., Noppa, H., and Sigurdsson, J. 1980. Sleep disturbances, nightmares and other possible central nervous disturbances in a population sample of women with special reference to those on antihypertensive drugs. *European Journal of Clinical Pharmacology* 17:173–177.

Lesse, S. 1959. Experimental studies on the relationship between anxiety, dreams and dream-like states. *American Journal of Psychotherapy* 13:440–445.

Lester, D. 1968. The fear of death of those who have nightmares. *The Journal of Psychology* 69:245–247.

Leveton, A. F. 1961. The night residue. *International Journal of Psycho-Analysis* 42:506–516.

Leuzzi, L. 1990. Nightmares can be good for you. *Ladies' Home Journal* March:64.

Levitan, H. 1984. Dreams which culminate in migraine headaches. *Psychotherapy and Psychosomatics* 41:161–166.

Levitan, H. L. 1976/77. The significance of certain catastrophic dreams. *Psychotherapy and Psychosomatics* 27:1–7.

Liddon, S. C. 1967. Sleep paralysis and hypnagogic hallucinations: Their relationship to the nightmare. *Archives of General Psychiatry* 17:88–96.

Marks, I. 1978. Rehearsal relief of a nightmare. *British Journal of Psychiatry* 133:461–65.

Maybruck, P. 1986. An exploratory study of the dreams of pregnant women. *Dissertation Abstracts International* 47(362-B) University Microfilms No. 86-05, 318.

Morris, J. 1985. Bad dreams: How to take control even while you sleep. *Glamour* August:177–180.

Miles, M. B. 1936. Banishing Dreams. *The Parents' Magazine* December:83.

Miller, W. R., and DiPilato, M. 1983. Treatment of nightmares via relaxation and desensitization: a controlled evaluation. *Journal of Consulting and Clinical Psychology* 51(6):870–877.

Moore, M. 1945. Recurrent nightmares: A simple procedure for psychotherapy. *The Military Surgeon* 97:282–285.

Moss, C. S. 1973. Treatment of a recurrent nightmare by hypnosymbolism. *The American Journal of Clinical Hypnosis* 16(1):23–30.

Mouze-Amady M., Sockeel, P., and Leconte, P. 1986. Modification of REM sleep behavior by REMs contingent auditory stimulation in man. *Physiology and Behavior* 37:543–548.

Neidhardt, J. 1982. Treatment of insomnia: a behavioral approach. *British Columbia Medical Journal* 24(10): 460–462.

Neidhardt, J. 1982. Guest Editorial—Behavioral Medicine. *British Columbia Medical Journal.* 24(10):453.

Neidhardt, J., Krakow, B., Kellner, R., and Pathak, D. The beneficial effects of one treatment session and recording of nightmares on chronic nightmare sufferers. *Sleep* (in press).

Neidhardt, J., Krakow, B., Kellner, R., and Pathak, D. 1992. A single treatment session for chronic nightmare sufferers. *Sleep Research* 21:137.

Nowlin, J. B., Troyer, W. G., Collins, W. S., Silverman, G., Nichols, C. R., McIntosh, H. D., Estes, Jr., E. H., and

Bogdonoff, M. D. 1965. The association of nocturnal angina pectoris with dreaming. *Annals of Internal Medicine* 63(6):1040–1046.

Ohaeri, J. U., Odejide, A. O., Ikuesan, B. A., and Adeyemi, J. D. 1989. The pattern of isolated sleep paralysis among Nigerian medical students. *Journal of the National Medical Association* 81(7):805–808.

Parco-Zuliani, N. 1986. The progression of hypnagogic images. *Indian Psychological Review* 30(4):53–55.

Pavlides, C., and Winson, J. 1989. Influences of Hippocampal Place Cell Firing in the Awake State on the Activity of These Cells During Subsequent Sleep Episodes. *The Journal of Neurosciences* 9(8):2907–2918.

Pearlman, C. A., and Greenberg, R. 1970. Medical-psychological implications of recent sleep research. *Psychiatry in Medicine* 1(4):261–275.

Perlis, M. L., Warbasse, C. P., and Bootzin, R. R. 1990. Self-reported dream affect and nightmare frequency. *Sleep Research* 19:140.

Raschka, L. B. 1979. The incubus syndrome: A variant of erotomania. *Canadian Journal of Psychiatry* 24:549–53.

Reed, H. 1976. Dream incubation: A reconstruction of a ritual in contemporary form. *Journal of Humanistic Psychology* 16(4):54–70.

Reynolds III, C. F. 1987. Sleep and affective disorders: A minireview. *Psychiatric Clinics of North America* 10(4):583–591.

Richmond, J. S., and Beck, J. C. 1986. Posttraumatic stress disorder in a World War II veteran. (letter) *American Journal of Psychiatry* 143(11):1485–1486.

Robert, R., Jansson, B., and Wager, J. 1989. Dreams of pregnant women: A pilot study. *Journal of Psychosomatic Obstetric Gynaecology* Supplement 10:21–33.

Robinson, W. J. 1916. Coitus and nightmares. *American Journal of Urology and Sexology* 12:471–473.

Ross, R. J., Ball, W. A., Sullivan, K. A., and Caroff, S. N. 1989. Sleep disturbance as the hallmark of posttraumatic stress disorder. *American Journal of Psychiatry* 146(6):697–707.

Scharf, M. B., Fletcher, K. A., and Jennings, S. W. 1988. Current pharmacologic management of narcolepsy. *American Family Physician* 38(1): 143–148.

Schenck, C. H., Bundlie, S. R., Ettinger, M. G., and Mahowald, M. W. 1986. Chronic behavioral disorders of human REM sleep: A new category of parasomnia. *Sleep* 9(2):293–308.

Schenck, C. H., Bundlie, S. R., Patterson, A. L., and Mahowald, M. W. 1987. Rapid eye movement sleep behavior disorder: A treatable parasomnia affecting older adults. *Journal of the American Medical Association* 257(13):1786–1789.

Schenck, C. H., Milner, D. M., Hurwitz, T. D., Bundlie, S. R., and Mahowald, M. W. 1989. A polysomnographic and clinical report on sleep-related injury in 100 adult patients. *American Journal of Psychiatry* 148(9):1166–1173.

Schindler, F. E. 1980. Treatment by systematic desensitization of a recurring nightmare of a real life trauma. *Journal of Behavior Therapy and Experimental Psychiatry* 11:53–54.

Schlosberg, A., and Benjamin, M. 1978. Sleep patterns in three acute combat fatigue cases. *Journal of Clinical Psychiatry* 39:546–549.

Schneck, J. M. 1969. Henry Fuseli, nightmare, and sleep paralysis. *Journal of the American Medical Association* 207(4):725–726.

Schneider, D. E. 1973. Conversion of massive anxiety into heart attack. *American Journal of Psychotherapy* 27:360–378.

Schwartz, J. L. ed.-in-chief 1989. Better outcomes in panic disorders. *The Psychiatric Times* January(supplement):1–8.

Smith, R. C. 1984. A possible biologic role of dreaming. *Psychotherapy and Psychosomatics* 41:167–176.

Smith, R. C. 1987. Do dreams reflect a biological state? *The Journal of Nervous and Mental Disease* 175(4):201–207.

Snyder, F. 1966. Toward an evolutionary theory of dreaming. *American Journal of Psychiatry* 123(2):121–142.

Spero, M. H. 1975. Anticipations of dream psychology in the Talmud. *The Journal of History and Behavioral Sciences* 11(4):374–380.

Stam, H. J., and Spanos, N. P. 1982. The Asclepian dream healings and hypnosis: A critique. *International Journal of Clinical and Experimental Hypnosis* XXX(1):9–22.

Stampfl, T. G. 1975. Implosive therapy: Staring down your nightmares. *Psychology Today* 2:66–70.

Stoddard, F. J. 1982. Body image development in the burned

child. *Journal of the American Academy of Child Psychiatry* 21(5):502–507.

Terr, L. C. 1983. Chowchilla revisited: The effects of psychic trauma four years after a school-bus kidnapping. *American Journal of Psychiatry* 140(12):1543–1550.

Terr, L. C. 1981. Psychic trauma in children: observations following the Chowchilla school-bus kidnapping. *American Journal of Psychiatry* 138:14–19.

Thorpy, M. J., and Glovinsky, P. B. 1987. Parasomnias. *Psychiatric Clinics of North America* 10(4):623–639.

Tokar, J. T., Brunse, A. J., Castelnuovo-Tedesco, P., and Stefflre, V. J. 1973. An objective method of dream analysis. *Monthly Psychoanalytic Quarterly* XLII:563–578.

Van Bork, J. J. 1982. An attempt to clarify a dream-mechanism. Why do people wake up out of an anxiety dream? *International Review of Psychoanalysis* 9:273–277.

Vogel, G. W. 1978. An alternative view of the neurobiology of dreaming. *American Journal of Psychiatry*. 135(12):1531–1535.

Weber, F. P. 1932. Nightmares and Freudian explanations. *The Medical Press* 133:329–330.

Wile, I. S. 1934. Auto-suggested dreams as a factor in therapy. *American Journal of Orthopsychiatry* 4:449–463.

Winget, C., and Kapp, F. 1972. The relationship of the manifest content of dreams to duration of childbirth in primiparae. *Psychosomatic Medicine* 34(4)313–320.

Winson, J. 1990. The meaning of dreams. *Scientific American* November: 86–96.

Wood, J. M., and Bootzin, R. R. 1990. The prevalence of nightmares and their independence from anxiety. *Journal of Abnormal Psychology* 99(1):64–68.

Wood, J. M., Bootzin, R. R., Klink, M., and Quan, S. F. 1989. Nightmare prevalence among patients with obstructive airways disease: A preliminary report. *Sleep Research* 18:364.

Zarcone, V., Gulevich, G., Pivik, T., and Dement, W. 1968. Partial REM phase deprivation and schizophrenia. *Archives of General Psychiatry* 18:194–202.

Drugs and Nightmares

Many drugs associated with nightmares have been written up in scientific case reports. These reports, however, are not controlled research studies. In other words, for many of these medicines there is no proof that they *cause* nightmares. Rather, an association is suggested because patients described nightmares occurring after using the medication. With some drugs, bad dreams were noted as a frequent side effect, while in others there may have been only a few cases.

For research purposes, drugs are placed into various classes. Interestingly, we find that drugs from the same or similar classes are linked with nightmares. For example, in the following list of 31 medicines, 11 drugs treat hypertension or high blood pressure, 5 drugs prevent cardiac chest pain or angina, 4 drugs improve the symptoms of Parkinson's disease, 4 are painkillers, and 2 fight depression.

If you suffer from disturbed dreams which you feel are caused by a medication, check the list below. If the medicine is not listed but falls into one of these classes we've just mentioned, such as hypertension or angina drugs, it still may be affecting your dreams.

Remember, however, many drugs *cannot* be stopped abruptly without causing serious side effects. If you believe these medications are affecting your dreams, then consult your physician before altering your use of the medicines.

Each drug is listed in alphabetical order by generic name. Following the generic is a brand name(s). Then, some uses of the medicine are listed.

amantadine (*Symmetrel*): Parkinson's;
   influenza A
atenolol (*Tenormin*): angina; hypertension

baclofen (*Lioresal*): spastic muscles from multiple sclerosis or spinal injuries

bromocriptine (*Parlodel*): acromegaly; hyperprolactinemia; Parkinson's; reduction in pituitary tumors

butorphanol (*Stadol*): narcotic painkiller

cimetidine (*Tagamet*): ulcers

ciprofloxacin (*Cipro*): antibiotic for various infections

clonidine (*Catapres*): hypertension; withdrawal from narcotics, cocaine, and nicotine.

digoxin (*Lanoxin*): heart failure; irregular rapid heartbeats

encainide (*Enkaid*): life-threatening irregular heartbeats

fenfluramine (*Pondimin*): appetite suppressor

folic acid (in numerous vitamin supplements or separately): treatment and prevention of folic acid deficiency

ketamine (*Ketalar*): anesthetic agent

labetalol (*Normodyne; Trandate*): hypertension

levodopa (*Larodopa, Sinemet*): Parkinson's

methyldopa (*Aldomet*): hypertension

metoprolol (*Lopressor*): angina; hypertension

morphine (*numerous brand names*): narcotic painkiller

nadolol (*Corgard*): angina; hypertension

nalbuphine (*Nubain*): narcotic painkiller

nifedipine (*Adalat; Procardia*): angina; hypertension

pentazocine (*Talwin*): painkiller

pergolide (*Permax*): Parkinson's

pindolol (*Visken*): hypertension

prasozin (*Minipress*): hypertension

protriptyline (*Vivactil*): depression

reserpine (*numerous brand names*): hypertension

timolol (*Blocadren*): angina; hypertension
       (*Timoptic*): glaucoma

trimipramine (*Surmontil*): depression

triprolidine (in combination decongestant, cold and sinus remedies): antihistamine effects

valproate (*Depakene*): seizures